Rethinking Education for Sustainable Development

Also Available from Bloomsbury

Ecopedagogy, *Greg William Misiaszek*
The Bloomsbury Handbook of Global Education and Learning, *edited by Douglas Bourn*
Education for Social Change, *Douglas Bourn*
Education and International Development, *edited by Tristan McCowan and Elaine Unterhalter*
Education in Radical Uncertainty, *Stephen Carney and Ulla Ambrosius Madsen*
Educating for Durable Solutions, *Christine Monaghan*
Sustainability Education, *Stephen Scoffham and Steve Rawlinson*
Leadership for Sustainability in Higher Education, *Janet Haddock-Fraser, Peter Rands and Stephen Scoffham*

Rethinking Education for Sustainable Development

Research, Policy and Practice

Radhika Iyengar and
Ozge Karadag Caman

BLOOMSBURY ACADEMIC
LONDON • NEW YORK • OXFORD • NEW DELHI • SYDNEY

BLOOMSBURY ACADEMIC
Bloomsbury Publishing Plc
50 Bedford Square, London, WC1B 3DP, UK
1385 Broadway, New York, NY 10018, USA
29 Earlsfort Terrace, Dublin 2, Ireland

BLOOMSBURY, BLOOMSBURY ACADEMIC and the Diana logo are trademarks of
Bloomsbury Publishing Plc

First published in Great Britain 2023
This paperback edition published 2024

Copyright © Radhika Iyengar and Ozge Karadag Caman and contributors, 2023

Radhika Iyengar and Ozge Karadag Caman and contributors have asserted their right under the Copyright, Designs and Patents Act, 1988, to be identified as Author of this work.

Cover image © Witthaya Prasongsin/ Getty Images

All rights reserved. No part of this publication may be reproduced or transmitted in any form or by any means, electronic or mechanical, including photocopying, recording, or any information storage or retrieval system, without prior permission in writing from the publishers.

Bloomsbury Publishing Plc does not have any control over, or responsibility for, any third-party websites referred to or in this book. All internet addresses given in this book were correct at the time of going to press. The author and publisher regret any inconvenience caused if addresses have changed or sites have ceased to exist, but can accept no responsibility for any such changes.

A catalogue record for this book is available from the British Library.

A catalog record for this book is available from the Library of Congress.

ISBN: HB: 978-1-3502-5612-5
PB: 978-1-3502-5616-3
ePDF: 978-1-3502-5613-2
eBook: 978-1-3502-5614-9

Typeset by Deanta Global Publishing Services, Chennai, India

To find out more about our authors and books visit www.bloomsbury.com and sign up for our newsletters.

*"Dedicated to our earth warriors—
Asmi, Swara, Arjun, and Destan"*

Contents

List of Illustrations	ix
List of Contributors	xi
Foreword *Jeffrey D. Sachs*	xx
List of Abbreviations and Acronyms	xxii

1 Introduction
  Radhika Iyengar and Ozge Karadag Caman — 1

2 Action for a Sustainable Future: The Key Role of Civic Education
  Tara Stafford Ocansey — 7

3 Citizen Science to Educate and Empower a Community Exposed to a Toxicant: A Case Study Concerning Well-water Fluoride in Alirajpur District of Madhya Pradesh, India
  Radhika Iyengar, Alexander Van Geen, and Charlotte Munson — 21

4 Building Capacity for Geospatial Data-driven Education Planning: Lessons from Nigeria
  Tara Stafford Ocansey, Emilie Schnarr, Anela Marie Layugan, and Annie Werner — 35

5 GIS and Storytelling for Sustainable Development Education
  Ismini Ethridge and Maryam Rabiee — 53

6 Lifelong Learning for All: Lessons from the Columbia Climate School
  Cassie Xu — 75

7 Building Cross-sectoral Education Programs for Sustainable Development: Design and Challenges
  Niyati Malhotra and Yanis Ben Amor — 89

8 Embedding Climate Science Research into Policy and Practice: IRI's Climate Services Academies Approach
  Mélody Braun, Zain Alabweh, Ashley Curtis, Carmen González Romero, Amanda Grossi, Ezequiel González Camaño, Ángel G. Muñoz, Andrew Kruczkiewicz, Tufa Dinku, and John Furlow — 103

9 Financial Education and Games in Weather-Index Insurance
  Rahel Diro, Mélody Braun, Juan Nicolas Hernandez-Aguilera, Souha Ouni, Max Mauerman, Yohana Tesfamariam Tekeste, Nitin Magima, and Daniel Osgood — 119

10 Building Child-focused Community Resilience Utilizing a
    Community-based, Multi-Modal Educational Approach
    Jeff Schlegelmilch and Jonathan Sury   141
11 Spaces for Youth Perspectives through Communication and Arts
    for Education for Sustainable Development
    Haein Shin   161
12 Conclusion *Radhika Iyengar and Ozge Karadag Caman*   173

Index   177

Illustrations

Figures

2.1	Civic-literacy framework	8
3.1	Map of wells tested for fluoride in Alirajpur	27
3.2	Close-up of a tested area shows the mixed spatial distribution of high- and low-fluoride wells	28
4.1	Timeline of research activities	39
4.2	Example distribution of primary school-aged children and nearby schools	41
4.3	Distance from schools to the nearest health facility	42
4.4	Distribution of primary schools with no early childhood care and education	43
4.5	Percentage of children aged 1–4 years within 2 kilometers of ECCE schools at the ward level	46
4.6	School Placement Optimization Tool for Kano State	46
5.1a b c	Selected images from ArcGIS StoryMap: "Nature-Based Climate Solutions. A Roadmap to Accelerate Action in California" by The Nature Conservancy	59
5.2a b c	Selected images from ArcGIS StoryMap: "Call to Action: End environmental racism now" by Harvard and Esri	60
5.3a b c	Selected images from ArcGIS StoryMap: "Space, shelter and scarce resources—coping with COVID-19" UNHCR, the UN Refugee Agency	61
5.4	ArcGIS StoryMap Collection: Exploring SDG 14 Life Below Water	64
5.5	From Esri Case Study "High School Students Learn Real-World STEM Skills with GIS": "A still interactive map used in the 'Students Search for Sustainability' narrative map shows a drive-time analysis of donation locations in the vicinity of the nonprofit organization, Food Forward"	65
5.6	Selected image from ArcGIS StoryMap: "The Quest for Arctic Power"	65

5.7	Selected image from ArcGIS StoryMap: "Dual Threat: The Impact of Black Carbon on Arctic Warming"	66
5.8	Selected image from ArcGIS StoryMap: "Innovation and Adaptation in the Urban Arctic"	67
5.9	The My School Today Dashboard	69
8.1	Decision-making flowchart model	106
8.2	BACS training dialogue modules	107
8.3	BACS training dialogue reciprocal learning approach	108
8.4	MTA implementation activities	111
8.5	ACToday-Ethiopia CSE initiative	114
8.6	Example of a co-produced curriculum and topics	115
9.1	Crowdsourcing climate risk data with gamification and digital tools. iKON WhatsApp version	132
10.1	Integrated Disaster Literacy Model (Çalışkan and Üner 2020)	146
10.2	RCRC Initiative key stakeholders and Community Resilience Coalition (CRC) Reach	149
10.3	The RCRC Initiative Model	150
10.4	Composite Community Preparedness Index (CPI) scores from six RCRC communities ($n = 6$) by sector depicted using a Box and Whisker chart	156
11.1	Elements observed across youth work presented in the summit merging learning styles and potential motivation	166

Tables

6.1	E.I. LIVE K12 Sessions	80
7.1	*Eminyeeto* Curriculum SEL Components and Descriptions	92

Contributors

Zain Alabweh is Staff Associate at the International Research Institute for Climate and Society, USA. She works on translating climate science into action; developing and managing partnerships to connect climate scientists to decision-makers in the fields of agriculture, food security, energy, and health. She focuses on reducing the impacts of climate risks through a circular exchange of information between producers of climate information, end-users, and everyone in between. She is a coordinator and researcher for the Latin American and the Caribbean team for the Columbia World Project "Adapting Agriculture to Climate Today for Tomorrow" (ACToday) project. She contributed to Latin America and the Caribbean: a community-based decentralized roundtable approach section in this book.

Yanis Ben Amor is Executive Director of the Center for Sustainable Development, Columbia University, USA. He launched the youth programs *Eminyeeto* in Uganda and *Yuva Nestham* in India to develop Social and Emotional Learning curricula for children and adolescents. He regularly develops cross-cutting initiatives between health and education. He created mental health and sexual education programs for school children in low-resource settings. He has launched Digital Health and Digital Education tools to monitor children's school absenteeism in India using fingerprint technology, and for refugees in Turkey, Lebanon, and Jordan to provide health information and access.

Mélody Braun is Senior Staff Associate at the International Research Institute for Climate and Society, USA. She works with climate scientists, development practitioners, and policy makers to co-develop transdisciplinary climate services approaches to improve the integration of climate information into decision-making processes and increase resilience. She is particularly interested in inclusive, participatory, and bottom-up approaches supporting decision-makers and locally led efforts. She is the Bangladesh country lead for the Columbia World Project "Adapting Agriculture to Climate Today for Tomorrow" (ACToday) project, through which she worked with partners to co-develop the Bangladesh Academy for Climate Services (BACS), and co-designed the BACS training approach described in this book.

Ashley Curtis is Senior Staff Associate at the International Research Institute for Climate and Society, USA. She is IRI's training lead, and Bangladesh country manager for "Adapting Agriculture to Climate Today for Tomorrow" (ACToday), a Columbia World Project. She oversees training activities at IRI, advancement of the IRI institutional training strategy, and development of IRI's Climate Services Academies, including the Bangladesh Academy for Climate Services (BACS). She also contributes to project management and research.

Dr Tufa Dinku is a Senior Research Scientist at the International Research Institute for Climate and Society (IRI), Columbia Climate School. He has PhD degree in civil engineering/hydrometeorology from the University of Connecticut. Dr Dinku's main research interest is improving availability and quality of climate data and derived information products. He has over 25 years of national and international experience in climate science and applications. Currently Dr Dinku leads IRI's ENACTS (Enhancing National Climate Services) program, which is a unique multi-faceted initiative designed to bring climate knowledge into local decision-making, as well as the development of IRI's Climate Data Tool(CDT).

Rahel Diro is an associate specializing in Disaster Risk Finance at Tetra Tech. Her work focuses on risk financing, climate-risk analytics, and insurance. She is a recognized leader in applying private sector risk finance tools to solve development challenges. Before joining Tetra Tech, she worked at Columbia University's International Research Institute for Climate and Society (IRI) as a senior research associate. She has extensive experience working with smallholder farmers as well as policy-level decision-makers. Rahel also worked at Oxfam America where she managed a holistic risk management program in Ethiopia. She holds a master's degree in Public Administration in Finance and Economic Policy from Columbia University's School of International and Public Affairs (SIPA) and Science in Agricultural Economics from Ghent and Humboldt Universities.

John Furlow is Director of the International Research Institute for Climate and Society, USA. His focus is on connecting complex climate science to decision-making to improve lives and livelihoods in developing countries. He is interested in policy reform that reflects the value of climate information in supporting important socioeconomic sectors, such as agriculture and public health. Prior to coming to IRI, he designed and led the Climate Change Adaptation Program in USAID's climate change office. He helped a number of governments develop approaches for adapting their economies to the impacts of climate variability and change.

Ezequiel González Camaño is a contributor and former translator for the International Research Institute for Climate and Society, USA. He supported the development of the Spanish version of the curricula of the agro-meteorological training material and data for use in local agricultural development in Guatemala and Colombia as part of the Latin American division of the first Columbia World Project, ACToday: Adapting Agriculture to Climate Today for Tomorrow. An interdisciplinary writer and anthropologist, he specializes in the cultural production and ecological politics of the Southern Cone and has been published internationally in English, Spanish, and French.

Carmen González Romero is a staff associate at the International Research Institute for Climate and Society, where she co-leads the Latin American component of the Columbia World Project "Adapting Agriculture to Climate Today, for Tomorrow" (ACToday). She has a multidisciplinary academic background and is interested in the co-development and co-design of climate services with local stakeholders, with a focus on food security (involving models for undernutrition and human migration) and vector-borne diseases. She co-led the Academy of Climate Services in Guatemala and Colombia and has supported the development of the locally led agroclimatic round tables in both countries.

Amanda Grossi is Senior Staff Associate and the "Adapting Agriculture to Climate Today, for Tomorrow" (ACToday) project country manager for Ethiopia and Senegal at the International Research Institute for Climate and Society (IRI), Columbia Climate School. She is a development practitioner with more than a decade of experience working with various agricultural and education-focused NGOs, research centers, and local and international development organizations targeting rural communities in both East and West Africa.

J. Nicolas Hernandez-Aguilera is an Associate Research Scientist at Yale School of the Environment, USA, and a former Columbia Earth Institute postdoctoral research fellow. He received his Ph.D. in Applied Economics and Management from Cornell University, and his research focused on sustainable agricultural systems for smallholders. In particular, he has evaluated the impact of direct business models in coffee and modeled profitable agroecological cropping systems to incentivize bird conservation. More recently, he has designed digital tools and games to motivate and scale smallholders' generation, translation, and use of climate information, improving climate-risk adaptation strategies, land-use practices, and financial instruments.

Radhika Iyengar is a Research Scholar and Director of Education at the Center for Sustainable Development, Earth Institute, Columbia University, USA. Dr. Iyengar has extensive experience in designing and managing international education research projects in South Asia and sub-Saharan Africa. She is the chair of the Environmental and Sustainability Special Interest Group at the Comparative International Education Society. She received the Distinguished Early Career Award from Teachers College, Columbia University, for her service to the field of international education development in 2020.

Ozge Karadag Caman works as Senior Research Scholar at the Center for Sustainable Development of the Earth Institute at Columbia University, USA. She earned her Medical Doctor degree from Istanbul University, and her MSc and PhD degrees in Public Health from Hacettepe University. She holds a postgraduate degree in health promotion from LSHTM and has more than fifteen years of public health research and teaching experience in different higher education settings. She is a member of The Lancet COVID-19 Commission Scientific Secretariat and one of the experts of the Global Happiness Council, where she chairs the Vulnerable Populations Thematic Group.

Andrew Kruczkiewicz works at Columbia University, USA. He is based at the International Research Institute for Climate and Society and is Faculty Lecturer within the Climate School. He is Co-Director of the Sustainable and Resilient Living in an Era of Increasing Disasters Network. Andrew is also science adviser for the Red Cross Red Crescent Climate Centre, The Netherlands. His background is in meteorology and remote sensing, focusing on disaster risk assessment, forecasting and early warning.

Anela Marie Layugan is Geographic Information Science (GIS) Analyst at the UN Sustainable Development Solutions Network (SDSN), USA, on the SDGs Today team where she visualizes, manages, and creates real-time and timely data on the Sustainable Development Goals. Prior to SDSN, she was a researcher at the Center for International Earth Science Information Network at Columbia University on the GRID3 Program creating geospatial data and visualizations for sustainable development work at the country level. She holds a Master of Science degree in GIS from Clark University where she researched changes in Arctic sea ice melt while working part-time on a flower farm called Fivefork Farms.

Nitin Magima is Staff Associate at the International Research Institute for Climate and Society, USA. He is part of the Financial Instruments Sector Team.

He works with climate scientists, development practitioners, and policy makers to help protect smallholder farmers around the world from climate risk through forecast-based climate action and climate insurance approaches. Nitin holds a master's in Public Administration in Development Practice from the School of International and Public Affairs, Columbia University, and a bachelor's degree in Mathematics from St. Stephen's College, Delhi University.

Niyati Malhotra is currently Research Fellow with the Development Impact Evaluation Unit of the World Bank Group, USA. She was previously a research analyst at the Center for Sustainable Development at the Earth Institute, Columbia University. She has worked on operational impact evaluations targeting the integration of early learning with other child development-focused interventions in low-income settings. Her current work focuses on understanding the potential of game-based literacy apps for improving learning outcomes for children in school and non-school environments. Niyati holds a master's in Public Administration degree from Columbia University and a bachelor's degree in Economics from McGill University.

Max Mauerman is Staff Associate on the Financial Instruments Sector Team at IRI, USA, and holds an MPA in Development Practice from Columbia University SIPA, USA. His roles at IRI include the development of decision support tools for climate-risk management as well as research on economic decision-making. Prior to joining IRI, Max worked for Innovations for Poverty Action (IPA), where he co-managed a multi-year evaluation of a pastoralist assistance program in Namibia. He has also worked as a consultant for the World Food Programme on research topics related to climate resilience and conservation agriculture.

Charlotte Munson is Program Coordinator for the Dean's Office at the Columbia Climate School, USA. While studying sustainable development and business management at Columbia University, she held an internship at the Center for Sustainable Development. Research interests include international education development, sustainable communities, and climate adaptation.

Ángel G. Muñoz Solórzano is Associate Research Scientist in IRI's Climate Program, USA, focusing on climate variations and prediction at multiple timescales. He leads the Latin American component of the Columbia World Project "Adapting Agriculture to Climate Today, for Tomorrow" and holds a BS in physics (2002, numerical general relativity), a Master of Arts and Philosophy, and a PhD in climate sciences (2014–16), Columbia University and a postdoc at the Atmospheric and Oceanic Sciences (AOS) Program, at Princeton University. He presently serves as co-chair of the Climate Information for Decision Making (I4D) project in the World Climate Research Programme (WCRP) Working Group on Subseasonal-to-Interdecadal Project (WGSIP); in the Research-to-Operations (R2O) group of the WWRP/WCRP S2S Prediction Project; in NOAA's Model Diagnostics Task Force (MDTF); in the WMO's Ad-Hoc Task Force on Regional Climate Forecast; and in NOAA's Modelling, Analysis, Predictions and Projections (MAPP) S2S Task Force until August 2020 (the end of that Task Force). He is also a reviewer of US-based and international projects.

Daniel Osgood leads the Financial Instruments Sector Team at the International Research Institute for Climate and Society (IRI), USA. He has an agricultural economics PhD from UC Berkeley. His team drives forecast-based action and insurance efforts around the world, supporting many of the index insurance projects that have gone to scale, ranging from national-level insurance to the millions of smallholder farmers purchasing index insurance contracts built through farmer-driven, science-based crowd at core processes. He has been involved in global policy processes such as the UNFCCC, with projects he works on highlighted by Ban Ki-moon in the opening speech at the 2015 Paris COP and has had press coverage in venues spanning Voice of America, Al Jazeera, the Guardian, Nature, New York Times, and Reuters.

Souha Ouni has an multidisciplinary background in environmental sciences and international development. Her work focuses on the design and implementation of Financial Instruments such as index-based insurance and forecast-based financing. Souha has been working on projects focusing on West Africa, developing interactive online tools that foster transparency and participatory financial instruments design.

Jeff Schlegelmilch is Research Scholar and Director of the National Center for Disaster Preparedness, Columbia Climate School, Columbia University, USA. Before becoming director, he served as the center's deputy director. Prior to his work at Columbia, he was the manager for the International and Non-Healthcare Business Sector for the Yale New Haven Health System Center for Emergency Preparedness and Disaster Response. He was also previously an epidemiologist and emergency planner for the Boston Public Health Commission. He is also the author of Rethinking Readiness: A brief guide to twenty-first-century megadisasters published by Columbia University Press. He holds a master's degree in Public Health from UMASS Amherst in Health Policy and Management, and a master's degree in Business Administration from Quinnipiac University.

Tara Stafford Ocansey is Executive Director of the Children's Environmental Literacy Foundation (CELF), USA, which aims to make sustainability and civic engagement integral components of every child's K-12 learning experience. Prior to joining CELF, she spent a decade with the Center for Sustainable Development at Columbia University's Earth Institute, where she managed education programs across the lifelong learning spectrum in eleven sub-Saharan African countries, India, and Myanmar. She holds a Master of Arts degree in Comparative and International Education from Teachers College, Columbia University.

Emilie Schnarr is Senior Staff Associate at the Center for International Earth Science Information Network (CIESIN), USA. She works with countries to generate, validate, and use geospatial data on population, settlements, infrastructure, and boundaries through the Geo-Referenced Infrastructure and Demographic Data for Development (GRID3) program. GRID3 combines the expertise of partners in government, the United Nations, academia, and the private sector to design adaptable and relevant geospatial solutions based on the capacity and development needs of each country. Prior to working on GRID3, she researched, analyzed, and documented climate change trends and model projections for the African and Latin American Resilience to Climate Change (ARCC) project and West Africa Biodiversity and Climate Change (WABiCC) program. She holds a Master of Science degree in Earth and Environmental Engineering and a Master of Arts degree in Climate and Society from Columbia University.

Haein Shin is Education Technical Adviser at the Center for Sustainable Development of Columbia University's Earth Institute, USA. For over ten years, she has worked on the implementation, management, monitoring and evaluation, and content development of projects in Myanmar, India, Morocco, Saudi Arabia, and ten countries in sub-Saharan Africa. The aim of these projects, mainly focusing on literacy, digital literacy, gender equality, employment readiness, life skills, and environmental activism, is to build sustainable and resilient communities. She received her Master of Arts in International Educational Development from Teachers College, Columbia University.

Jonathan Sury a Project Director at the National Center for Disaster Preparedness Columbia Climate School, Columbia University. He holds a master's degree in public health in Environmental Health Sciences with a concentration in Environment and Molecular Epidemiology from the Mailman School of Public Health, Columbia University. He is currently a doctoral student in public health at the Mailman School of Public Health focusing on Leadership in Global Health and Humanitarian Systems. He has a keen interest in Geographic Information Systems (GIS) and their use in disaster preparedness and recovery and has over ten years experience in qualitative and quantitative research with significant emphasis on field research and study design, implementation, management, and data architecture and analysis. Presently, he contributes to a variety of disaster-related research at NCDP including community coalition building, child-focused community resilience, disaster recovery research, and project communications. He also has significant experience evaluating the unanticipated consequences of pandemic flu, determining racially and ethnically appropriate emergency messaging, and analyzing the long-term disaster resiliency and recovery issues in the Gulf Coast following Hurricane Katrina, Superstorm Sandy, and the Deepwater Horizon Oil Spill.

Alexander van Geen is Research Professor at Lamont-Doherty Earth Observatory, USA, and a faculty member of the Earth Institute at Columbia University, USA. His research focuses on ways to reduce the impact of the environment on human health, specifically in the case of heterogeneously distributed contaminants. Such patterns complicate prediction but often also point the way to mitigation when a hazard can be mapped, which is often possible using simple field kits. For his work on well-water arsenic in South Asia, he received the International Service Award (US National Chapter) of the International Association of Hydrogeologists in 2019.

Cassie Xu is Associate Director of Non-Degree Programs and Outreach at the Columbia Climate School, USA, where she is responsible for managing educational and outreach activities at the K12 levels and continuing education learners. She also oversees the Office of Education and Outreach (E&O), an office she led efforts to establish, at Lamont-Doherty Earth Observatory. The office offers an ideal mix of educational research, authentic learning experiences and programs, a centralized administrative and operational hub for E&O activities, and enthusiasm for innovation. Before joining Columbia University, she was a classroom teacher.

Annie Werner is Project Coordinator for the Geo-Referenced Infrastructure and Demographic Data for Development (GRID3) program at the Center for International Earth Science Information Network (CIESIN), USA. She works with government, non-governmental, and academic partners to develop geospatial solutions for development planning. Prior to GRID3, she worked in research and coordination on agricultural development projects in Sierra Leone. She holds a BA in International and Area Studies from Washington University in St. Louis and is a Masters of International Affairs candidate at the School of International and Public Affairs, Columbia University.

Yohana Tesfamariam Tekeste is Staff Associate at the Financial Instruments Sector Team (FIST) at the International Research Institute for Climate and Society (IRI), USA. She holds an MA in Biotechnology from Columbia University, USA. She is responsible for leading various Anticipatory Action programming (AA) in Djibouti and Lesotho where she works with decision-makers and stakeholders to make climate-informed decisions through the co-design, and co-generation of decision-making tools. She is also involved in a number of index insurance projects in Southern Africa, she supports the scaling of insurance-based climate-risk mitigation programs and centers vulnerable communities in these processes. She is also involved in some research projects that investigate the active participation of smallholder farmers in index insurance programs.

Ismini Ethridge is currently a master's student at the Yale School of Environment where she focuses on land use, sustainable food systems, and climate change mitigation strategies. Prior to Yale, she worked at Columbia University's Center for Sustainable Development, supporting the director on a number of programs and initiatives on policy implementation and advocacy for the Sustainable Development Goals. She was a founding member of the SDGsToday team, supporting their GIS and storytelling initiatives, and led collaboration with Esri for the 2020 ArcGIS StoryMaps Competition for the SDGs.

Maryam Rabiee is a manager at the UN Sustainable Development Solutions Network, USA, working across two data programs, SDGs Today and the Thematic Research Network on Data and Statistics (TReNDS). Her work focuses on exploring new methods and approaches to strengthen the data ecosystem for sustainable development and integrating geospatial knowledge and technologies in the implementation of the Sustainable Development Goals (SDGs).

Foreword

We live in a time of massive and complex changes that challenge the very fabric of our society. Technologies are developing at an unprecedented speed. Environmental crises continue to worsen. The world is more interconnected than ever before, but also deeply divided by cultures, ideologies, and competing interests. To surmount these challenges, we need a global citizenry that understands these complexities and has the tools and skills to address the world's challenges in a cooperative manner.

In short, we need a new kind of education that empowers people around the world to achieve sustainable development. This education is for all of us. Today's workers need to master fast-changing technologies. Older people who grew up in the pre-digital world need new digital skills to safely and happily navigate the new environment. Young people who will be tomorrow's leaders need to understand the world they will inherit: a crowded, interconnected world facing multiple environmental crises that demand urgent attention and solutions.

I am proud, edified, and inspired by this volume on rethinking education in the age of sustainable development. The book is guided by the Sustainable Development Goals (SDGs), and notably by SDG Target 4.7, which directs the entire world community to a new kind of education for sustainable development. This target is as challenging as it is inspiring.

Target 4.7. By 2030, ensure that all learners acquire the knowledge and skills needed to promote sustainable development, including, among others, through education for sustainable development and sustainable lifestyles, human rights, gender equality, promotion of a culture of peace and non-violence, global citizenship and appreciation of cultural diversity and of culture's contribution to sustainable development.

Target 4.7 recognizes that Education for Sustainable Development (ESD) entails a thrilling combination of technical knowledge (such as about the science of climate change), cultural awareness and appreciation, and what the ancient Greeks called the virtues, meaning the excellences of character to enable each of us to live harmoniously and happily with others. We are, for example, inspired to help young people appreciate cultural diversity and cultivate a culture of peace and non-violence, so urgently needed in our world today.

The case studies in this volume open our eyes to the remarkable range of innovations in education that can and should become central in the coming years. Some of the case studies cover formal education in the classroom; others consider education in the community. Some use new GIS tools for analysis and storytelling; others deploy games to help communities to understand and apply challenging new concepts (such as weather-index insurance). Some are aimed at youth; others are aimed at working parents. All emphasize the challenge of designing new ESD curricula that are science-based, intelligible for the intended community, and useful and relevant in local contexts.

In our work at the Columbia University Center for Sustainable Development and the UN Sustainable Development Solutions Network, we are inspired by opportunities to help solve global problems through innovative education, and we are deeply moved by the number of schools, universities, civil society organizations, businesses, and governments that are making strong commitments to ESD and to remarkable innovations in pedagogy. This inspiring set of case studies will help key stakeholders around the world to take new and bold steps to meet the high aspirations of Target 4.7 as a key step to achieving all of the SDGs and the Paris Climate Agreement.

The ancient Greeks knew well that the path to healthy and happy societies lies in virtuous citizens benefiting from an education in science, arts, and ethics. This book helps us to find the path to wellbeing in our own time through education for sustainable development.

Jeffrey Sachs, University Professor,
Columbia University.

Abbreviations and Acronyms

Chapter 1: Introduction

ESD	Education for Sustainable Development
GIS	Geographic Information System
GRID3	Geo-Referenced Infrastructure and Demographic Data for Development
NAEP	The National Assessment of Education Progress
NCDP	National Center for Disaster Preparedness
RCRC	Resilient Children/Community
SEL	Social, emotional learning
STEM	Science, technology, engineering, and math
STC	Save the Children
UNESCO	United Nations Educational, Scientific, and Cultural Organization

Chapter 2: Action for A Sustainable Future: The Key Role of Civic Education

CSD	Center for Sustainable Development
EAD	Educating for American Democracy
ESD	Education for Sustainable Development
GC	Generation Citizen
NAEP	National Assessment of Education Progress
SEL	Social, emotional learning
STEM	Science, technology, engineering, and math

UNESCO	United Nations Educational, Scientific, and Cultural Organization
XR	Extinction Rebellion

Chapter 3: Citizen-science to Educate and Empower a Community Exposed to a Toxicant: A Case Study Concerning Well-water Fluoride in Alirajpur District of Madhya Pradesh, India

INREM	India National Resource Economics and Management
PHED	Public Health and Engineering Department

Chapter 4: Building Capacity for Geospatial Data-driven Education Planning: Lessons from Nigeria

CIESIN	The Center for International Earth Science Information Network
ECCE	Early Childhood Care Education
GRID3	The Geo-Referenced Infrastructure and Demographic Data for Development program
ITU	The International Telecommunication Union
LGA	Local Government Area
MBSSE	The Ministry of Basic and Senior Secondary Education
NASRDA	The National Space Research and Development Agency
NMIS	The Nigeria Millennium Development Goal Information System
NPAs	National Personnel Audits
PHED	Public Health and Engineering Department
SDGs	Sustainable Development Goals
SPOT	The School Placement Optimization Tool
SUBEBs	The State Universal Basic Education Boards
SDSN	The United Nations Sustainable Development Solutions Network
UBEC	The Nigerian Universal Basic Educational Commission
UNESCO	United Nations Educational, Scientific, and Cultural Organization

Chapter 5: GIS and Storytelling for Sustainable Development Education

CTE	Career and Technical Education
CMHS	Clark Magnet High School
GIS	Geospatial Information Systems
SDGs	Sustainable Development Goals
SDSN	The Sustainable Development Solutions Network's

UNITAR-UNOSAT The United Nations Satellite Centre at the United Nations Institute for Training and Research

UNHCR	The UN Refugee Agency

Chapter 6: Lifelong Learning for All: Lessons from the Columbia Climate School

ESD	Education for Sustainable Development
STEM	Science, technology, engineering, and math
UNESCO	United Nations Educational, Scientific, and Cultural Organization

Chapter 7: Building Cross-sectoral Education Programs for Sustainable Development: Design and Challenges

CASEL	The Collaborative for Academic, Social, and Emotional Learning
MCB	My Changing Body
SEL	Socio Emotional Learning
SHPI	School-based health promotion interventions
SRH	Sexual and reproductive health

Chapter 8: Embedding climate science research into policy and practice: IRI's Climate Services Academies approach

ACToday	Adapting Agriculture to Climate Today for Tomorrow
ATVET	Agricultural Technical Vocational and Training

BACS	Bangladesh Academy for Climate Services
BMD	Bangladesh Meteorological Department
CIMMYT	Center for Wheat and Maize Improvement
COMPAS	Connecting Earth Observations to Decision-makers for Preparedness Actions
CSE	Climate Services Education
DMF	Decision-Making Flowcharts
DRR/M	Disaster Risk Reduction and Management
ICCCAD	International Center for Climate Change and Development
IRI	International Research Institute for Climate and Society
MTA	Mesas Técnicas Agroclimáticas (Agricultural roundtables)
NASA	National Aeronautics and Space Administration
NDRMC	National Disaster Risk Management Commission
NGO	Non-Government Organization
NMA	National Meteorological Agency
SDGs	Sustainable Development Goals
ToT	Training of Trainers
UN	United Nations

Chapter 10: Building Child-Focused Community Resilience Utilizing a Community-Based, Multi-Modal Educational Approach

CBPR	Community-Based Participatory Research
CEM	The Community Empowerment Model
COOP	Continuity of Operations Planning
CPI	The Community Preparedness Index
CRC	The Community Resilience Coalition
FEMA	Federal Emergency Management Agency

GSK	GSK (formerly GlaxoSmithKline)
NCDP	The National Center for Disaster Preparedness
PAR	Participatory Action Research
RCRC	The Resilient Children/Resilience Communities
STC	Save the Children

Chapter 11: Spaces for youth perspectives through communication and arts for education for sustainable development

| CSD | The Center for Sustainable Development |
| LDEO | Lamont-Doherty Earth Observatory |

Chapter 12: Conclusion

COP26	The United Nations Climate Change Conference
ESD	Education for Sustainable Development
SDGs	Sustainable Development Goals

1

Introduction

Radhika Iyengar and Ozge Karadag Caman

The one thing that Education for Sustainable Development (ESD) calls for most centrally is inter-sectorality. Agenda 2030 for Sustainable Development agreed upon by almost all United Nations Member States shared a blueprint for peace and prosperity for the people and the planet. This called for an ambitious agenda that was reflected in seventeen Sustainable Development Goals (SDGs). The post-2015 agenda was made with the intention of breaking the sector silos that existed in the Millennium Development Goals. The foundation of the SDGs was based on the four pillars of sustainable development; environmental sustainability, peace and security, inclusive social development, and inclusive economic development. Addressing the four pillars of sustainable development through strategies, interventions, and goals requires inter-sectoral collaborations.

Research has shown many benefits of inter-sectoral strategies. UNESCO (2011) notes that each extra year of a mother's schooling reduces the probability of infant mortality by 5 percent to 10 percent. An extra year of female schooling reduces fertility rates by 10 percent. In sub-Saharan Africa, an estimated 1.8 million children's lives could have been saved in 2008, if their mothers had at least a secondary education. These are not new facts to the development sector. However, planning and executing inter-sectoral strategies require (un)learning at the governmental level, community level, and individual level.

SDG 4 states the importance of lifelong learners. ESD is for all ages. Therefore this book uses the concept of lifelong learning and applies it to various contexts both in and out of formal education across all ages. The book has a specific focus on SDG 4.7. "By 2030, ensure all learners acquire knowledge and skills needed to promote sustainable development, including among others through education for sustainable development and sustainable lifestyles, human rights, gender equality, promotion of a culture of peace and non-violence, global citizenship, and appreciation of cultural diversity and of culture's contribution to sustainable development."

In order to accomplish this target, ESD must be more outward-looking. The education sector needs to be the bridge between all SDGs. It needs to learn about various sectors and translate the learnings into lesson plans for all educational settings. It needs to urgently take all the action messages and reach the communities having the hardest impact of climate change. But first, ESD must look at the sources of structural inequalities and become the tool to ask critical questions. It must address climate change and injustices at the same time.

The authors of this book bring in their years of practice and research to suggest a new take on ESD. The book suggests approaches that will empower individuals, communities, and countries to make ESD a lever of change toward justice and sustainability. The chapter authors come from various fields including informal educators, nonformal educators, geophysicists, public health experts, disaster-preparedness experts, GIS-based storytellers, art-based educators, and agriculture insurance educators. This wide range of expertise forms the unique aspect of this book. The book is able to redefine ESD as it pertains to a much wider use of education than the way it is traditionally perceived.

Stafford Ocansey's framing of ESD forms the core of this book. She asks the question "what is the civic mission of schools?" Stafford Ocansey's framework of civic literacy is the intersection of knowledge, skills, values, and agency to mobilize for change through civic spaces. The author uses the intersection of Global Citizenship Education and ESD as an empowering framework that creates agents of social change. Often seen as siloed dimensions of SDG4.7, Stafford Ocansey brings both Global Citizenship Education and ESD together. The author uses Social Emotional Learning (values), ESD (knowledge), twenty-first-century skills (skills), Global Citizenship Education (values, attitudes, and behaviors), Peace Education (knowledge and questioning assumptions), Human Rights Education (knowledge of legal rights) in addition to Environmental Justice and Anti-racist Education (critical thinking and building agents of change). This book uses these pillars of ESD as we read through different chapters. In the conclusion section, we come back to reflect on these pillars to see if we were able to gain a better understanding of the progress made toward these aspirational goals.

Shin discusses youth climate activism, keeping communication as the focus. Through the example of the Center for Sustainable Development's Eco-ambassadors, Shin puts forward communication and arts, partnerships in the community, and knowledge and information on environmental realities. She reminds us that art as a way of communicating environmental stories has a wide impact on building a movement. Another form of storytelling is through Geographic Information System (GIS) Story Maps. Ethridge and Rabiee's chapter uses geospatial mapping as a powerful tool to reconnect with the local environmental issues as well as to connect to the global goals. The authors also expand the capabilities of technology and discuss the role of real-time data collection and its role in educational planning. Through various case studies and examples, the authors demonstrate the role that technology can play in ESD. Their topics range from plastic pollution in the ocean to finding a safe place during the COVID-19 pandemic. A wide array of examples used in the chapter makes education a powerful tool to learn about the localization of the problem and at the same time connect to larger global issues.

In this book, GIS is not only used as a storytelling tool but as an educational planning tool as well. Stafford Ocansey, Schnarr, Layugan, and Werner derive lessons from Nigeria in their geospatial planning tool. They discuss basic population-based indicators that form a part of the national measurement for tracking the SDGs. The number of children of school age, the number of children in nonformal education, and the number of children attending school are some of the indicators that help to track SDG 4. However, this data is usually hard to find and more often not in a user-friendly format. The authors use the Geo-Referenced Infrastructure and Demographic Data for Development (GRID3) program to show the potential of using basic indicators to form the basis of workshops with educational planners. Using geo-referenced maps, the chapter investigates whether the current educational practices are in compliance with the national education policy in Nigeria. The maps also help to analyze the progress toward inter-sectoral SDG tracking. The chapter uses various case studies to demonstrate the potential of geo-reference planning and shows that ESD that is data-driven at the subnational level has the potential of demonstrating cross-sectoral strategies that could meet multiple SDGs.

Data-driven planning across all sectors is critical. Braun et. al. focus on strengthening national and global policies by local-level adaptation. They focus on decision-makers in various sectors as a part of the government or in communities to be able to rely on the most updated scientific knowledge for climate adaptation strategies. The authors note that there is a mismatch between national policies and on-the-ground realities. The authors address the theme of the book by discussing the need to focus and strengthen ground-level cross-sectoral strategies and provide field-based processes in Bangladesh, Ethiopia, Latin America, and the Caribbean that were followed to expand the cross-sectoral dialogue and learning.

The chapter yet again brings to our notice that climate crises need cross-sectoral collaborations.

In a similar vein, Malhotra and Ben Amor use health interventions in schools to highlight the much-needed cross-sectoral strategies at an institutional level. ESD requires the holistic development of children. Thus cross-sectoral strategies need to address all aspects (e.g., intellectual, mental, physical, emotional, and social abilities) of a child's growth. The authors provide field-based interventions that target Social Emotional Learning, sexual and reproductive health awareness, and provide student-centered counseling to help students stay in school. The authors situate their arguments in their designed and implemented programs in Uganda and India. The findings support the claim that the Social Emotional Learning needs of the youth are better served with cross-sectoral collaborations included in their formal education (through schools). The authors also note that such interventions should be student-centered, culturally relevant, and need a long-term commitment.

There is no doubt that communities need to be included in any educational planning. As an extension of Braun et al.'s chapter on local adaptation of national policies, Schlegelmilch and Sury's chapter on disaster preparedness note that each community is different and having only one disaster-preparedness plan will not work for all communities. Community members need to own and co-create a resilience and preparedness plan that is inclusive and science-driven. The chapter focuses on child-centered resilience plans as many times the children get left behind in important dialogues. The authors discuss the Resilient Children/Community (RCRC) Initiative of the National Center for Disaster Preparedness (NCDP) at Columbia University and Save the Children (STC). The initiative aims to create a model of child-focused community resilience by strengthening community-based preparedness plans. Through this example, the authors focus on the effective communication of evidence-based concepts in disaster research and humanitarian response. The intervention shows us the potential that the community has in building disaster literacy and preparedness through education, outreach, and communication. The book includes disaster preparedness using another community-based education approach by educating the farmers on weather-related risks. Diro et al. use educational games with scenarios that help the farmers to measure their risk. They then introduce weather-index insurance, a financial product which without education has concepts difficult to understand. The authors using their gamification methodology are able to break this information barrier and are able to find a way through educating the masses. Financial literacy related to climate risk needs continuous reinforcement. On the back end, sophisticated data-driven modeling is required for weather prediction. Educating the farmers in international contexts also requires knowledge of their cultures that need to be included in creating educational activities to explain difficult concepts such as weather-index insurance.

The same thread of community involvement and empowerment is continued in Iyengar, van Geen, and Munson's chapter. The authors use a citizen-science approach to support the government system and get the youth empowered to understand the local sustainable development problems. They were able to demonstrate that cross-collaboration is needed at the local government level which makes the community involvement more streamlined. The chapter also narrates that ESD could use the citizen-science model to build individual agency. The students in this case are empowered and develop a sense of community ownership to collectively tackle the fluoride problem. The chapter demonstrates that confidence-building, and challenging the gender power dynamics need to be incorporated into the science-based training. This community-based education model also has links to higher education institutions as well as governmental support which helps the youth to get the support needed to get organized for water testing. The chapter demonstrates that for a long-lasting impact, interdisciplinary approaches are needed to tackle sustainable development problems at the local level.

With the COVID-19 pandemic, ESD has got an opportunity to "Build-Back Better" and rethink strategies that have not been traditionally explored to the fullest. Xu's chapter provides insight into ESD's future, a future that prepares all learners to explore lifelong learning opportunities. E.I. LIVE provides the outreach and potential of technology to reach the masses. The chapter shows how ESD can connect with science in a way that is digestible so that the wider audience understands the larger phenomenon of climate change and connect it to their local environment. Educating the masses to connect the SDGs to local issues needs to be an ongoing "free" education.

As the readers go through this book, it is important to keep in mind the authors' treatment of cross-sectoral strategies. The book includes many case studies and field-based examples. The focus of the book is to provide the reader with detailed information on the processes that were followed in these cross-sectoral strategies. The book illustrated different ways of making cross-sectoral strategies a priority in ESD. A key takeaway from the book is the use of interdisciplinary approaches to design and implement ESD strategies—fluoride mitigation, disaster preparedness, and health education to name a few. The readers are asked to keep a keen eye on the ways interdisciplinary work could be made possible through ESD. Community buy-in or community collaboration is a theme that runs throughout the book. It is easier said than done. This book hopes to provide a plethora of ways in which the community becomes the center of decision-making to have a long-lasting impact on the intervention. In this age of sustainable development, it is important that we use this book to make all learners lifelong learners of sustainability. How we do that is explained in Stafford Ocansey's framework of civic literacy. The readers are asked to keep the civic-literacy conceptual framework in mind to ask critical questions about the purpose of ESD and the type of education we need to strive toward a greener and healthier future.

Reference

UNESCO (2011). *Education Counts Towards the Millennium Development Goals UNESCO*. http://unesdoc.unesco.org/images/0019/001902/190214e.pdf. Date Accessed May 25, 2022.

2

Action for a Sustainable Future

The Key Role of Civic Education

Tara Stafford Ocansey

Introduction

We are living in one of the most tumultuous times in history. As countries struggle to control a deadly pandemic, many are reckoning with historically oppressive and discriminatory systems of colonization, globalization/corporatization, criminal justice, and more. Education is often exalted as a panacea to our myriad problems, and indeed a quality education holds much potential for contributing to a more just, sustainable society. Yet globally, dominating education systems are still largely based on Western models first developed during the Industrial Revolution, focused on preparing productive workers to contribute to never-ending economic growth. Gaudelli (2020) describes this dominating model of education as viewing "environment as a resource trove/limitless dump," resulting in today's climate crisis, an intersecting culmination of the impacts of oppressive, discriminatory systems that have created a relative handful of people enjoying extreme wealth as half the world lives in poverty (World Bank, 2018).

The urgency of the climate crisis and contributing systems of inequality demand an education that equips learners to understand and address these intersecting challenges, notably through civic participation. Within the Sustainable Development Agenda 2030 Education Goal 4, Target 4.7 aims to "ensure all learners acquire knowledge and skills . . . to promote sustainable development, including . . . through education for sustainable development and sustainable lifestyles, human rights, gender equality, promotion of a culture of peace and non-violence, global citizenship, and appreciation of cultural diversity and of culture's contribution to sustainable development." This goal calls for a renewal of what Jamieson et al. (2011) calls the "civic mission" of schools to prepare learners for participation in public life.

If universal access to education is to equip learners to play roles in pursuit of a more equitable, sustainable world, the cultivation of civic knowledge, skills, values, and agency to mobilize for change, or what together can be called "civic literacy," must be key. Numerous education frameworks introduced and evolved in recent decades can be considered under the umbrella of schools' civic mission and a broad definition of civic literacy, offering enriching, intersecting approaches to teaching civic education through the lens of issues in learners' lives and our shared local and global challenges. Figure 2.1 helps visualize how these frameworks work together to inform a rich framework for civic literacy.

One contributing framework, Education for Sustainable Development (ESD), as outlined in SDG Target 4.7, grows out of the field of environmental education dating back to the 1960s, evolving from discourse based on the natural sciences toward socioecological explorations of environmental concerns and their

Figure 2.1 Civic-literacy framework.

intersections with poverty and injustice along the lines of race, gender, and class (Hume and Barry, 2015).ust society.

The early twenty-first century has also seen a new emphasis on frameworks for twenty-first-century skills, global citizenship, and Social Emotional Learning (SEL), all of which can be facilitated through action-oriented civic education. An early framework of twenty-first-century skills from the US Department of Education (2002) calls for education connected to learners' lives and reflects how people learn by emphasizing media literacy, communication skills, critical and systems thinking, ability to frame, analyze, and solve problems, creativity, and social responsibility. This framework further calls for content that applies twenty-first-century skills to collaboratively understand and address global issues and exercise rights and obligations of citizenship at local to international levels.

Similarly, Education for Global Citizenship, also outlined in SDG 4.7, is defined by UNESCO as "empowering learners . . . to become active promoters of more peaceful, tolerant, inclusive, secure and sustainable societies."[1] The recent elevation of frameworks for SEL, particularly in light of COVID-19, offers the potential to promote ethics of empathy, resilience, and understanding of one's beliefs, biases, and emotional responses. In their briefing paper on civic education, Levine and Kawashima-Ginsburg (2017) include SEL as part of an extended civic education framework, yet, as Simmons (2019) notes, many popular SEL frameworks do not explicitly confront societal inequities, and SEL teaching is often divorced from larger sociopolitical contexts.

Education frameworks that explicitly confront societal inequities and injustices include peace and human rights education frameworks. Peace education seeks to dismantle all forms of violence—including structural violence such as colonialism, imperialism, and racism—and build a more just, peaceful, and happier world (Hantzopoulos and Bajaj, 2021). Human rights education invokes a vision that centers on human dignity within an ethical framework primarily concerned with addressing societal inequality and oppression, drawing on an ethos of duties within the community and human rights legal standards (Tibbits, 2017). In recent years, human rights have embraced the principle of collective rights—not just individual rights—as well as the pursuit of environmental justice.

With regard to the human right to health and well-being, Feldheim (2017) argues that civic health (i.e., civic engagement, social capital, and political participation) is a key component to building healthy communities and promoting strong public health ecosystems. Education frameworks such as peace and human rights education can equip learners with skills to interrogate social determinants of health, which according to the World Health Organization (n.d.), can be defined as "the conditions in which people are born, grow, live, work and age, including the health system." Considering the disparate impacts of the COVID-19 pandemic on communities of color in countries like the United States, a civic education approach that includes these critical aspects of peace and human rights education can guide learners to explore the root causes of these disparate health impacts and to reflect on their roles in promoting public health based on their own social determinants of health.

This overview of contributing frameworks is not exhaustive. Still, it highlights how these frameworks share an ethos of educating about rights and duties within communities, exploring root causes of inequalities and injustices, and promoting individual and collective agency to promote solutions and social change. When facilitated in ways that guide learners through problem identification and understanding of civic structures within which learners can engage to promote change, civic education offers a broader framework within which these more nuanced approaches can find a home.

While civic education holds great promise for enabling learning in these broad, interconnected areas for twenty-first-century citizenship, in the United States and other parts of the world, civic education has been neglected over the past half-century, as concerns over global competitiveness and security have spurred science, technology, engineering, and math (STEM) into the upper echelons of education investment. At the same time, increasingly polarized societies struggle to find consensus on what should be taught in civics (EAD, 2021). The politically contentious nature of civic education has meant twenty-first-century US Federal education reforms, including No Child Left Behind and Race to the Top, failed to address it (EAD, 2021). Low investment and prioritization over the past half-century have contributed to record low levels of basic civic literacy and vast inequities in who participates in civic life. The National Assessment of Education Progress (NAEP) in Civics data show that the percentage of high school seniors in the United States reaching proficiency has flatlined around 23 percent in recent decades (NAEP, 2014), that low average masking vast inequities. Students in eighth grade with college-educated parents not qualifying for free/reduced lunch were over five times more likely to be proficient in civics than students whose parents have up to a high school diploma and do qualify for free/reduced lunch (NAEP, 2014). This translates to disparities in civic engagement activities like voting. In 2016, young adults who had attended college were 20 percent more likely to vote than those who had not (Levine and Kawashima-Ginsburg, 2017).

This chapter considers civic literacy a crux where these frameworks for an expanded civic mission of education intersect by equipping learners to identify the connections between challenges they see in their communities and globally and to understand the systems they can influence through inclusive forms of civic engagement. The chapter offers a brief discussion of the literature on contemporary frameworks for inclusive, equitable civic education and some common barriers to more transformational implementation of civic education in today's education systems. The chapter explores select civic education programs in formal and nonformal settings that promote learner agency to mobilize for change. The chapter concludes with recommendations for how education systems can transform to effectively develop learners' civic literacy and agency toward a more equitable, sustainable world, and improved well-being for all.

Common Challenges in Civic Education

Even in established democracies, deciding what knowledge, skills, and attitudes should form the basis of civic education can often become contentious. Civic education curriculum—and learners by extension—are influenced by every major societal institution—family, economy, religion, media, and government, while also facing pressures from political and social movements to reflect societal concerns and challenges, with individual actions having the potential to influence the greater society (Torney-Purta et al., 1999). This political nature of civic education is a primary challenge, with decisions about what content should be taught embedded in debates about who should have citizenship and other rights (Beadie and Burkholder, 2021). For example, many contemporary civic education resources still gloss over Black history without interrogating the ways slavery and legacies of discrimination continue to deny Black humanity and equal rights. Pushes to tell more accurate, integrative histories like the NY Times' *1619 Project* have faced immense backlash, with some states in the United States, such as Texas, taking legislative measures to prevent teachers from discussing current events in classrooms (Agnew, 2021).

Quigley (2000) notes that a common challenge of civic education globally is "the gap between ideas and reality." Democratic ideas enshrined in founding documents often fail to translate to the realities of marginalized groups within democratic nations. Research has shown that civic education can promote civic equality (Gould, 2011), yet, as Mirra and Garcia (2017) discuss, civic education often prioritizes the instillation of patriotism and admiration of national heroes and virtues of the form of government without discussing the current national challenges. Further, standard definitions of citizenship seldom recognize alternative forms of engagement more commonly used among young people and people of color—social media, music, poetry, and public art—as expressions of active citizenship (Levinson, 2010; Greer, 2021).

Beadie and Burkholder (2021) explain how those who do not face the threat of their rights being suppressed may feel less compelled to understand their rights than marginalized groups who fear suppression of rights. This is evidenced by Sirin, Valentino, and Villalobos (2017) in their exploration of "Group Empathy Theory," which looks at how members of disadvantaged minority groups come to support the rights of other disadvantaged minority groups, even when they are in direct competition for rights and resources, while those in the dominant majority show less support for disadvantaged groups. The authors explain that individuals are more likely to experience greater quantity and quality interactions with people from different backgrounds in schools than in other contexts. Therefore, education can boost empathy for people outside of one's own group as characterized by race, class, religion, immigration status, or other demographic factors. Such research shows how social-emotional skills like empathy overlap with civic education that builds skills for listening and understanding across differences.

Scholars of civic education broadly conceptualize civic education as a composite of three interrelated areas—civic knowledge, civic skills, and civic virtues/dispositions (Quigley, 2000; Gould, 2011; EAD, 2021). Further Levine and Kawashima-Ginsburg (2017) outline "six proven practices":

- Civics, government, and related courses implemented with effective pedagogies
- Deliberation of current, controversial issues to cultivate skills and dispositions for fostering productive conversations across political and social differences
- Service-learning that includes community engagement, reflection, and study of implicated issues
- Student-led voluntary associations
- Student voice in schools
- Simulations of adult civic roles

Adding onto this, Levine and Kawashima-Ginsburg (2017) note that civic learning must address unequal distribution of education resources and opportunities across communities, start early as a priority from K-12, and prepare students to navigate today's civic climate, where viral disinformation on social media makes it difficult to navigate complex social and environmental challenges in increasingly polarized, diverse societies.

Exploring Applications of an Action-oriented Civics Education Framework

A comparative desk review of in-school programs and community-based Action Civics initiatives was conducted to identify common features among the approaches and practices of effective programs. For some programs, key informants were interviewed to share their civic education experiences in school and/or discuss the curriculum and activities of their nonformal civic education programs. Gray literature such as program reports, organizational documents, and web and multimedia content were reviewed to understand program features, including educator training, curriculum, classroom practice, learner engagement, and community connection.

Levine and Kawashima-Ginsburg (2017) note that Action Civics shares many characteristics with the proven service-learning practice, helping learners develop citizen identities. Generation Citizen (GC) is a US-based nonprofit organization addressing discrepancies in civic engagement by delivering Action Civics education in low-income schools and promoting state policy for Action Civics curriculum. GC defines Action Civics education as "a student-centered, experiential approach to civics education in which young people learn about democracy by actively working to address issues in their communities" (GC, 2019). GC conducted interviews with a racially and geographically diverse group of youth from underserved communities across the United States on what they see to be transformative kinds of civic learning experiences (GC, 2019). Based on their findings, GC designed a toolkit to support youth civic engagement in underserved communities that builds on the three commonly conceived civic education areas of civic knowledge, skills, and values, adding a fourth building block of civic efficacy—or cultivation of learners' belief in their ability to make a difference—which GC sees as key for promoting civic equality. Based on their literature review, research, and visioning process with youth, GC proposes that any solution aimed at supporting civic education and empowerment of youth from underserved communities should be youth-centered, contextually grounded, emotionally supportive, activating, and courageously resilient, acknowledging the connection between civic empowerment and learner's social-emotional support and skills. GC's curriculum is facilitated by teachers who receive professional development support from GC. The curriculum begins by engaging students in a democratic process to choose an issue to address, validating young people's experiences and perceptions. Learners are then guided to research root causes and potential solutions, build goal-setting skills, identify decision-makers, and develop tactics to influence decision-makers. Students then implement their action plans, with each term culminating in a student conference where participating classes come together to share projects. To help equip more teachers beyond GC's capacity for direct school support with skills for facilitating the Action Civics curriculum, GC developed a free online teacher professional development course.[2]

While GC sets a high standard for in-school Action Civics, the organization operates separately from school systems, identifying where GC curriculum overlaps with official curricula and filling gaps where existing curricula fail to promote civic efficacy. Where schools fall short—largely due to concerns over politicization of curriculum and teachers' concerns over lack of issue expertise (Simmons, 2019), community-based, nonformal approaches can engage young people in direct, empowering ways.

In the case of GC's program in New York, GC's advocacy played an influential role in the New York City school district's adoption of their Civics for All program in 2018, equipping educators with a K-12 curriculum, resources, and experiential learning opportunities to facilitate with their students. Activities of the Civics for All program include partnering with the city government every year to register eligible high school students to vote. Since its 2018 launch, the program has helped register over 60,000 students to vote. The program also aims to promote student voice through activities such as participatory budgeting. Students allocate portions of their school budgets toward community projects and other student-identified priorities. Further, the program engages the community and civics-focused organizations like GC as school partners to bring civics learning and action beyond the classroom to address community challenges (NYC DoE, 2021).

As Educating for American Democracy (2021) notes, civil society and higher education institutions can do more to translate the best scholarship in relevant fields into K-12 content, pedagogical guidance, and collaborative learning opportunities to help equip education systems and educators to teach effective civic education. One example of higher education supporting K-12 ESD with an emphasis on civic skills is the Eco Ambassador initiative of the Center for

Sustainable Development at Columbia University's Earth Institute (CSD). The program blends an Action Civics approach to addressing sustainability challenges through the lens of the SDGs, connecting K-12 learners with leading earth, climate, and social scientists. The program builds learners' skills for conducting research on sustainability issues and advocating for solutions to decision-makers. The program partners with interested schools, educators, and civil society organizations to engage students and teachers in supplemental learning activities that build skills for problem identification, data analysis, storytelling, and community organizing. The program also engages global youth leaders and educators to help develop content for teaching action-oriented lessons to address sustainability challenges. Like GC's approach to building a teacher professional development platform to extend their reach, CSD launched a free online teacher training course to integrate action-oriented ESD across subjects.

Civically inclined youth have also helped fill the gap through engagement in various kinds of youth activism. For example, recent years have seen a steep rise in youth climate activism. Many organizations engage in community-based civic education as part of their organizing, educating youth participants in the science of climate change and its ecological and social impacts and training youth in civic skills to promote desired policy solutions. Many youth organizations focus on traditional civic lobbying, petitioning, and media campaigning. In contrast, others focus more on nonviolent direct action and use art, music, and social media to build support.

While these programs operate separately from schools, many outreach to schools to share opportunities for young people. *Our Climate* is one such organization that empowers youth to "analyze and advocate for science-based and equitable climate policies that secure a living planet."[3] *Our Climate* organizes a multitiered leadership development program to build students' skills to coordinate their peers and communities in climate advocacy initiatives, build public support, and engage with lawmakers. To make students aware of their opportunities, organizers reach out to administrators of area public schools. One high school student involved in the Our New York, *Our Climate* chapter got involved after receiving an email from her public school and participated in their week-long Summer Policy Camp, where she took part in training on the science of the climate crisis, climate policy, lobbying, storytelling, writing media content, and organizing rallies. When discussing the differences between her civic education in school and her activism, she explained, "When I started getting involved outside of school, I realized how much I was missing in school," including how climate connects to racism and socioeconomic issues.

Treeage, a New York-based, youth-led climate justice organization, organizes youth through "The Hive," their network of students organizing their classmates and other youth in their communities to push their schools and elected representatives to enact legislative change for climate justice and racial equality. These youth leaders go through similar training in traditional civic engagement skills, recruiting local political candidates to champion their platforms, and helping turn out voters for their endorsed candidates.

While many youth-led organizations focus on these more traditional skills for civic engagement, others include less conventional forms. Sunrise Movement has "art and banner drops" as one of their key tactics alongside protest rallies and other more traditional letter-writing methods and voter turnout. Extinction Rebellion (XR) takes this further, viewing strategies that help build a "regenerative culture" as core to achieving their aims. XR's core value of creating a regenerative culture is an example of how social-emotional competencies can be facilitated through civic engagement, with XR defining regenerative culture as "mutually support categories" of self-care, care for each other during actions, interpersonal care, community care, and people and planet care.[4] These approaches offer ideas for how K-12 classes in the arts can support the development of learners' civic identity through creative expression.

While strategies and tactics differ among these examples of youth-led organizations engaging in nonformal Action Civics education, what they share is strategically designed leadership development pathways for youth participants and a training curriculum that blends issue content knowledge with skills for civic engagement that immediately encourage youth participants to put to use through actions.

These organizations also see schools as key hubs for engagement and change. Schools are places where such organizations recruit youth participants and where youth participants turn to encourage their peers to become more civically active. Through Our Climate's model, in 2020, they recruited and trained 1,299 youth leaders across six US states and Washington, DC, who in turn engaged with 354 elected officials, and held 309 events (including virtual events) (Our Climate, 2020). In the case of GC, their internal monitoring conducted using pre-and post-surveys of teachers and students participating in their programs found that, according to teachers participating in the 2016–17 academic year, 80 percent of students increased in civic knowledge, 72 percent in civic skills, and 62 percent in civic motivation, while 90 percent of surveyed students believed they could make a difference in their community (GC, n.d.). But what happens in the schools that don't help facilitate connections between these opportunities for civic education outside the classroom? Bridging the civic engagement gap requires all students to have access to civic education and opportunities to learn and explore ways to harness their voice and power to create change. How can schools facilitate meaningful civic learning and empowerment opportunities for all?

Way Forward

The report *Educating for American Democracy* (EAD, 2021) argues, "The time has come to recommit to the education of our young people for informed, authentic, and engaged citizenship" (p. 8). The "ideologically, philosophically, and demographically diverse historians, political scientists, and educators" (p. 8) who contributed to the report note that civic education must be rooted in local cultures and the needs of communities. The authors, therefore, describe the report not as a curricular prescription but as a roadmap for inquiry-based pedagogical practices and learning opportunities that can promote "skills and virtues for productive, civil disagreement" (p.8). The roadmap seeks to promote depth over breadth, correcting current models that rapidly cycle through the same history year after year by encouraging education decision-makers to consider how they can "support instructors in helping students move between concrete, narrative, and chronological learning and thematic and abstract or conceptual learning" (p. 17). Key Content Themes include civic participation, contemporary debates and possibilities, and responsibility to the natural world, while Pedagogical Principles facilitate growth mindset, inquiry, and student agency.

Some US states and districts are putting forth mandates for civic education that is honest about history while preparing youth with skills for building more equitable, sustainable futures, yet mandates alone are inadequate. Policies must also support teacher professional development, invest in quality curriculum and assessments, and use data to continually assess and improve civic education implementation (Levine and Kawashima-Ginsburg, 2017). To guide education decision-makers in developing civic education that is relevant and responsive to local needs, EAD (2021) proposes five design challenges that attempt to balance honest exploration of historical and contemporary national failings with belief and pride in a democratic system in which learners' can use their voice to make an impact. By using these challenges as a guide, education decision-makers are encouraged to consider questions like "How can we help students pursue civic action that is authentic, responsible, and informed?" and "How do we simultaneously teach the value and the danger of compromise for a free, diverse, and self-governing people?" (p. 17). These questions can help educators develop civics education that engages students in the requisite research, foundational understanding of the issues they care about, and facilitation of discourse across differences that can inform their civic action to be most impactful.

In September 2021, New York City's Department of Education became the first school district in the United States to commit to the EAD roadmap to strengthen its approach to K-12 civic education. The district's commitment to EAD builds on the district's Civics for All program outlined earlier. While this example from New York offers hope that progress is being made, EAD (2021) explains that even well-resourced schools operate with outdated standards and inadequate curricula. Historians and political scientists have made significant gains in incorporating historically marginalized voices and innovative approaches in historical narratives and analysis of political systems. Yet, few examples of that work are being translated to help create integrative historical narratives and frameworks to support K-12 social studies education. Governments can incentivize higher education institutions and civil society organizations to partner with education systems to develop a more inclusive, participatory curriculum, teacher pedagogical skills, and collaborative learning opportunities.

While civic education as a subject requires investment, civic engagement opportunities and exploration of connected concepts like ESD can also be woven across disciplines, including languages, sciences, and the arts (Matto et al., 2017). Therefore, curriculum developers and educators across disciplines must identify opportunities for integrating civic engagement and ESD opportunities across subjects to help fulfill schools' civic mission for a more sustainable, equitable future for all.

Notes

1 https://en.unesco.org/themes/gced
2 https://www.kickstartactioncivics.org/
3 https://ourclimate.us/policy-principles/
4 https://rebellion.global/about-us/

References

Agnew, D. (May 5, 2021). GOP Lawmakers Want to Ban "woke philosophies" Like Critical Race Theory in Texas Schools. *Texas Tribune*. https://www.texastribune.org/2021/05/05/texas-critical-race-theory-schools-legislature/. Date Accessed May 25, 2022.

Beadie, N., & Burkholder, Z. (2021). From the Diffusion of Knowledge to the Cultivation of Agency: A Short History of Civic Education Policy and Practice in the United States. *Educating for Civic Reasoning and Discourse*. National Academy of Education, pp. 109–55.

Department of Education (2002). Learning for the 21st Century: A Report and MILE Guide for21st Century Skills. Prepared by the Partnership for 21st Century Skills. www.21stcenturyskills.org.

Educating for American Democracy (EAD) 2021. Educating for American Democracy: Excellence in History and Civics for All Learners. *iCivics*, March 2. www.educatingforamericandemocracy.org.

Feldheim, M.A. (2017). Developing Healthy Communities: Civic Health Symposium. *Journal of Health and Human Services Administration*, 39(4), pp. 427–35.

Gaudelli, W. (2020). The Trouble of Western Education. *On Education: Journal for Research and Debate*. https://www.oneducation.net/no-07_april-2020/the-trouble-of-western-education/. Date Accessed May 25, 2022

Generation Citizen (n.d.). *By The Numbers*. https://generationcitizen.org/our-impact/by-the-numbers/. Date Accessed May 25, 2022.

Generation Citizen (2009). https://www.mightycause.com/organization/Generation-Citizen.

Gould, J. (Ed.). (2011). Guardian of Democracy: The Civic Mission of Schools. Campaign for the Civic Mission of Schools and The Leonore Annenberg Institute for Civics of Annenberg Public Policy Center at the University of Pennsylvania.

Greer, M. (2021). Civic Engagement and Inclusion Through Art. *National Civic Review*, 109(4), pp. 30–4. National Civic League.

Hantzopoulos, M., & Bajaj, M. (2021). *Educating for Peace and Human Rights: An Introduction*. New York: Bloomsbury Publishing.

Hume, T., & Barry, J. (2015). Environmental Education and Education for Sustainable Development. In *International Encyclopedia of Social and Behavioral Sciences*, 2nd ed. (pp. 733–9). Elsevier. https://doi.org/10.1016/B978-0-08-097086-8.91081-X.

Jonathan, Kathleen Hall Jamieson, Peter Levine, Ted McConnell, & David B. Smith, eds. (2011). *Guardian of Democracy: The Civic Mission of Schools*. Rep. Philadelphia: Leonore Annenberg Institute for Civics of the Annenberg Public Policy Center at the University of Pennsylvania, 2011. Print. https://www.carnegie.org/publications/guardian-of-democracy-the-civic-mission-of-schools/. Date Accessed May 25, 2022.

Levine, P., & Kawashima-Ginsberg, K. (2017). The Republic Is (still) at Risk–and Civics Is Part of the Solution. Briefing Paper for the Democracy at a Crossroads National Summit, September 17. Jonathan M. Tisch College of Civic Life, Tufts University,

Medford, MA. https://civxnow.org/wp-content/uploads/2021/08/Equity-in-Civic-Eduation-White-Paper_Public.pdf. Date Accessed May 25, 2022.

Levinson, M. (2010). The Civic Empowerment Gap: Defining the Problem and Locating Solutions. In Lonnie Sherrod, Judith Torney-Purta, & Constance A. Flanagan (Eds.), *Handbook of Research on Civic Engagement* (pp. 331–61). Hoboken, NJ: John Wiley & Sons.

Matto, E., McCartney, A.R.M., Bennion, E., & Simpson, D. (2017). *Teaching Civic Education Across the Disciplines*. Washington DC: American Political Science Association.

Mirra, N., & Garcia, A. (2017). Civic Participation Reimagined: Youth Interrogation and Innovation in the Multimodal Public Sphere. *Review of Research in Education*, 41, pp. 136–58. American Educational Research Association.

National Center for Education Statistics (2014). NAEP 8th Grade Data Tabulation by CIRCLE. https://nces.ed.gov/nationsreportcard/naepdata/report.aspx.

New York City Department of Education (2021). Civics for All Info Hub. https://infohub.nyced.org/in-our-schools/programs/civics-for-all.

Our Climate (2020). Our Climate 2020 Annual Report: The Stories of Our Impact. https://drive.google.com/file/d/1H6YjqiSFiOzjPmqZdlBieIxgJJDVB31k/view.

Quigley, C. (2000). *Global Trends in Civic Education*. Bandung: Center for Civic Education.

Simmons, D. (2019). Why We Can't Afford Whitewashed Social-Emotional Learning. A.C.S.D. https://www.ascd.org/el/articles/why-we-cant-afford-whitewashed-social-emotional-learning.

Sirin, C.V., Valentino, N.A., & Villalobos, J.D. (2017). The Social Causes and Political Consequences of Group Empathy. *Political Psychology*, 38(3), pp. 427–48. International Society of Political Psychology. https://www.jstor.org/stable/45094364.

Tibbitts, F.L. (2017). Revisiting "Emerging Models of Human Rights Education". *International Journal of Human Rights Education*, 1(1). https://repository.usfca.edu/ijhre/vol1/iss1/2.

Torney-Purta, J., Schwille, J., & Amadeo, J.A. (1999). *Civic Education across Countries: Twenty-Four Case Studies from the IEA Civic Education Project*. Amsterdam: International Association for the Evaluation of Educational Achievement (IEA).

UNESCO (n.d.). What is Education for Sustainable Development? https://en.unesco.org/themes/education-sustainable-development/what-is-esd.

World Bank (2018). *Piecing Together the Poverty Puzzle: Poverty and Shared Prosperity 2018*. Washington, DC: The World Bank. https://openknowledge.worldbank.org/bitstream/handle/10986/30418/9781464813306.pdf.

World Health Organization (n.d.). *Social Determinants of Health*. https://www.who.int/health-topics/social-determinants-of-health.

3

Citizen Science to Educate and Empower a Community Exposed to a Toxicant

A Case Study Concerning Well-water Fluoride in Alirajpur District of Madhya Pradesh, India

Radhika Iyengar, Alexander Van Geen, and Charlotte Munson

Toxicants are usually heterogeneously distributed in the environment. Heterogeneity complicates prediction, but a toxicant can often be avoided once a distribution is known. This simple idea set the stage in late 2019 for engaging a rural community of Madhya Pradesh to test its public wells for potentially toxic fluoride levels in the water. Ingesting some fluoride prevents tooth decay, but drinking water containing too much fluoride can cause skeletal deformation and affect intellectual function. Over three months, a class of sixty master's students in social work from a local college sought out over 1,000 wells in their villages, tested them for fluoride using a field kit, painted the pump heads blue or yellow according to the result, and encouraged users of unsafe wells to seek a nearby safe well instead. This chapter describes the citizen-science project and the experience that students had while on the project.

This case study is from the Alirajpur district in rural Central India. This primarily rural district is located in the western corner of Madhya Pradesh, a state in Central India. The district's socioeconomic indicators are among the weakest in the country. According to the 2011 Census, the district had the lowest adult literacy rate. The government, therefore, has a special responsibility to serve a population that is grappling with hunger, poverty, and lack of employment opportunities.

The present chapter addresses sustainable development through education via citizen science and community involvement. The chapter first provides a background to the government structure to understand the context; it then explains the citizen-science model applied to this study. This is followed by the preliminary results from this exploratory study. The following section discusses the educational approaches attempted to change peoples' behavior and promote safe water source use. The final section draws the key lessons from this approach on education for sustainable development, ending with a conclusion and a forward-looking research agenda.

Governmental Structure

The government's Public Health and Engineering Department (PHED) is responsible for providing water for the district in India (equivalent to a county in the United States). PHED works under the supervision of the district collector, a civil servant of the Indian Administrative Services. This structure is a prototype of all the rest of the districts in the country. PHED is responsible for water management, including purification, sanitation, sewage, drilling tube wells, connecting the villages to piped water through significant rivers, and its treatment. PHED needs to consider equity issues since it is responsible for providing water to all 729,000 residents of the District irrespective of their economic status. However, Alirajpur's PHED struggles with lack of funding, bureaucratic delays, and lack of human power and therefore works to meet the villagers' expectation of an essential commodity such as water. PHED has its own set of challenges with a lack of adequate funds and a vast set of unmet needs. It has to implement the national water-related strategies in a district that has a crippling economic situation and impoverished population to serve.

PHED is run mainly by engineers hired through a lengthy process at the district level. Therefore, the staff is outstanding in resolving technical issues but are not necessarily community mobilizers. PHED is headed by a chief engineer, followed by an assistant engineer who helps take all decisions as directed by the collector/magistrate of the district. Each block (a sub-division under the district; Alirajpur has six blocks) has its own PHED representative responsible for all the waterworks in the block. Each block contains roughly 115 villages.

In principle, anyone should have access to safe water, but sadly this is all too often not the reality on the ground. In Alirajpur district, hundreds of wells installed by the government provide drinking water that, by and large, should be free of microbial pathogens. Unfortunately, natural geologic processes cause some of these wells to yield water that does not meet the World Health Organization's guideline for fluoride of 1.5 milligrams per liter. Elevated fluoride levels impact wells in other parts of India, some much more so than in Alirajpur (Podgorski et al., 2018). Regular consumption of water that does not meet this guideline can cause dental fluorosis, weakening of the bones, and neurological ailments but health impacts also vary considerably from one person to the next. PHED has been aware of the problem for decades and is expected to regularly test these thousands of government-provided water sources, an almost impossible task. PHED needs to gather such data manually and is the designated custodian of an up-to-date database of all high-fluoride tube wells. PHED is also supposed to inform the residents of the district to stop drinking and cooking with the water from these tube wells (washing does not pose a risk) and find the nearest alternative. However, since the education level is low and behavior change requires strategic interventions, many residents continue to consume water from high-fluoride water sources. Poor communication and lack of human power at PHED lead to inaction at the ground level. This causes many village residents, especially children, to have dental fluorosis, a severe health ailment.[1] High fluoride in well water is not new in the district. Groundwater is likely to have been elevated in fluoride for decades if not centuries. What has probably changed is that a growing proportion has switched from drinking surface water that is low in fluoride to groundwater that can be high in fluoride. The Health Department and the Water Department are supposed to work together to educate the villagers and ensure that they don't drink water from high-fluoride sources. Both departments also set up health camps at schools to identify dental fluorosis cases and conduct training for all the community-preschool teachers (Aaganwadis) and community health nurses (ASHA workers). However, many challenges remain due to the lack of an updated database, no geo-referenced maps accessible in digital form, and a lack of coordination with the Education Department. Many short-lived attempts have not led to a sustained effort.

In 2018, a new district collector and magistrate were appointed. Ms. Surbhi Gupta, a young female, came with a keen ear to hear about local problems and try to resolve them. Aware of this fluoride issue for a long time, the research team from Columbia University decided to do a preliminary needs assessment in the district. The district collector supported our interest and opened many doors for us. The district collector's support and Columbia University's technical assistance were critical for this chapter.

In our initial needs assessment,[2] Columbia University researchers went to community preschool centers, spoke to community health workers, visited district colleges, and found out that there were many rumors and misconceptions about the issue.[3] We presented the initial report to the district collector and decided on an action plan. The district collector invited PHED experts and the district's college officials to the meeting. We embarked on a new path to understand and mitigate the impact of high fluoride in the target population together.

Citizen-science Approach

The district collector and Columbia University agreed to enroll a batch of sixty social work students from Alirajpur District College in a well-testing and education program (Iyengar, 2020). Columbia University researchers trained the students to conduct fluoride tests, record data on their smartphones to create a digital map that can be navigated, color paint the tube well according to the content of the fluoride (blue if safe; yellow if high fluoride), and also talk to the village residents and show posters on the ill-effects of fluoride.[4] Using this citizen-science approach, the government's PHED had support from multiple people, and the department did not have to rely on its own ten personnel. They could get help from sixty students who had a defined field-based internship on fluoride awareness.

There was more intergovernmental partnership to address this issue. The District Education Department also joined hands because college students were involved. The Health Department continued to conduct dental fluorosis detection health camps, but now with new energy since the village residents were much more aware. The student interns had made the other residents aware of the problem, and they were more receptive to the Health Department when they conducted their health camps. The villagers also cooperated with the Water Department/ PHED much more than in previous years, as they had heard the same message from their college-going students belonging to the same village.[5]

Literature-driven Models of Citizen Science

The Department of Life Sciences of the Open University defines a citizen scientist as a volunteer who collects and/or processes data as a part of a scientific inquiry (Silvertown 2009). Resnik et al. (2015) define citizen science as "a range of collaborative activities between professional scientists and engaged laypeople (citizens) in the conduct of research" (p. 476).

Trumbull et al. (2000) note that citizen-science projects help the participants in a thinking process that is similar to conducting science investigation. McKinley et al. (2017) suggest that over the last ten years, citizen-science work has grown immensely in the United States and many other countries. Apart from the environmental impact, there are also social implications of citizen-science projects that are worth mentioning (Bonney et al., 2014). Citizen-science projects are a collaboration between scientists, communities, and agencies and these are able to have a wider social local impact to protect the biodiversity in the region. Citizen-science participants usually look for the following outcomes in these projects: interest in science and nature; self-efficacy for science and environmental action; motivation for science and environmental action: skills of science inquiry; data interpretation skills; knowledge of the nature of science; environmental stewardship (Bonney and Phillips (2016).

The Department of Life Sciences of the Open University explains three reasons for the explosion of citizen science. First, easily available technical tools for disseminating information about projects and gathering data from the public (Newman et al., 2012). Collection of field data, including GPS coordinates, with smartphones, are a major improvement over paper-based forms. Second, there is a recognition among the research community that the public can provide free labor, skills, and even finance for research projects. Third, it is based on a requirement from the National Science Foundation in the United States and the Natural Environment Research Council in the United Kingdom that the research projects funded by them should have a science outreach component. Newman et al. (2012) also add that existing databases such as Citizen Science Central, SciStarter, and the Citizen Science Alliance along with training materials and searchable databases will help more citizen-science teams to be formed. Concurrently there is an expanded data computational and storage enhancement using grid and cloud computing (Newman et al., 2012). The authors narrate that the dissemination of results using virtual forums and communities has expanded.

The Department of Life Sciences of the Open University shares some practices that have emerged from these scientific explorations. The department suggested the following practices: (1) data collected by the public must be validated by a process, (2) assumptions must be laid out, (3) methods must be well designed and standardized, (4) it is good practice to have a hypothesis in mind, and (5) volunteers must receive feedback on their contribution. Resnik et al. (2015) explain that citizen participation can provide a valuable resource to scientists in terms of time, effort, and labor. Resnik et al. (2015) note that citizens can provide advice on conducting research that can help the community directly. Public involvement in the development and implementation of science projects will help to build contextual factors in the project, thus making it more relevant to the community. These projects also engage the public through education and outreach which could help in data-driven decision-making (Resnik et al., 2015). However, there are still unresolved practices regarding data quality, data sharing and intellectual property, conflicts of interest, and exploitation (Resnik et al., 2015). Ellwood et al. (2017) add to the list by emphasizing that communicating the insights of the projects not just locally, but in a wider capacity will help to share knowledge and experience and grow the field. The authors also mention that creating interdisciplinary teams will result in the deliberation of various types of strategies. Finally, improving coordination among investments in citizen-science projects is an area that needs much attention.

Results to Date

The students used a reagent to add to well water provided with PHED's standard field kit for fluoride. The reagent is one of several variants of organo-metal dyes that are bleached in proportion to fluoride concentration (Levin et al. 2016). Rather than using the provided color cards as a reference, the students were instructed to analyze a reference sample containing 1.5 milligrams per liter fluoride together with the unknown and compare the two colors. A stronger pink color relative to the reference was interpreted as a lower fluoride concentration; a lighter yellowish color was higher. Test results were recorded along with the well's other characteristics, including a photo of each painted well on the students' smartphones using the SurveyCTO Collect app (surveCTO.com). The app stores the data when the phone is not connected to the network until it can be uploaded to a central server.

Testing over 1,600 wells in one block of Alirajpur district showed that the fluoride content of 9 percent of wells exceeded the WHO guideline (Figure 3.1). The good news was that the geo-referenced data confirmed a high degree of spatial variability in fluoride concentrations in well water. This implied that not all water points were high in fluoride in one village. The next available safe water point was often within walking distance from the high-fluoride water point (Figure 3.2).

Some villages had higher fluoride intensity than the rest of the villages. However, not 100 percent of the water points were high in fluoride in any one

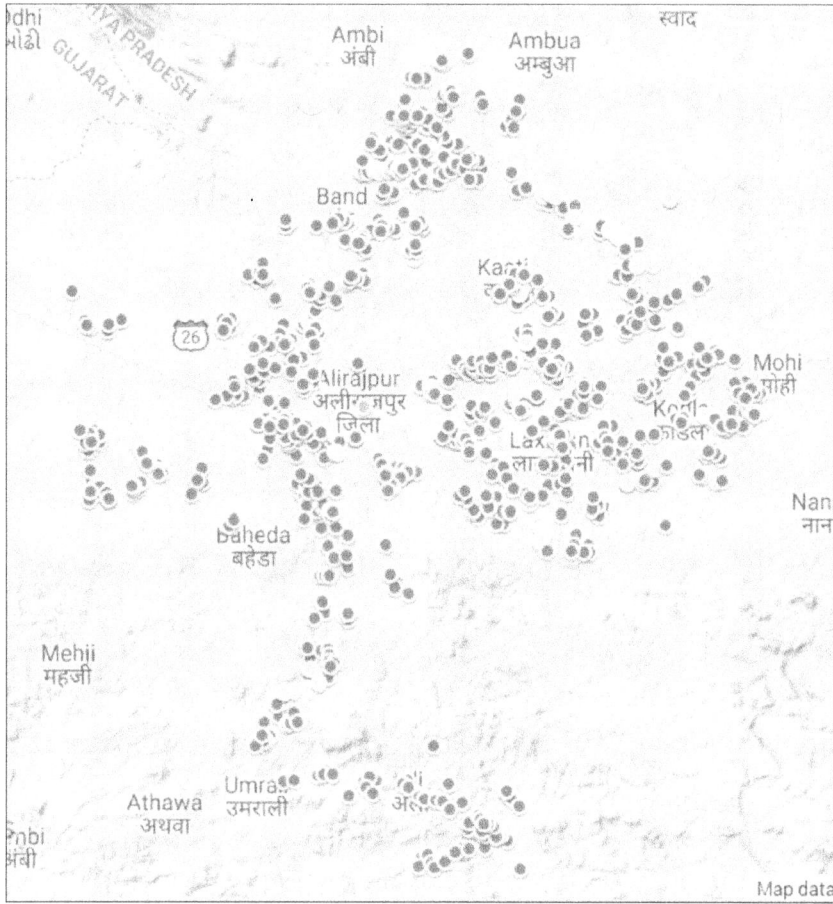

Figure 3.1 Map of wells tested for fluoride in Alirajpur. Wells with a fluoride content <1.5 mg/L are shown with darker dots and >1.5 mg/L are lighter dots.

village. Therefore, the results implied that behavioral interventions would be essential to increase the likelihood that residents are making an effort to obtain their water from a safe well.

The three days training covered fluoride detection and communication of the results to the village results. There was also another element to this study. Sixty percent of the student interns were women. This was the first time young women had to explain a social issue to their village elders and the rest of their families. They were very hesitant at first but soon realized that this information would benefit the rest of the village. They were empowered[6] by their new skill of testing the water from the tube wells, which no one else in their village knew. With this

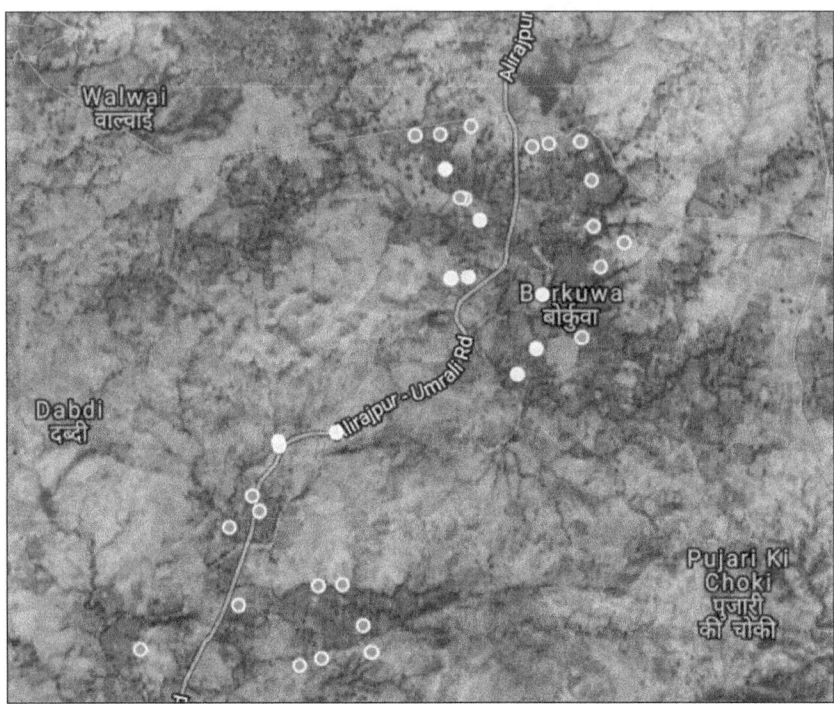

Figure 3.2 Close-up of a tested area shows the mixed spatial distribution of high- and low-fluoride wells. Wells with a fluoride content <1.5 mg/L are shown with darker dots and >1.5 mg/L are lighter dots.

unique skill, they gained new respect in their village, and many people started asking them questions regarding the water fluoride issue.

A lot of the testing and education-related work was now on the students. The college professors and the Columbia University research team started calling this citizen-science army "Fluoride Warriors." The work of "Fluoride Warriors" seems more relevant not just to conduct water testing and inform the village residents about the harmful effect of fluoride, but also to convince them to use water from only the safe sources.

Promoting Safe Water Behaviors Through Posters, Local Theater, and WhatsApp Messaging

The citizen-science approach was likely beneficial in terms of reducing exposure to excessive fluoride, although this has yet to be demonstrated systematically. Many students hailed from the same villages where they were surveying. Therefore, the villages gained a resident fluoride expert through the project. The social work students became trained fluoride testers and were able to explain the harmful effect of fluoride to the village residents. The government officials, often understaffed, were not able to be present in the village regularly. However, they now had a village resident who had the basic minimum training on fluoride detection. Since the messages on fluoride came from their village with a graduate student who was educated and whom the village residents knew personally, it was more likely to be trusted than messages from external people they had not seen before.

Interviews with the social work students revealed that it was challenging to convince the village elders who did not think that fluoride was a major health hazard. Some village elders noted that they have been drinking the same water since they were kids, and they were alive and took it as proof that the water was not harmful. A few others had dismissed communication on fluoride by saying that this was the only source of water close to their house and the most convenient. In discussions with the students, a group of women said that older men especially were not convinced with what they had to share on fluoride. Some of the students noted that they were young and not considered as reliable as the village elders. Therefore, the age and gender of the students also played a role in trusting their message. However, because women were responsible for the family's water supply in most households, and these women were more receptive to communication coming from other women, female students were often more impactful messengers for driving actual behavior change where it counts. Some of the students noted that they were young.

Much work needs to be done systematically measuring all factors that influence individual behavior before anything can be said more conclusively about influencing behavior. The intervention study used various other mediums such as local theater and local songs in multiple locations to pass on the message of high fluoride in the water pumps painted yellow by the students. This managed to draw a lot of attention from the village residents. Theaters were conducted in three locations, two at the village clusters and one in the leading marketplace in the Alirajpur district. Many village residents reached the spot to listen to the theater perform. Many people came forward to ask questions at the market and show the damage the fluoride had done to their teeth. There was considerable interest in the theater. However, since this was only a preliminary round of using theater as a medium, we are uncertain of the impact it created. Also, after the feedback front his first round, the theater group decided to finetune their messaging and act. The study also used pictorial posters and small vehicles with a loudspeaker at marketplaces to narrate simple messages in the local language to make the fluoride issue a public topic. WhatsApp was also used to record these theaters and songs and shared with various lists. However, there is a need for a systematic review of multiple interventions to understand these impacts on behavior change.

Discussions and Future Research Agenda

The study helped the residents to start realizing their social capital. The citizen-science model has the potential of utilizing the community's rich social capital for actional sustainable development agenda. The arts' role in sustainable development needs to be explored further.[7] The study included street theater to make people aware of the fluoride problem in water. Communicating a scientific issue in an accessible form using local language and arts helped have a far wider reach with a long-lasting impact. This aspect needs to be systematically studied.

Formal education systems such as schools and colleges need to have more field-based exploration that affects their lives. Initial needs assessment for the study revealed that school and college students were aware of the symptoms (browning of teeth), but all were unaware of what caused it. Many rumors about fluoride came up as a part of the initial interviews. This included that the browning of the teeth was caused by children not brushing their teeth correctly or because adults consumed a lot of tobacco. At the time of the study, there were no existing modules in the K-12 system or higher education that included any information on fluoride. Education for sustainable development needs to be integrated into the formal school and college curriculum, and most importantly, localized health issues need to be addressed in the syllabus. PHED engineers who are local experts on the topic could be invited as guest speakers to talk about the health hazards of high fluoride. Connecting local issues to education is a priority, and this can only happen with inter-sectoral collaboration at the local level. The community health workers (ASHA) need to talk to the government preschools (Aaganwadis) to talk about the fluoride issue. Most often, national programs are priorities and funding, leaving out local issues that are not prevented in all districts to be left out. This creates a big disconnection with the lived realities of the village residents.

Technology played a significant role in making the topic known at scale relatively quickly. With smartphones, the students could collect the data themselves and view the map to get a bigger picture. In about three months, over

1,600 wells were tested and their fluoride levels were made publicly available. All the different stakeholders could see the map and see the magnitude of the problem. All students, the PHED, and other government departments such as rural development could see the map and look at the villages severely impacted by fluoride.

A forward-looking research agenda should focus on system-wide cross-collaboration of local and state agencies. It should also look at curriculum integration of various sustainable development topics at the schools and colleges.

Implications for Education for Sustainable Development

Some key lessons concerning education in sustainable development emerged from this intervention study and are summaized by Iyengar(2019) and Ghosh (2019). First, sustainable development problems, like the case of high fluoride, need a multidisciplinary approach toward understanding its complexities. To tackle the issue of fluoride detection, we need the science that can quantify the extent of the problem. The problem also needed social science to educate and make people aware of the problem. Second, Education in Sustainable Development is a multi-sectoral issue. The research team had to work with many government departments such as water, rural development, tribal welfare, education, and health. Therefore, inter-departmental collaboration is key to holistic planning interventions. Third, local problems require local solutions to make a dent in long-term sustainable practices. The fluoride kits detection and the solutions were all procured from the Water Department. Imported kits may be more accurate but the approach is not sustainable in the long run. The procedures and solutions need to be integrated into the government machinery to make scale possible. On the technical side, PHED adopted the technique used in this chapter for their work.[8] PHED helped with conducting the training for the students and helped to supervise the students when Columbia University researchers came back. Fourth, this study also validated that external agents cannot drive sustainable change and that involving a wide range of stakeholders is a key recipe for local development. The external agents, in this case, the Columbia University research team, were able to bring in the technical expertise; however, without the support of the local government, the social work college students, local NGOs such as India National Resource Economics and Management (INREM), and other more informal stakeholders, significant scale detection of fluoride would not have been possible. Fifth, Education for sustainable development often neglects informal educational approaches toward educating the masses. This category is very relevant for bringing community-wide change to a social issue. Sixth, international evidence on citizen science is weak, and this area has a lot of future potential that could be further explored to boost community-based social issues. Seventh, literature suggests that art has effectively raised awareness about social issues. However, art could be explored further to promote education in sustainable development. Eight, technology played a vital role in data collection and result dissemination across various departments and with the students who were village residents themselves. Data were collected on smartphones owned by the students; data were shared widely on all WhatsApp lists down to the local village councils. Technology was also used to share videos of local songs via WhatsApp to promote safe water behaviors. Nine, involving educational institutions like the School of Social Work was very beneficial since the students were mandated to work on a field study. There was accountability as the school faculty was also supervising their role.

Notes

1 Process Documentation for the Fluoride Awareness Campaign in Alirajpur https://www.youtube.com/watch?v=4_liFIDtpgk
2 Glimpses of Day 1 https://www.youtube.com/watch?v=PDDiEDe8zWU
3 Education brings sectors together to address Fluorosis in Alirajpur Education needs to learn to do sustainable development https://blogs.ei.columbia.edu/2019/08/12/education-interventions-high-fluoride-india/
4 Explaining the Fluorosis problem using pictorial posters https://www.youtube.com/watch?v=jAPoZAD3yYQ
5 Explaining the Fluorosis problem using pictorial posters https://www.youtube.com/watch?v=jAPoZAD3yYQ
6 Women in Science https://www.youtube.com/watch?v=QMhJjbobX9Y
7 Street Theater to make people aware about Fluorosis https://www.youtube.com/watch?v=lKQBCDOi-D8
8 Process documentation about testing fluoride in Alirajpur https://www.youtube.com/watch?v=6eW3Vi9XOEc

References

Bonney, R., & Phillips, T. (2016). Can Citizen Science Enhance Public Understanding of Science? *Public Understanding of Science*, 25, pp. 2–16.

Bonney, R., Shirk, J., Phillips, T., Wiggins, A., Ballard, H., Miller-Rushing, A., & Parrish, J. (2014). Next Steps for Citizen Science. *Science*, 343(6178), pp. 1436–7.

Ellwood, E., Crimmins, T., & Miller-Rushing, A. (2017). Citizen Science and Conservation: Recommendations for a Rapidly Moving Field. *Biological Conservation*, 208, pp. 1–4.

Ghosh, Sahana. (2019). Madhya Pradesh's "Fluoride warriors" Unleash Citizen Science to Empower Community. *Mongabay India*. https://india.mongabay.com/2020/03/madhya-pradeshs-fluoride-warriors-unleash-citizen-science-to-empower-community/, Accessed May 5, 2020.

Iyengar, Radhika. (2019). The Treatment of Education for Sustainable Development in India: Review of Two Case Studies. https://www.youtube.com/watch?v=7shVOE8onxo, Accessed May 5, 2021.

Iyengar, Radhika. (2020). Testing Fluoride Levels in Indian Wells. https://blogs.ei.columbia.edu/2019/09/16/testing-fluoride-levels-indian-wells/, Accessed May 5, 2020.

Levin, Saurabh, Krishnan, Sunderrajan, Rajkumar, Samuel, Halery, Nichal, & Balkunde, Pradeep. (2016). Monitoring of Fluoride in Water Samples Using a Smartphone. *Science of the Total Environment*, 551–552, pp. 101–7.

McKinley, D., Miller-Rushing, A., Ballard, H., Bonney, R., Brown, H., Cook-Patton, S., Evans, D., French, R., & Parrish, J. (2017). Citizen Science Can Improve Conservation Science, Natural Resource Management, and Environmental Protection. *Biological Conservation*, 208, pp. 15–28.

Newman, G., Wiggins, A., Crall, A., Graham, E., Newman, S., & Crowston, K. (2012). The Future of Citizen Science: Emerging Technologies and Shifting Paradigms. *Frontiers in Ecology. The Ecological Society of America*, 10(6), pp. 298–304.

Podgorski, J.E., Labhasetwar, P, Saha, D., & Berg, M. (2018). Prediction Modeling and Mapping of Groundwater Fluoride Contamination throughout India. *Environmental Science & Technology*, 52(17), pp. 9889–98. doi: 10.1021/acs.est.8b01679. PMID: 30052029.

Resnik, D., Elliott, K., & Miller, A. (2015). A Framework for Addressing Ethical Issues in Citizen Science. *Environmental Science & Policy*, 54, pp. 475–81.

Silvertown, Jonathan. (2009). A New Dawn for Citizen Science. *Trends in Ecology & Evolution*, 24(9), pp. 467–71.

Trumbull, D., Bonney, R., Bascom, D., & Cabral, A. (2000). Thinking Scientifically during Participation in a Citizen-Science Project. *Informal Science*, 84(2), pp. 265–75.

4

Building Capacity for Geospatial Data-driven Education Planning

Lessons from Nigeria

Tara Stafford Ocansey, Emilie Schnarr, Anela Marie Layugan, and Annie Werner

A Case for Data-driven Decision-Making

In September 2015, countries adopted the 2030 Agenda for Sustainable Development, along with its 17 Sustainable Development Goals (SDGs), 169 specific targets, and 232 indicators across a broad range of interlinked sectors. Along with these goals, there has been extensive dialogue on the need for increased capacity for data-driven monitoring and decision-making. Even with an abundance of data availability, for data to be useful in decision-making, stakeholders must have direct access to training and tools that make analyzing and using data more accessible and must foster a culture of data use and teamwork (Dunlap and Weber, 2009, p. 452).

While there has been extensive global dialogue on defining the SDGs, how to implement them, and the role of data-driven decision-making, there has been less focus on the critical role geospatial information can play in monitoring progress and targeting solutions to the geographic areas that need them most urgently (Scott and Rajabifard, 2017). It has been estimated that as many as 20 percent of the SDG indicators can be measured using geospatial data—either alone or integrated with statistical data (Arnold, Chun, and Eggers, 2019). According to UNESCO's International Institute for Educational Planning, when education planners are equipped to cross-reference data from the education system with geo-referenced information, they can develop highly contextualized policies that are more responsive to the needs of local communities, helping to promote more equitable distribution of educational opportunities, better adaptation of educational opportunities to local community needs, and more efficient use of education resources (IIEP, n.d.). This last benefit is of particular importance in countries where resources are limited, and out-of-school and underserved school-aged populations remain high, such as in the case of Nigeria. However, there exist great differences among the capacities of countries to generate high-resolution geospatial data, and those countries that stand to benefit most from geospatial data are often the same countries that lack adequate ability to implement a robust program of geospatial data collection and data-driven decision-making (Arnold et al., 2019).

The purpose of the present chapter is to provide an overview of the geospatial data landscape within the Nigerian education sector, present analyses and outcomes from a geospatially focused education workshop that took place in Abuja in June 2019, describe the current state of the Ministry of Education's application of geospatial data for evidence-based decision-making in Nigeria, and discuss applications of lessons learned in Sierra Leone and beyond.

Overview of Geospatial Data Landscape Within the Nigerian Education Sector

Nigeria is one of the world's most populous countries, with an estimated 206 million people, 43 percent of whom are fourteen years old or less (World Bank, 2022). Nigeria also struggles with the world's largest out-of-school population, estimated to be 10.5 million children aged five to fourteen years old, with girls constituting 60 percent of that number. Among children enrolled in primary school, only 61 percent regularly attend. In the north, the picture is bleaker, with primary-aged children having a net attendance rate of just 68 percent (NPS, 2015). Several factors drive this trend, including early marriages and the nonformal system of Islamic education known as the Almajiri system, poor investment in education, teachers with limited training, as well as armed conflicts that parts of the north have faced over the past decade, have all hampered progress toward universal enrollment and improved quality education.

Nigeria's top-down education system includes different management structures at each level that often overlap responsibilities. At the state level, while the state Ministry of Education is the umbrella structure and is mainly responsible for secondary education, the State Universal Basic Education Boards (SUBEBs) manage primary education. Local Government Education Authorities monitor and support basic education at the local level, under the SUBEBs, which report to the state ministries of education. These intersecting roles contribute to competing ideas on where information and data should be centralized and which sources should be considered the gold standard. This type of structure also contributes toward a general lack of confidence in the validity of data sources, which could be addressed through transparent, accessible geospatial data platforms.

In Nigeria, stakeholders from national to Local Government Area (LGA) levels have made significant strides in building local capacity to use geospatial data in making data-driven education decisions in recent years. Iyengar et al. (2015) describe the development of the Nigeria Millennium Development Goal Information System (NMIS) from 2011 to 2013. Enumerators were trained to collect data using a mobile platform uploaded to an online platform that mapped local education data to specific schools. Technical specialists were then provided training and support to use the data to formulate proposals and plans for school infrastructure and other improvements. While this experience demonstrated the great potential of data-driven decision-making in education, it also revealed that such progress requires ongoing training and support to teach the cultural shift to data-driven planning and decision-making, and also requires data to be readily available and understandable, that is, data visualization tools available through an online portal, with local capacity to manage the data portal. Challenges in sustaining data use in planning and decision-making include low ability to use technology, inaccurate data, insufficient capacity to use data in planning and decision-making, and a lack of funding to support building capacity and regularly updating an online data portal. In Nigeria, there is plenty of education data available through the NMIS, but the level of effort put into collecting the data is not matched by the effort and funding put into using that data to drive decision-making (Iyengar et al., 2014).

The Nigerian Universal Basic Educational Commission (UBEC) has developed a range of policies to address school attendance issues and established the Universal Basic Education Commission Act in 2004. This act states that periodic National Personnel Audits (NPAs) of teaching and non-teaching staff should be carried out in all basic primary educational institutions for policy-making purposes. In 2018, UBEC released its first NPA dataset that contained geospatial information, with assistance from the National Space Research and Development Agency (NASRDA). The NPA dataset contains geo-located national school data that includes details on each school, classifying school type, facilities available, number of teachers, and attendance figures broken down by age group. The release of the NPA data was an essential milestone for UBEC and Nigeria. It marked the first time a Nigerian government institution conducted country-wide geospatial data collection, capturing all school locations and relevant characteristics (GRID3, 2020).

Background on GRID3

Since 2018, the Geo-Referenced Infrastructure and Demographic Data for Development (GRID3) program have made a substantial effort and impact in various sub-Saharan African countries to generate, validate, and use geospatial data on population, settlements, infrastructure (including schools), and boundaries. GRID3 combines the expertise of partners in government, the United Nations, academia, and the private sector to design adaptable and relevant geospatial solutions based on each country's capacity and development needs.

In Nigeria specifically, GRID3 has facilitated a series of workshops, training, and other support for Nigerian education officials to fully adopt geospatial data analysis practices to make education data more transparent and use it to drive decision-making. In April of 2019, GRID3 supported NASRDA in establishing a GRID3 Nigeria geodatabase and portal, which contains freely available geospatial datasets for the entire country. Since then, NASRDA has been hosting and managing the geodatabase and portal and working closely with various ministries, including UBEC and the SUBEBs, to enhance the quality of the datasets and enable the government and public to use such data for improved decision-making purposes freely.

A Participatory Approach to Capacity Building for Data-driven Decision-Making

To engage a broad group of education stakeholders and decision-makers in understanding the top priorities for how geospatial data can be used and start creating plans for building capacity to use geospatial data in their education planning, GRID3 and the Center for Sustainable Development (CSD) at Columbia University facilitated a three-day workshop in Abuja in June 2019. Workshop participants included thirty government and education leaders from Adamawa, Gombe, and Kaduna states, as well as from the national level, with eighteen of them working in the education sector at various local, state, and national agencies, three working with a higher education institution in Adamawa, and nine coming from various GRID3 partners, including workshop facilitators. In addition to collecting data, the workshop's outcome was to develop a use case work plan describing what kinds of geospatial analyses would be most helpful, and how GRID3 data will be utilized within various education offices for planning and decision-making.

The workshop was designed to use qualitative, social assessment methods including participant surveys, interviews, and focus group discussions to engage education leaders in discussion of their current decision-making processes, use of geospatial data and the role of data in their decision-making, the challenges they face in using data for decision-making, and staff capacity for data-driven decision-making. Rietbergen-McCracken and Narayan define social assessment as a process that "provides a framework for prioritizing, gathering, analyzing, and incorporating social information and participation into the design and delivery of development operations" (p. 19). Within the social assessment framework, the workshop was designed first to present the premise and guiding questions for the workshop, which were:

- Are current educational practices in compliance with policies at the state and national level?
- How can data inform policy planning and implementation monitoring?
- Effective pathways to meet the SDGs are based on strategic inter-sectoral linkages. How do other sectors, such as health, support the education sector? (Figure 4.1).

Stakeholders were then presented with relevant policy scenarios mapped using GRID3 data and engaged in the discussion of relevant policy scenarios that could be visualized. They also discussed how their institutions could support the mapping of identified scenarios through harmonization, provision, and/or

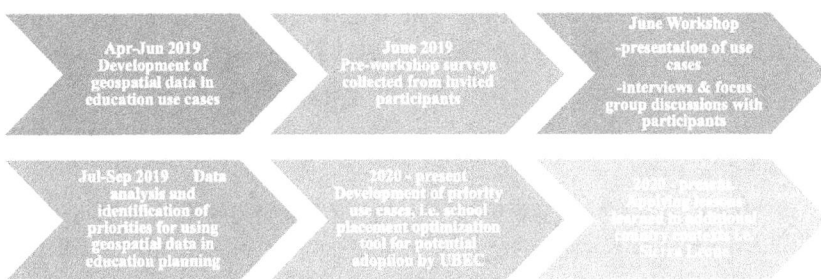

Figure 4.1 Timeline of research activities.

collection of additional data. Based on identified scenarios, stakeholders were asked to think of key policy issues to prioritize for mapping GRID3 data and develop action plans to enable data mapping in their decision-making.

Presentation of Education Use Cases

The beginning of the workshop was dedicated to presenting a series of geospatial data analysis use cases designed to help answer a set of education research questions targeting common education priorities and challenges in developing country contexts. The use cases were developed by the Center for International Earth Science Information Network (CIESIN), GRID3's managing partner, with input from the CSD's education experts based on their experience implementing education programs in sub-Saharan Africa.

Education Research Question 1: What is the geographical distribution of the primary school-age population, and are there enough schools located near this population? (Figure 4.2).

The Nigeria National Education Policy (2004) states that primary education should be conducted at a 1:35 teacher-pupil ratio. The UBEC Minimum Standards for Basic Education (2010) says that students shouldn't need to walk more than 2 kilometers to reach a school. While not a complete solution, mapping school-aged population data alongside or overlaid with school catchment area data using the 2 kilometers standard could show adequate or inadequate infrastructure to support the school-aged population. It was discussed that additional datasets to answer this research question further could include the number of classrooms and teachers.

Education Research Question 2: What is the female to male ratio of school-age populations? What are the differences in trends between female and male students?

The Nigerian National Policy on Gender in Basic Education calls to increase girls' access to basic education, promote high retention, and create a favorable environment supporting planning, management, implementation, and actualization of the gender policy in basic education. Therefore, strategies for addressing the barriers to girls' enrollment and retention must consider the needs based on the gender makeup of specific populations and their enrollment and retention trends.

This research question did not yield as much immediate interest, perhaps because it was unclear what to do with this data on its own. The facilitators suggested that this data could be overlaid with school attendance and/or performance disaggregated by gender.

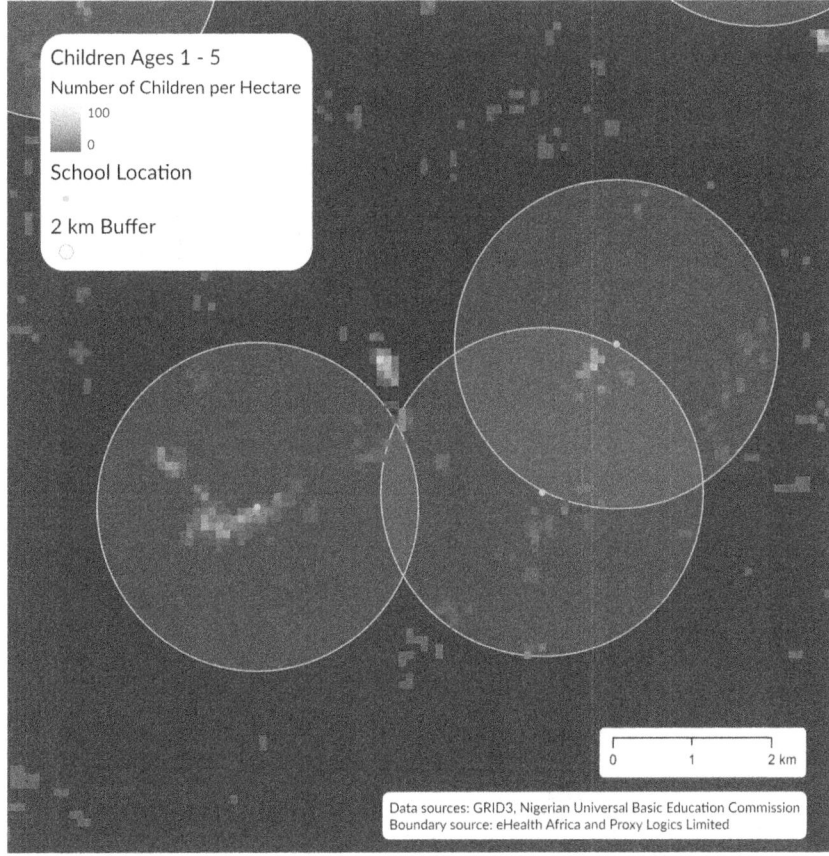

Figure 4.2 Example distribution of primary school-aged children and nearby schools.

Education Research Question 3: Is there a basic health facility within walking distance of each school?

While this use case did not come directly from a Nigerian Education Policy, it served as an example of how geospatial data can explore the cross-sectoral linkages impacting progress in education. In this use case, the proposition is that each school should have a functional health facility within proximity for:

- Access to health care services
- Students with health-related issues to have access to health services easily
- Association between access to health care and quality of education (Case, Fergin, and Paxson, 2005)
- Ensuring children are healthy to support their learning

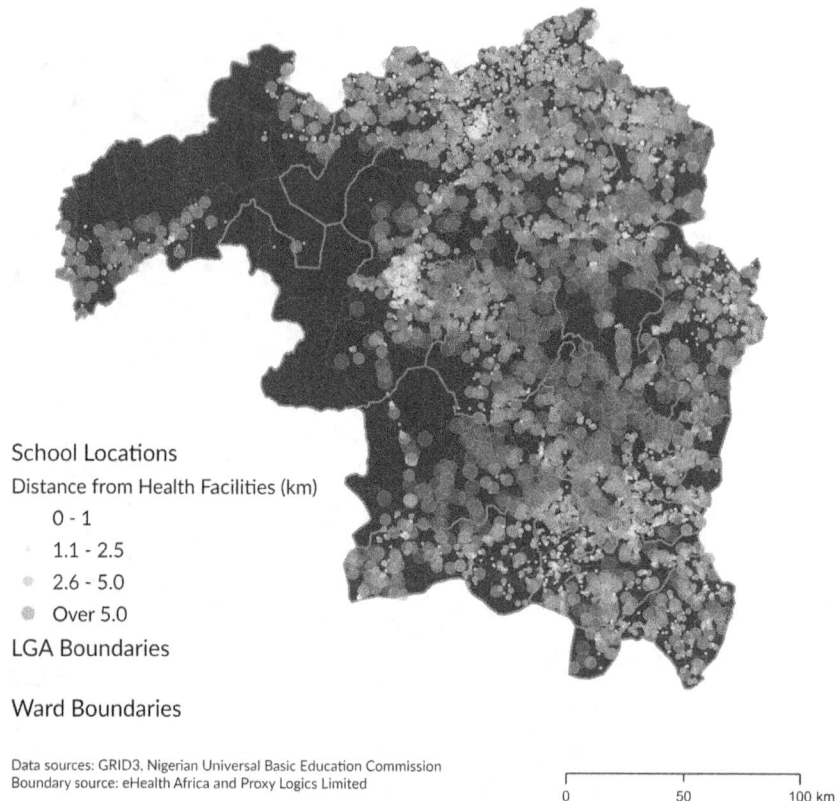

Figure 4.3 Distance from schools to the nearest health facility.

Figure 4.3 shows school locations in Kaduna state and how far away the closest functioning health facility is from each school. The clusters of schools with a health facility within 1 kilometer reveal that more schools in urban locations have health facilities within proximity than schools in rural locations. This pattern can be extrapolated across the country, indicating the need for more health facilities within walking distance of rural schools.

Education Research Question 4: Where are unmet preprimary education needs most severe?

According to Nigerian Education Policy, all primary schools should offer Early Childhood Care Education (ECCE). Figure 4.4 shows the distribution of primary schools that do not provide ECCE. The participants were struck by the overall need for further investment in preprimary education, particularly outside urban areas.

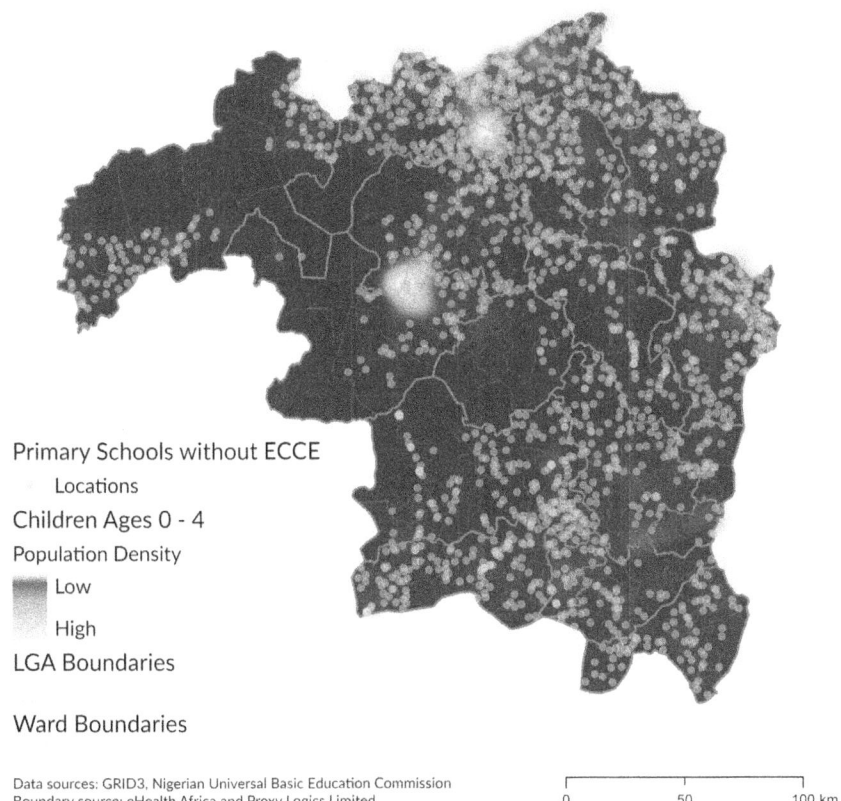

Figure 4.4 Distribution of primary schools with no early childhood care and education.

Priorities Identified by Education Leaders

Findings from discussions facilitated during the workshop were organized into four areas: (1) Education priorities generally (not relating to geospatial data), (2) main challenges faced in addressing those priorities, (3) perceived benefits to geospatial data mapping, and (4) priorities for using geospatial data to support education planning and decision-making.

Education Priorities

Stakeholders tended to agree across states that increasing access and bringing out-of-school children to school was a top education planning priority. To help facilitate that increased access, the second most cited priority was to improve/

increase education facilities. Improving the capacity to use data to inform education planning through monitoring and evaluation was the third most cited area. Increasing girls' enrollment/gender equity and improving the quality of education were also frequently cited priorities.

Challenges to Achieving Education Priorities

After sharing education priorities, stakeholders were asked to discuss what they perceived to be the most significant challenges to addressing them. The two most frequently discussed challenges were lack of political will/politically motivated decision-making and lack of reliable data. Following closely was the lack of capacity for managing data. Other frequently discussed challenges included inadequate and/or delayed funding from the government, the relationship between data on enrollment and federal funding, lack of human resource capacity, and cultural norms, including traditional gender roles.

Benefits of Geospatial Mapping of Education Data

Participants were asked, "If it becomes available, how do you envision geospatial data being useful in your education planning role?" The two most frequently discussed areas were identifying community needs and increasing accountability among education stakeholders by significant margins. Other benefits included increasing the efficiency and ease of data analysis and data-driven decision-making and reducing political interference in education decision-making processes. Many participants discussed the potential of geospatial mapping as a helpful tool in data validation, helping to address concerns of unreliable data and build trust in the education data system. Stakeholders also discussed how geospatial data could support grassroots education advocacy, help make cross-sectoral links, and identify remote village names where such data was lacking.

Priorities for Geospatial Data Analysis

During the workshop, participants broke into small groups by the state to develop action plans for using geospatial data to address specific education planning priorities. Noting that many priorities overlapped with each other, the top priority discussed during breakout discussions was to use geospatial data to "Identify infrastructure needs," followed by "Verify enrollment figures," and "Identify out-of-school populations." Other priorities discussed included

"Identify early childhood care and development needs," "Support girls' enrollment," "Identify inter-sectoral opportunities," "track dropout trends," and "Determine catchment areas."

Participants expected that the maps would help education stakeholders verify and build trust around the data to use the verified data and then drive decision-making in other areas. Some participants alluded to how geospatial data can eliminate some uncertainty around how some education decisions are made, including potentially politically motivated decisions.

In line with assessing how geospatial data can support the achievement of the SDGs, several participants noted how geospatial data could help identify inter-sectoral linkages. Some participants drew a link between health and education by highlighting how the maps could help identify schools where school gardens could be established and highlighting schools lacking sanitation and hygiene facilities.

The workshop fostered debate on how best to represent school infrastructure needs based on population, considering the policy that says no child should travel more than 2 kilometers to reach a school. During the workshop, this use case was mapped using 2-kilometer radius circles color-coded based on population density. However, concerns were raised by participants that this way of presenting the data did not realistically account for geography and accessibility. Informed of these concerns, the accessibility map has been reconfigured by GRID3 to show the percentage of the school-aged population within 2 kilometers of a school. Examples of this improved map are included in Figure 4.5, and further iterations that consider the time required to travel to school are discussed in the next section.

Carrying the Work Forward in Nigeria and Beyond

During the interviews conducted during the workshop in Abuja, stakeholders were asked to identify individuals that GRID3 could train to perform geospatial analysis to build local capacity to carry this work forward. Since the workshop, UBEC has established a small technical group that will receive training by GRID3 on geospatial data management and uses case development. One such use case that has been developed and is currently being implemented in the School Placement Optimization Tool (SPOT), which enables the government to determine optimal locations where new primary schools should be built in the country, based on population density. The NPA dataset serves as the basis for

46   *Rethinking Education for Sustainable Development*

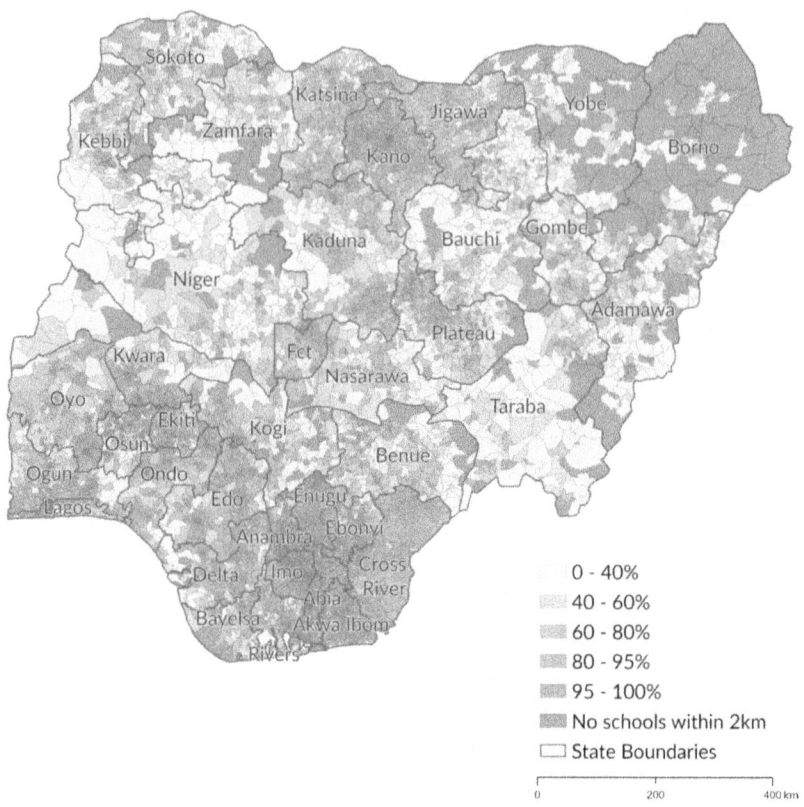

Figure 4.5 Percentage of children aged one to four years within 2 kilometers of ECCE schools at the ward level.

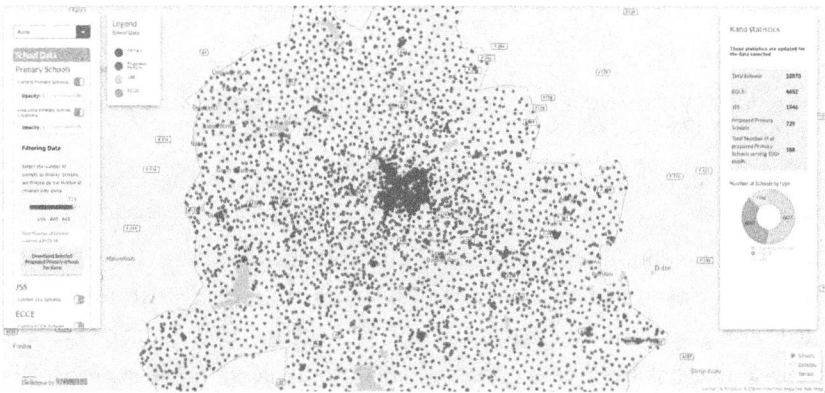

Figure 4.6 School Placement Optimization Tool for Kano State.

observing current school locations. Figure 4.6 is an image of existing primary school locations (blue dots) in Kano state and proposed locations of new schools (red dots) is shown according to the principle that all primary school-aged children should be within a 2-kilometer walking distance of a school. Although UBEC and the SUBEBs have yet to adopt the SPOT officially, conversations are underway, and the value and importance of this tool are recognized.

Applying Lessons Learned Beyond Nigeria

Understanding the value of geospatial data and specific use cases within the education sector in Nigeria, the Ministry of Basic and Senior Secondary Education (MBSSE) in Sierra Leone, together with GRID3, investigated analogous questions concerning population coverage and accessibility to schools to inform the Ministry's school catchment and infrastructure planning and accompanying policy throughout 2020. Disaggregated by school level, age, and several other relevant factors detailed in the Education Coverage Report, GRID3 calculated the percentage of each school-age cohort that falls within a 3-mile radius of the appropriate school type (benchmark set by the MBSSE). A major finding from the analysis was that almost all children aged six to eleven were within 3 miles of a primary school, in stark contrast to preprimary, junior secondary, and senior secondary students, due to a more significant number and distribution of primary schools across all sixteen districts in Sierra Leone.

While informative, education stakeholders' experience and research told a somewhat different story of the challenges that geography, roads, and infrastructure pose to traveling to school, echoing the findings reported in Nigeria. To understand accessibility more pragmatically, the exploratory benchmark was then adapted from a 3-mile straight-line distance to a time-based approach—the number of children under sixty minutes from the nearest age-relevant school. Using a novel method and procedure that takes land cover, roads, and elevation into account, GRID3 developed a friction surface layer[1] and catchment algorithm which identifies and delineates all areas to the closest school and the average time it takes from any given 100-meter site to reach it. The initial results paint a more nuanced picture, demonstrating that coverage and accessibility may, in fact, be lower or even higher than initially thought when taking physical and natural features into account and varying by mode of travel. Carrying this work forward, MBSSE, implementing education partners, and GRID3 will continue to explore how to improve the time-based approach to answer further questions around accessibility and the construction and optimized placement of new schools and classrooms.

Democratizing Geospatial Data Collection for Education Equity

The lessons learned by GRID3 in Nigeria and Sierra Leone are being applied to data-driven geospatial solutions led by other organizations conducting tangential work. The *My School Today!* call to action was launched in July 2021 by SDGs Today, an initiative by the United Nations Sustainable Development Solutions Network (SDSN). In response to the lack of reliable and inconsistent datasets on school locations at the regional level limiting leaders' ability to make data-driven decisions, this call to action mobilizes citizens, ministries of education, and other SDG stakeholders to map schools within their communities in Africa. The goal of *My School Today!* is to improve the analysis of geographic access to schools by making sure no school is left unmapped. These crowdsourced data complement the dataset produced by SDGs Today that calculates walking time to schools at Administrative Level 1 on a daily basis using open-source data. Open-source mapping allows for geospatial data to promptly reflect changes on the ground and puts the power of mapping into the hands of the community. These two traits make open-source mapping just one of many solutions to the outdated datasets and lack of trust in data that GRID3 has come across in their work.

In addition to physical access to schools, geospatial technologies also advance digital access to schools. Giga was launched in 2019 by the International Telecommunication Union (ITU) and UNICEF to connect all schools to the internet and close the digital divide between young learners without internet access and digital educational resources. As of October 2021, their map displays connectivity to the internet in over 900,000 schools in over 35 countries in real-time, and those numbers are increasing rapidly. This project once again highlights the need for reliable geospatial data on schools to show where reliable internet is located and to expose infrastructure gaps. Digital access to educational materials also opens up a wealth of opportunities, especially for students who do not have physical access to schools or unforeseen emergencies requiring physical school closures.

The importance of reliable and timely geospatial data was also highlighted most recently during the COVID-19 pandemic. The UNESCO has been tracking school closures caused by COVID-19 and the students affected by them since February 2020. Their dataset on school closures, length of closures, and the number of students affected by those closures is based on information collected from ministries of education and UNESCO enrollment figures between 2000 and 2019, and it is updated on a weekly basis. This undercurrent of the need for validated and timely enrollment figures to lessen the effects of unexpected current events is present in both UNESCO's digital access research and GRID3's work.

Closing

The cases from Nigeria, Sierra Leone, and the three initiatives described earlier highlight the need for reliable geospatial data to support the development of education systems. They show that technology and analyses are being developed, but results are based on how well schools are mapped. As evidenced by data brought forth through these use cases, geospatial data can play a key role in building confidence in education systems through verification of enrollment and out-of-school figures compared to geographic distributions of school-aged children and dissemination of these figures with education stakeholders at all levels. While discussed outright in many instances, the undercurrent woven through many of the responses summarized from the GRID3 workshop in Abuja was that geospatial data could help overcome the pervasive problem of unreliable data, often caused by politically motivated decision-making at various levels.

It must be emphasized, though, that this perceived challenge of politically motivated decision-making can only be addressed through geospatial data analysis if grassroots stakeholders are engaged in using data to hold leaders accountable and if every rung of the education system ladder is empowered to use geospatial data to conduct analysis and make recommendations to their leaders. It is also worth noting that overcoming current assumptions of unreliable data will be difficult due to years of distrust. Therefore consistent availability and use of geospatial data must continue over time to minimize this overwhelming concern eventually. The thread that connects the geospatial data priorities identified by the education leaders during the Abuja workshop discussions is the value of using geospatial data for data validation and building trust in data collected by the education system. Innovative geospatial analysis tools like the SPOT tool consider the realities of impacted populations' experiences of going to school (i.e., travel time), along with initiatives promoting open-source geospatial data and crowdsourced data collection such as *My School Today!* have great potential to help build this trust and transparency. Continuing to collect and utilize reliable, transparent, and widely accessible geospatial data can help create a foundation upon which many other decisions can be made to improve education systems and build trust among education stakeholders.

Note

1 A friction surface layer is a raster file that has "costs" associated for each cell, in this case representing travel time. We created this layer by calculating slope, land cover, roads, and rivers with information on mode of transport and speed. Each calculation per cell then has a cost and the shortest time traveled is the sum of these "least cost cells."

References

Arnold, A., Chen, J., & Eggers, O. (2019). *Global and Complementary (Non-Authoritative) Geospatial Data for SDGs: Role and Utilisation*. United Nations. https://ggim.un.org/documents/Report_Global_and_Complementary_Geospatial_Data_for_SDGs.pdf. Date Accessed May 25, 2022.

Case, A., et al. (2005). The Lasting Impact of Childhood Health and Circumstance. *Journal of Health Economics*, 24, pp. 365–89.

Dunlap, D.M., & Weber, R.E. (2009). When Data Are Insufficient to Make Group Decisions: A Case Study in Community College Administration. In T.J. Kowalski & T.J. Lasley II (Eds.), *Data-Based Decision-Making in Education* (pp. 441–54). New York: Taylor & Francis.

GRID3 (2020). *How Geospatial Data Can Help Solve Nigeria's Educational Challenges*. Geo-Referenced Infrastructure and Demographic Data for Development (GRID3). https://grid3.org/news/how-geospatial-data-can-help-solve-nigerias-educational-challenges. Date Accessed May 25, 2022.

International Institute for Educational Planning (n.d.). *Geospatial Data in Educational Planning and Management*. UNESCO. http://www.iiep.unesco.org/en/our-expertise/geospatial-data-educational-planning-and-management. Date Accessed May 25, 2022.

Iyengar, R., Mahal, A., Aklilu, L., Sweetland, A., Karim, A., Shin, H., Aliyu, B., Park, J., Modi, V., Berg, M., & Pokharel, P. (2014). The Use of Technology for Large-scale Education Planning and Decision-Making. *Information Technology for Development*, doi:10.1080/02681102.2014.940267.

Iyengar, R., Mahal, A., Felicia, U., Aliya, B., & Karim, K. (2015). Federal Policy to Local Level Decision-Making: Data Driven Education Planning in Nigeria. *The International Education Journal: Comparative Perspectives*, 14(3), pp. 76–93.

National Population Commission, 2015 Nigeria Education Data Survey. Abuja, Nigeria (2015). https://ierc-publicfiles.s3.amazonaws.com/public/resources/2015-NEDS-National-011716.pdf, Accessed June 1, 2019.

Nigeria National Education Policy. (2004). https://educatetolead.files.wordpress.com/2016/02/national-education-policy-2013.pdf.

Scott, G., & Rajabifard, A. (2017). Sustainable Development and Geospatial Information: A Strategic Framework for Integrating a Global Policy Agenda into National Geospatial Capabilities. *Geospatial Information Science*, 20(2), pp. 59–76, doi:10.1080/10095020.2017.1325594.

World Bank. (2022). https://data.worldbank.org/country/nigeria. Date Accessed May 2022.

5

GIS and Storytelling for Sustainable Development Education

Ismini Ethridge and Maryam Rabiee

Our current global challenges undoubtedly require cutting-edge technologies, data-driven science communication, and a generation of leaders competent in both. This chapter will explore the use of technology in sustainable development education, highlighting the advantages of Geospatial Information Systems (GIS) and geospatial literacy in education, especially involving real-time data and storytelling. The chapter will also call attention to how students engage with and contribute to the GIS community, how partnerships have helped create an abundance of resources for including GIS in sustainable development curricula, and gaps and next steps.

Use of Technology in SDG Education and Advantages of GIS

Technology's Role in Education

Education is the foundation of development and prosperity for any nation. Education attainment can drive economic growth, improve health, and reduce poverty (Psacharopoulos and Patrinos, 2018). Investing in new technologies in the education sector can help narrow the gaps in the quality of learning and accessibility to education facilities.

The integration of technology in educational curricula allows students to access more information, fosters more opportunities for engagement with their peers and the educational lessons, and improves learning processes. In their analysis of technology's role in education in six developed countries, Rasinen reports that technology integration contributes to skill development, problem-solving skills, innovation, and applications of technology that are in line with social and environmental circumstances (Rasinen, 2003).

However, the digital divide between high-income and low- and middle-income countries can exacerbate educational disparities (Cruz-Jesus et al., 2018). For instance, the education sector was required to rapidly respond to the COVID-19 pandemic and minimize its impacts on students. Unfortunately, school closures affected over a billion learners during the pandemic, and not all of them could continue learning due to a lack of information and communications technologies. Societies and communities that could afford access to an internet connection offered educational services using virtual platforms.

In addition to increased accessibility, new technologies can equip students with the tools and skills needed to enhance their educational experience and play a part in building an equitable and sustainable future. Knowledge of programming languages, cloud architecture, GIS, and other emerging technologies empower learners with the skills to develop local solutions and respond to challenges in a timelier manner.

GIS and Its Advantages

A GIS is a framework for gathering, managing, analyzing, and integrating many types of data, and is rooted in the science of geography. Using GIS, one can analyze the spatial location and organize layers of information into visualizations using maps, which can give greater insight into patterns and problems driven or reinforced by geography (Esri n.d.). GIS is a potent tool in the case of sustainable development. For example, an urban planner trying to assess the accessibility and reach of public transportation in a city or a first responder looking for the shortest route to get to a population affected by a disaster will need reliable and timely geo-referenced data. GIS would enable them to run analyses that could answer questions about the location of people or an incident and how to enhance the well-being of communities and the environment. On a global register, GIS is also especially useful in efforts toward achieving the Sustainable Development Goals (SDGs), which rely heavily on knowing where critical resources and facilities (such as schools, hospitals, clean water, etc.) are and where they are not, where environmental disasters (such as deforestation, coral bleaching, drought) are occurring, and where populations are about all of that.

GIS applications are already being used in various scenarios involving sustainable development. The Lebanese Red Cross uses GIS to help with emergency readiness and response. The United Nations Satellite Centre at the United Nations Institute for Training and Research (UNITAR-UNOSAT) uses geospatial data to support the humanitarian community in Syria and provide them with critical information. The Geneva International Centre for Humanitarian Demining utilizes GIS applications for efficient and safe demining operations. The IUCN "Red List of Threatened Species" uses GIS to produce spatial mappings of species. As will be discussed throughout the chapter, combining storytelling with GIS can be particularly effective in communicating the urgency of specific data and issues in sustainable development. The UN Refugee Agency (UNHCR) uses Esri's ArcGIS StoryMaps, which combine interactive maps, media, and narrative text, to convey the extent and gravity of emergencies surrounding refugee crises (Bonaccorsi, 2018).

From participatory community mapping to global satellite data collection, GIS has quickly permeated the world of sustainable development as a critical tool to guide policy-making for meeting environmental, social, and economic development targets. As a global community, our technological and financial capacity to protect the natural environment and ensure all basic human needs are met have never been greater. Still, our potential for actionable solutions, policy-making, and monitoring progress relies critically on knowing where people and resources are and how to effectively use and relay this information.

Importance of Real-Time Data

To effectively track and monitor processes toward the SDGs, particularly SDG 4 (Quality Education), policymakers need to access data that provide insight into the current quality and accessibility of educational facilities and programs. However, the official data used to track progress are often outdated and rely on traditional data collection methods. In many low- and middle-income countries, data on education are not collected frequently enough (The World Bank, 2021). Advanced methods and data sources can complement conventional sources of data to develop data that can inform decision-making processes that are future-forward and sustainable.

Stakeholders from various sectors struggled to access and analyze real-time data that could inform immediate responses to the impacts of the pandemic on education. Understanding where students are located or what services are available requires a comprehensive ecosystem of timely data on student demographics, school amenities and infrastructures, teachers, and other information (Local Burden of Disease Educational Attainment Collaborators, 2020, Nature 2020). In recent years, efforts such as UNICEF's Giga Initiative

(Giga Connectivity, n.d.), the Sustainable Development Solutions Network's (SDSN) My School Today project—we aren't calling it a call to action anymore (My School Today, n.d.), and the World Bank's Global Program for Safer Schools (GPSS, n.d.) are using new methods to narrow the education data gap.

> *Excerpt from Esri blog post: Prof. Jeffrey Sachs, President of the Sustainable Development Solutions Network and Director of the Center for Sustainable Development at Columbia University, discusses the critical roles of GIS and storytelling in solving global challenges*
>
> **"Why is geospatial data important for the SDGs?"**
>
> When I was training in economics, we did not have modern GIS tools at hand. We may have looked at maps, but the data for our statistical models came mostly from national income accounts, or state and local data. Much public policy was therefore blind to geography. Policy decisions on poverty, schooling, healthcare, even infrastructure, was taken with far too little regard for the spatial distribution of real needs and opportunities.
>
> Now we can do vastly better because of the powerful GIS tools and massive digital data now available."
>
> "Indeed, to meet the SDGs, we absolutely need reliable, quality, and timely geo-spatial data, for example, to monitor environmental changes in real-time (climate change, deforestation, pollution) and to assess by region the most urgent economic needs (poverty, hunger, access to healthcare and education, access to safe water and sanitation, and so forth). Real-time geo-spatial data is crucial for implementing urgent policies such as controlling the COVID-19 epidemic and for holding governments accountable for their commitments." (Esri, 2020)

Importance of GIS and Geographic Literacy in Education

There's no doubt that technical training in GIS is critical to train the next generation of leaders in sustainable development effectively. Joseph Kerski, a geographer with a focus on the use of Geographic Information Systems in education, and former president of the National Council for Geographic Education writes:

> Today, the geographic perspective is more relevant than ever before, as issues of climate change, economic globalization, urban sprawl, biodiversity loss, sustainable agriculture, water quality and quantity, crime, cultural diversity,

energy, tourism, political instability, and natural hazards grow in importance on a global scale but also increasingly affect our everyday lives. To grapple with these issues requires a populace that has a firm foundation in geography, who can see the "big picture" but also who understands how different patterns and trends are related from a global scale down to the local community. The geographic perspective is concerned with all of the relevant issues of our time because all of these issues have a geographic component.(Kerski, 2018)

Studies have also shown that utilizing GIS in social sciences is a great way to improve students' engagement and critical thinking. GIS serves as an investigative tool that allows students to explore, interact, and interpret information from a spatial/locational perspective (Fitchett and Good, 2012). In a study evaluating the applicability of GIS in primary education in Turkey, Elif Aladag found that teachers saw the benefits of GIS in enabling visual learning, improving map skills, promoting retention, making the learning process fun, allowing easy access to numerical data, facilitating the learning process, developing creativity, achieving hands-on learning, making a comparison among various data, developing critical thinking, enabling spatial analysis, and increasing active participation in classes (Aladag, 2014).

Kerski emphasizes that GIS "helps students think critically, use real data, and connects them to their community" in informal, primary, secondary, and university settings. It also provides career pathways that are increasingly in demand (Kerski, 2018). He also draws attention to the fact that "the use of GIS is not simply about using technology and becoming proficient in using GIS tools—but rather, fosters a whole range of communication, data, media fluency, and critical thinking skills" (Kerski, 2018). At the end of the chapter, examples of school programs and curricula utilizing GIS are provided.

Importance of Data-Driven Storytelling for Sustainable Development Education

Role of Storytelling in GIS

The potential of maps and geospatial data to inform action-oriented solutions and policy-making is dramatically expanded when individuals can translate the information into compelling narratives around sustainable development. While advances in data visualizations and digital mapping have helped make geospatial data more accessible to a broader range of audiences, storytelling is yet another powerful tool for helping convey why certain data is important, what it means, and how we can use it for sustainable development. In many ways, storytelling can be seen as a pillar of science communication in the realm of mapping and GIS and beyond. In recognizing this, many leaders in GIS technologies have developed additional software and tools to explicitly combine geographic information with multimedia to help users build narratives around maps and geospatial data.

Esri's ArcGIS StoryMaps is one example of a highly popular tool that has been used globally and in very diverse capacities to expand the traditional use and audience of geospatial data. Especially in the case of sustainable development, ArcGIS StoryMaps can help contextualize data presented, tell meaningful stories that can advance awareness of the SDGs, and effectively guide policy-making. Allen Carrol, former art director and chief cartographer at National Geographic Maps, and founder of the StoryMaps team and program at Esri, emphasizes that "Maps add extra dimensions to multimedia stories. They pin a narrative to place; they place a story within a larger context; they provide additional, deeper insights" (Carroll, 2020).

Esri's ArcGIS StoryMaps tool is used to tell a range of location-based, action-oriented stories around sustainable development. For example, The Nature Conservancy of California's StoryMap on Nature-Based Climate Solutions: A Roadmap to Accelerate Action in California uses the platform to explain the benefits of nature-based climate solutions in California and uses interactive mapping features to highlight critical issues and policy opportunities specific to different geographies and communities (Figure 5.1).

Harvard and Esri collaborated on a story map titled, Call to Action: End environmental racism now to illustrate the potential of a new bill being introduced to address critical disparities in how pollution is harming black communities. The storymap utilizes geospatial data on air pollution in conjunction with demographic community data to highlight these disparities' urgency and articulate the policy solutions to help address them (Figure 5.2).

The UN Refugee Agency (UNHCR) has published several storymaps to show up-to-date geographic visualizations and statistics on global refugee crises. Their story "Space, shelter and scarce resources—coping with COVID-19," for example, utilizes multimedia to draw attention to the critical issue of displaced communities struggling to cope with COVID-19, especially under conditions of densely populated refugee camps with limited medical and social resources (Figure 5.3).

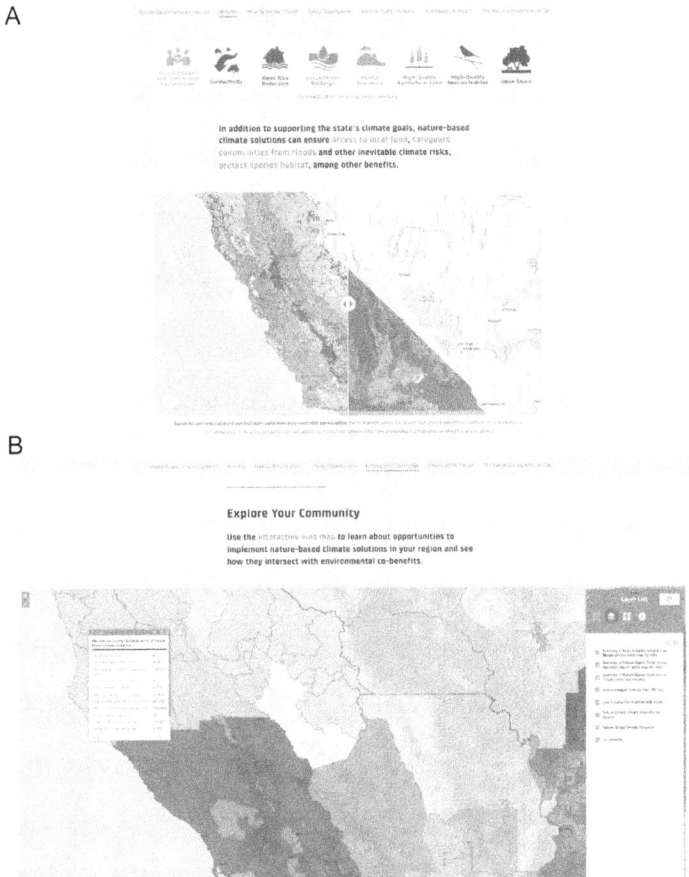

Figure 5.1a, 5.1b Selected images from ArcGIS StoryMap: "Nature-Based Climate Solutions. A Roadmap to Accelerate Action in California" by The Nature Conservancy. https://storymaps.arcgis.com/stories/a891b41520c343a582b845dcbb89e48b

Recognizing the power of storytelling with real-time geospatial data for sustainable development, the SDSN partnered with Esri and National Geographic to run an ArcGIS Storytelling Competition for the SDGs. Using ArcGIS StoryMaps, storytellers from forty-seven countries, including university students and professionals, submitted location-based, data-driven stories that addressed one or more SDGs. Guest judges whose expertise ranged from science communication, development economics to indigenous rights and activism selected first-, second-, and third-place winners in a student and professional track. The stories themselves included a remarkable span of topics. In the student track, "Hidden Realities" story took first prize for its "compelling infographics and personal narratives about

Figure 5.2a, 5.2b, 5.2c Selected images from ArcGIS StoryMap: "Call to Action: End environmental racism now" by Harvard and Esri. https://storymaps.arcgis.com/stories/da0df1524c704b488d79bb3e656addb3

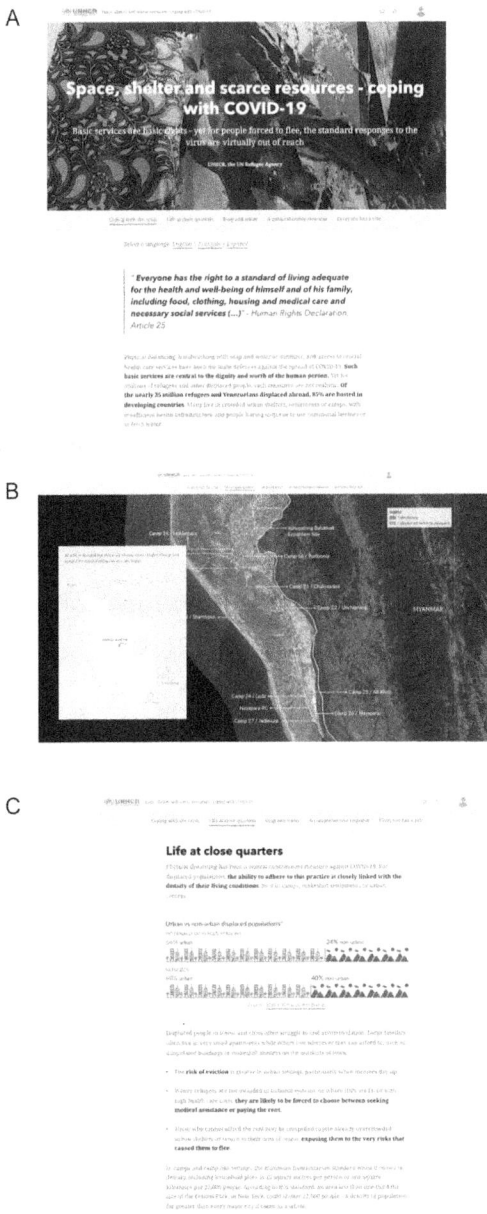

Figure 5.3a, 5.3b, 5.3c Selected images from ArcGIS StoryMap: "Space, shelter and scarce resources—coping with COVID-19" UNHCR, the UN Refugee Agency. https://storymaps.arcgis.com/stories/e1da7d80fbcf4ce8a3a954910c1e7f37

femicide in Turkey." Second place for the student category was won by students in Indonesia, who analyzed the impacts of weather and natural disaster on agricultural lands in their story, "iBanker Kendal Regency." What you CAN'T see in the Tennessee River was the third-place winner in the student track, examining pollution in the Tennessee River—a water source for recreation, power generation, drinking water, and biodiversity (Harrower, 2021).

One of the main attractive aspects of this tool is that it is incredibly user-friendly and intuitive to use, no matter your technical background in GIS and mapping. Storymaps are therefore authored by a wide variety of users, ranging from primary school students to researchers to professionals at major international development agencies. Their ease of use also makes them particularly effective entry points for working GIS and geo-literacy into education materials and curricula.

Examples of GIS and Storytelling in Sustainable Development Education

Many educators are already using GIS and storymaps to engage their students in sustainable development. A study assessing teachers' perceptions of ArcGIS StoryMaps as effective teaching tools reported that they "were user-friendly, interactive and engaging, enjoyable for students, and able to help in presenting material that meets academic standards" (Strachan and Mitchell, 2014). Technical education programs at the high school level have also seen inspiring success with GIS curricula and GIS technology, and these tools, including storytelling platforms, are being used in higher education as well. Debbie Stevens, an instructor at the Indian Hills Community College Geospatial Program, even uses ArcGIS StoryMaps as a platform to articulate how "GIS can be used to engage students across the curriculum in classroom instruction and field work" in K-12 education (Stevens, 2021). The following examples highlight the versatility of GIS and data-driven storytelling and its value in applied learning from grade school through university.

Middle School

Eco Ambassador Summer Curriculum

Mission 4.7 brings together leaders from government, academia, civil society, and business to accelerate the implementation of Education for Sustainable Development around the world. In an effort to integrate geospatial literacy and knowledge into educational curricula and support Mission 4.7, SDSN SDGs Today and the Eco Ambassadors Program at the Center for Sustainable Development at Columbia University joined forces to develop a GIS-oriented summer curriculum for middle school and highs school students concerned with sustainable development and climate challenges.

The 2021 summer curriculum combined ocean science and sustainability with GIS mapping and storytelling activities (Eco Ambassadors Program, n.d.). In collaboration with Esri, SDGs Today and the Eco Ambassador Program prepared collections of ArcGIS StoryMaps, Learn Lessons (ArcGIS guided lessons), and virtual workshops activities. These GIS resources provide students with a new skill set that can enable a network of youth to facilitate the exchange of ideas and empower students to use local data and information to inform solutions applicable to their communities and share their findings with other youth networks addressing similar challenges.

The program aims to serve as an educational model merging the SDGs with new data sources and technologies that can significantly enhance their ability to interact with data and provide data-driven outputs and produce geospatial analysis that can track change and progress over time and various geographies.

The program culminated with students publishing a stellar collection of ArcGIS StoryMaps featured on SDGsToday's homepage (Figure 5.4).

High School

The Glendale Unified School District's Career and Technical Education (CTE) program integrates technical skills with core academics to prepare students for college and careers. Through CTE, Dominique Evans-Bye, a biology teacher and certified GIS professional at Anderson W. Clark Magnet High School (CMHS) in La Crescenta, California, created a GIS curriculum where students are introduced to using and applying GIS to their coursework. The course teaches students how to use GIS to monitor and communicate data about the locations and conditions of natural disasters caused by geological processes (Esri, n.d.). Students work through college-level textbooks and GIS tutorials and have come up with impressive projects involving the analysis of heavy metal sediment between the Port of Los Angeles and the Los Angeles River, studies on water conservation at local school district campuses, global analyses on volatile organic compounds and air pollution levels, and food sustainability issues in their local areas (Esri, n.d.).

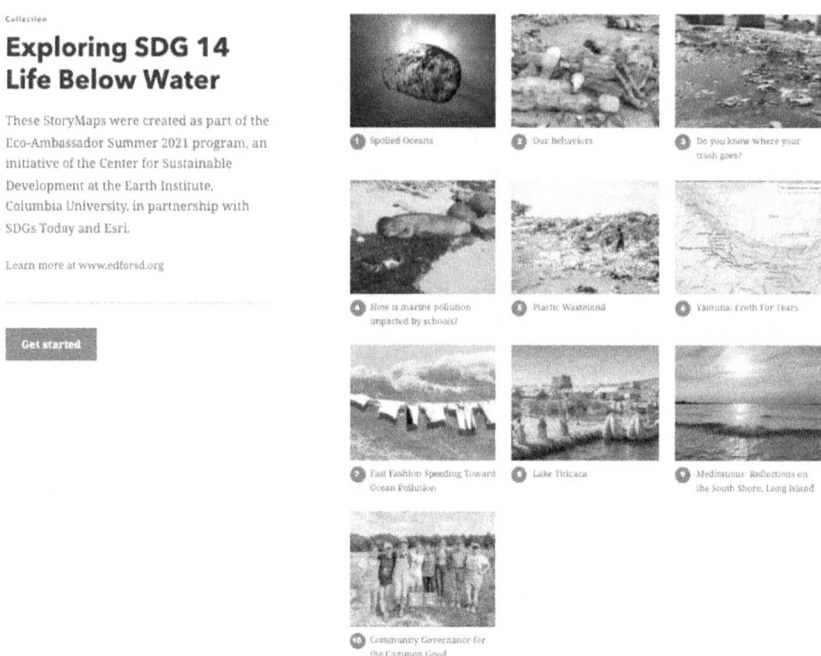

Figure 5.4 ArcGIS StoryMap Collection: Exploring SDG 14 Life Below Water. https://storymaps.arcgis.com/collections/fee26719ccf242b1b7dc9c096019c6df

Another project included a food sustainability program inspired by the previously mentioned 2020 ArcGIS StoryMaps Competition for the SDGs. Students used GIS to conduct drive-time analyses to find nearby donation locations, source bamboo utensil distributors for bulk purchase and used ArcGIS Survey123 to gather and display survey data to determine vegetarian meal option demand. The project effectively touched on ten of the seventeen SDGs, using GIS to address issues right at their own school: food waste, the use of single-use plastics, and a lack of vegetarian meal options (Esri, n.d.; Figure 5.5).

Higher Education

As highlighted by the 2020 ArcGIS StoryMap competition for the SDGs, storymaps are being used by university-level students in remarkable ways as well. The Arctic Data Stories workshop, for example, is an interdisciplinary intensive exposing students to issues at the intersection of Arctic science, policy, and communication. The workshop was started in partnership with the Belfer

GIS and Storytelling   65

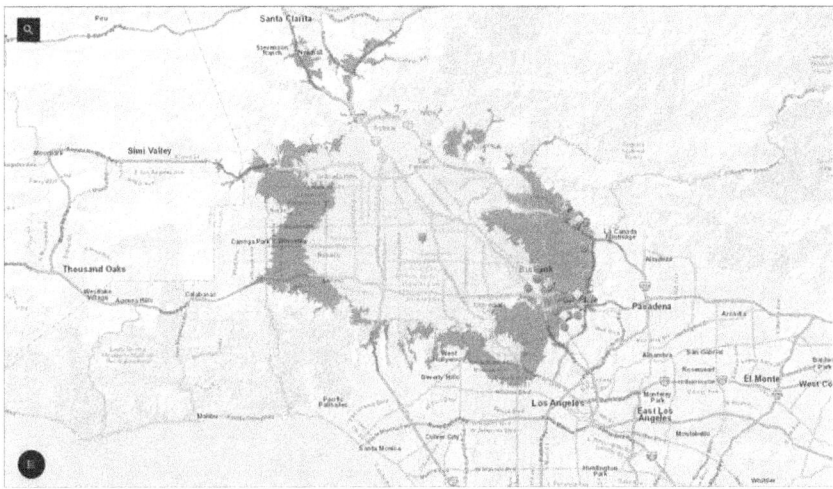

Figure 5.5 From Esri Case Study "High School Students Learn Real-World STEM Skills with GIS": "A still interactive map used in the 'Students Search for Sustainability' narrative map shows a drive-time analysis of donation locations in the vicinity of the nonprofit organization, Food Forward." https://www.esri.com/en-us/lg/industry/education/high-school-students-learn-stem-skills-with-gis

Figure 5.6 Selected image from ArcGIS StoryMap: "The Quest for Arctic Power." https://storymaps.arcgis.com/stories/c7c70a6b39a243f6a535403f25c666b7

Center's Arctic Initiative and Woodwell Climate Research Center to answer the question: How best should scientists target their visualizations to policymakers or the public? The organizations found that using storymaps as "[d]ynamic multimedia contextualization tools for maps [would be] the perfect way to

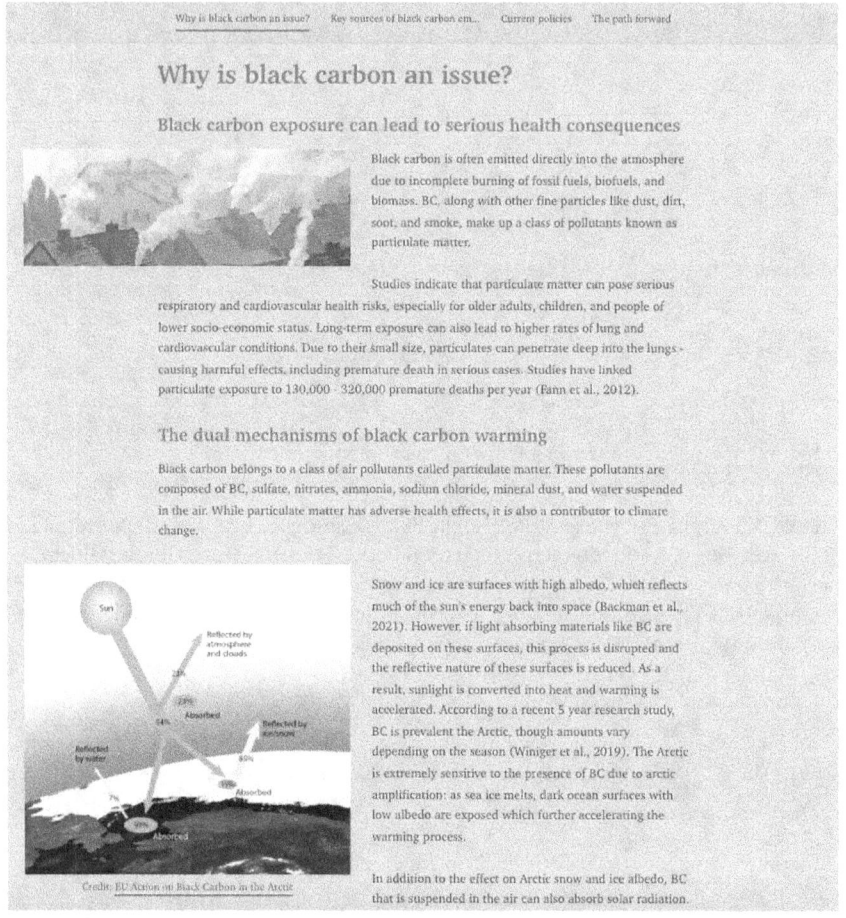

Figure 5.7 Selected image from ArcGIS StoryMap: "Dual Threat: The Impact of Black Carbon on Arctic Warming." https://storymaps.arcgis.com/stories/f7f4ea7a78234a8489f31a5c4aea0948

integrate science and policy in a clear and interesting narrative." Through the month-long, weekly virtual workshop, students from the Harvard Kennedy School, Harvard Law School, the Harvard Graduate School of Design, Harvard Divinity School, Tufts Fletcher School, Smith College, and others published awe-inspiring stories tackling issues ranging from black carbon to urbanization to international security (Dewey, 2021). During one of the workshops, Greg Fiske, a senior geospatial analyst at the Woodwell Climate Research Center, perfectly summed up the power of maps. "They distill a story out of a highly complex system, identify patterns in otherwise hidden data, and they invoke conversation" (Dewey, 2021; Figures 5.6–5.8).

Figure 5.8 Selected image from ArcGIS StoryMap: "Innovation and Adaptation in the Urban Arctic." https://storymaps.arcgis.com/stories/f94cad8aab5544a7ba724d8b5c81493f

How Students Are Contributing to and Engaging in the GIS Community

Students have a lot to gain from education programs involving GIS, but the interactive nature of GIS means that students can also play a meaningful role in contributing to the GIS community for sustainable development in many ways. Kerski highlights the value of GIS being interactive and collaborative by nature—"students can gather locations with GPS or smartphone apps such as Survey123 along with information about tree species, historical buildings, water quality, or other variables on a field trip or on their own school or university campus. The data can be gathered in citizen science mode by all students simultaneously populating a single online web map" (Kerski, 2018). Following are a few examples of the important role student engagement plays in actually contributing to the larger ecosystem of GIS and quality, timely, geo-referenced data.

Earthrise Education

Earthrise Media, a technology-led creative agency providing meaningful satellite imagery for news reporting and action on climate change and conservation, launched Earthrise Education. This classroom tool uses collaborative mapping and satellite imagery to support real-world investigations. The tool enables project-based learning in the natural and social sciences using mapping technology designed specifically for young learners (grades 7–11), and the outcomes provide "valuable information to scientists, activists, and journalists—people who need real-time information to support local change" (Earthrise Education, https://earthrise.education/).

Their lesson plans cover various topics and are based on real-world problems relating to sustainable development. Using data from satellite imagery, students can investigate the global impacts of climate change through a glacial retreat in the Hindu Kush Himalaya mountain belt or measure the scale of and identify causes of deforestation in the Peruvian Amazon.

One of the first Earthrise investigation lessons was a project on natural resources and uncontacted indigenous people. High school students in Massachusetts and Iowa were challenged to find and measure illegal gold mines in the Yanomami territory of the Amazon using high-resolution satellite imagery, and the geospatial data that Reuters and Survival International picked up the students generated through the exercise for a groundbreaking storymap-based news piece that garnered over 3 million views (Young and Hammer, 2020).

Cady Coleman, a former NASA Astronaut, has commended the program and tool, affirming that "Today's environmental challenges require many more people doing much more to protect our home planet" and that "[t]he Earthrise tool has the potential to engage a broad and inclusive group of students in environmentalism" (Young and Hammer, 2020).

My School Today

SDG 4 aims to ensure inclusive and equitable quality education for all, but access remains a significant challenge. While enrollment rates continue to increase, other quality barriers remain for many students and learners. Physical distance to educational facilities is one such barrier. A long commute to school can negatively impact students' learning outcomes, even if they are successfully enrolled. A one-minute increase in walking time can decrease a student's writing proficiency by one percentage point (Afoakwah and Koomson, 2021). Such a rate could prove extremely limiting for students in rural areas, particularly those without vehicular transportation.

The SDSN's SDGs Today program launched My School Today in July 2021, a call to action to support students, local communities, and ministries of education to geo-reference schools and education facilities as part of an effort to promote timely information on school locations in Africa. SDGs Today provides an accessible product to share national population counts within various travel distances and times from recorded educational facilities. Using open-source geo-referenced data and satellite data products, SDGs Today constructs travel-time isochrones from school locations and overlays subnational population counts to build a dataset of age-specific population counts within travel-time catchment areas in Africa. The resulting walk-time data can help support gaps in existing education data and highlight open-source methods

My School Today not only aims to promote geospatial literacy through GIS education resources and activities, but also, in fact, relies on the local participation of students, communities, and other actors in the ongoing development of the dataset (Mapping School Locations, n.d.). Students can access a collection of mapping guides, educational lessons, and material on the SDGs and GIS, map their school in OpenStreetMap or ArcGIS Online, and provide additional information about their schools that is made available to policymakers and other stakeholders (Figure 5.9).

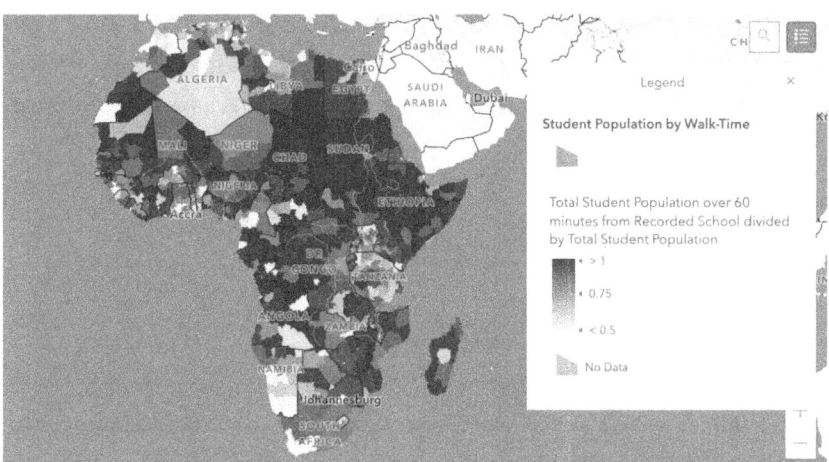

Figure 5.9 The My School Today Dashboard. https://sdgstoday.org/version-test/dataset/mapping-school-locations

Citizen Science for Clean Drinking Water

Educationalists at Earth Institute's Center for Sustainable Development and geochemists at Lamont-Doherty Earth Observatory at Columbia University in New York City collaborated on a citizen-science project in Alirajpur, India, to locate wells with safe drinking water. With more than 1,000 data points, the resulting map helps governmental departments make water quality decisions and brings the community closer to achieving SDG 6: ensure the availability and sustainable management of water and sanitation for all (Iyengar and van Geen, 2020).

Partnerships for GIS and Sustainable Development Education

Many of the programs mentioned earlier and initiatives were made possible by institutional partnership. Organizations beyond the education sector have recognized the importance for children and young professionals to have a strong grounding in geographic literacy to understand the increasingly interconnected world around them and have implemented programs and technologies that aid in this endeavor.

A noticeable trend of organizations pairing GIS tools and resources with education material reflects the desire to have constituents trained in these tools and skills. Professor Jeffrey Sachs has emphasized that our most significant challenges with sustainable development, such as deep transformations of our energy and land-use systems, are inherently geospatial and has advocated heavily for "students of sustainable development and businesses in key sectors [to] become highly proficient in GIS mapping, modeling, and design" (Kantor, 2020).

GIS Resources for All

Empowering educators and students with GIS knowledge and tools also require resources and funding to develop the infrastructure needed to integrate geospatial literacy into curricula. Several studies have been carried out (Kholoshyn et al., 2021; Mkhongi and Musakwa, 2020; Mzuza and Van Der Westhuizen, 2019; Akinyemi, 2015) to assess the gaps in GIS education. Poor funding, shortage of technical support, and inadequate infrastructures are some of the challenges schools, particularly in African countries, encounter. Various initiatives around the world are working toward making GIS educational resources more accessible to students:

- The Education Commission's GIS for Education Working Group in collaboration with the EdTech Hub explores new ways to support the education and non-education sectors with geospatial enablement.
- Esri offers free software through their Schools Program (Schools Program, n.d.) to all public, private, and home schools, in addition to youth clubs. The ArcGIS School package includes a collection of online tools and lessons to support K-12 students.
- QGIS is a free and open-source GIS software package accessible to students and teachers everywhere.
- Google Earth Education (Google Earth Education, n.d.) provides lessons and tutorials on how to use Google Earth and Google's mapping tools that can help teachers integrate geospatial technology into educational curricula.
- Mapbox gives students and teachers access to educational resources through Learn with Mapbox (Learn with Mapbox, n.d.) that can be integrated into the classroom.

Education systems and schools require increased funding and structural changes to curricula in order to develop to more robustly integrate GIS technology. Using resources already freely available to schools, however, will accelerate the introduction of GIS to students and provide an opportunity to develop analytical and spatial skills that will enhance not only their career paths, but also, their role in designing sustainable solutions to address social, environmental, and economic challenges.

Conclusion and Next Steps

Our ability to address some of the world's most pressing challenges in sustainable development will rely heavily on our ability to train and equip the next generation of leaders with the necessary tools and technologies. Youth are already showing their leadership in sustainable development, stepping up to challenges like the 2020 ArcGIS StoryMap Competition for the SDGs, and making valuable contributions to the geospatial data ecosystem that has inspired globally recognized journalism. Using GIS in the classroom and data-driven storytelling can be a powerful way to inform local, national, and global policies and decision-making processes that impact their future, and more broadly, help the global community track progress on the SDGs. Combining geospatial information and technologies with storytelling instruments enables students to engage with a broader audience and mobilize their peers and other stakeholders to propel the SDGs. The skills used and acquired through GIS and storytelling are applicable for any age group, as demonstrated by the wide range of programs used across education levels.

Recognizing this critical potential and need for utilizing technologies like GIS in sustainable development education, we must work to close the digital and educational divide that persists and has been significantly exacerbated by the COVID-19 pandemic. Students worldwide have the potential to engage with GIS and data-driven storytelling in a way that can help illustrate the dynamic nature of our challenges and connect communities across different locations working toward improving the state of sustainable development for all. To increase the chances of a more sustainable future, we must invest in building the skills and provide equitable access to the information and tools students need to bring change.

References

Afoakwah, C., & Koomson, I. (2021). How Does School Travel Time Impact Children's Learning Outcomes in a Developing Country? *Review of Economics of the Household*, 19, pp. 1–21. doi:10.1007/s11150-020-09533-8.

Akinyemi, F. (2015). An Assessment of GIS Use for Teaching in Rwandan Secondary Schools. *The Geography Teacher*, 12(1), pp. 27–40, doi:10.1080/19338341.2014.975144.

Aladag, E. (2014). An Evaluation of Geographic Information Systems in Social Studies Lessons: Teachers' Views. *Educational Sciences: Theory & Practice*, 14(4), pp. 1533–9.

Bonaccorsi, E. (2018). *GIS for a Sustainable World: Bringing the Power of Maps to the SDGs*. IISD. https://sdg.iisd.org/commentary/generation-2030/gis-for-a-sustainable-world-bringing-the-power-of-maps-to-the-sdgs/, Accessed December 27, 2021.

Carroll, A. (2020). Why Maps? *ArcGIS StoryMap*. https://storymaps.arcgis.com/stories/4c4b9cc3cba44e3a860b4a9c09accb87. Date Accessed May 25, 2022

Cruz-Jesus, F., Oliveira, T., & Bacao, F. (2018). The Global Digital Divide: Evidence and Drivers. *Journal of Global Information Management (JGIM)*, 26(2), pp. 1–26.

Dewey, S. (2021). "Arctic Data Stories: A Collection of Student-created StoryMaps from the Arctic Initiative and Woodwell Climate Research Center Arctic Data

Stories Workshop," featured in Belfer Center Spring 2021 Newsletter. Belfer Center for Science and International Affairs, Harvard Kennedy School. https://www.belfercenter.org/arctic-data-stories. Date Accessed May 25, 2022.

Earthrise Education (n.d.). https://earthrise.education/. Date Accessed May 25, 2022.

Eco Ambassadors Program. SDGs Today. www.sdgstoday.org/eco-ambassadors-program, Accessed December 30, 2021.

Esri (n.d.). High School Students Learn Real-World STEM Skills with GIS. https://www.esri.com/en-us/lg/industry/education/high-school-students-learn-stem-skills-with-gis. Date Accessed May 25, 2022.

Esri (n.d.). What is GIS? https://www.esri.com/en-us/what-is-gis/overview. Date Accessed May 25, 2022.

Esri (2020). Jeffrey Sachs Discusses the Critical Roles of GIS and Storytelling in Solving Global Challenges. *ArcGIS StoryMaps Blog*. https://www.esri.com/arcgis-blog/products/story-maps/constituent-engagement/jeffrey-sachs-discusses-the-critical-roles-of-gis-and-storytelling-in-solving-global-challenges/. Date Accessed May 25, 2022.

Fitchett, P.G., & Good, A.J. (2012). Teaching Genocide through GIS: A Transformative Approach. *The Clearing House: A Journal of Educational Strategies, Issues and Ideas*, 85(3), pp. 87–92.

Giga Connectivity, UNICEF. www.gigaconnect.org, Accessed December 30, 2021.

Google Earth Education. https://www.google.com/intl/en_in/earth/education/resources/, Accessed December 30, 2021.

GPSS, World Bank. www.gpss.worldbank.org, Accessed December 30, 2021.

Harrower, M. (2021). Seven Lessons from the 2020 ArcGIS StoryMaps Competition Winners. *ArcGIS StoryMaps Blog*. https://www.esri.com/arcgis-blog/products/arcgis-storymaps/constituent-engagement/seven-lessons/. Date Accessed May 25, 2022.

Iyengar, R., & van Geen, L. (2020). Enhancing the Impact of Well Testing for Fluoride: Raising Awareness by Local Participation. ArcGIS StoryMap. https://storymaps.arcgis.com/stories/20b91f66ec5f4bf3ae190111f7ca866b. Date Accessed May 25, 2022.

Kantor, M. (2020). Sustainable Business: A Conversation with Jeffrey Sachs. *Where Next Magazine, Esri*. https://www.esri.com/about/newsroom/publications/wherenext/sustainable-business-a-conversation-with-jeffrey-sachs/. Date Accessed May 25, 2022.

Kerski, J. (2018). Why GIS in Education Matters. *Geospatial World*. https://www.geospatialworld.net/blogs/why-gis-in-education-matters/. Date Accessed May 25, 2022.

Kholoshyn, I., Nazarenko, T., Bondarenko, O., Hanchuk, O., & Varfolomyeyeva, I. (2021). The Application of Geographic Information Systems in Schools Around the World: A Retrospective Analysis. *Journal of Physics: Conference Series*, 1840(1), p. 012017. doi:10.1088/1742-6596/1840/1/012017.

Local Burden of Disease Educational Attainment Collaborators (2020). Mapping Disparities in Education across Low-and Middle-Income Countries. *Nature*, 577(7789), p. 235. https://doi.org/10.1038/s41586-019-1872-1.

Mapping School Locations, SDGs Today. www.sdgstoday.org/dataset/mapping-school-locations, Accessed December 30, 2021.

Mkhongi, Felicity A., & Musakwa, W. (2020). Perspectives of GIS Education in High Schools: An Evaluation of uMgungundlovu District, KwaZulu-Natal, South Africa. *Education Sciences*, 10(5), p. 131. doi:10.3390/educsci10050131.

My School Today. SDGs Today. www.sdgstoday.org/myschooltoday, Accessed December 30, 2021.

Mzuza, M., & Van Der Westhuizen, C. (2019). Review on the State of GIS Application in Secondary Schools in the Southern African Region. *South African Geographical Journal*, 101(2), pp. 175–91, doi:10.1080/03736245.2019.1579110.

Nature. 2020. Education Must Fix its Data Deficit. *Nature Editorials*, 564, p. 564. https://doi.org/10.1038/d41586-020-01263-2.

Psacharopoulos, G., & Patrinos, H.A. (2018). Returns to Investment in Education: A Decennial Review of the Global Literature. *Education Economics*, 26(5), pp. 445–58.

Rasinen, A. (2003). An Analysis of the Technology Education Curriculum of Six Countries. 15(1). https://scholar.lib.vt.edu/ejournals/JTE/v15n1/pdf/rasinen.pdf. Date Accessed May 25, 2022.

Schools Program, Esri. https://esri.com/schools, Accessed December 30, 2021.

Stevens, D. (2021). GIS in K-12 Education. ArcGIS StoryMap. https://storymaps.arcgis.com/stories/ee191b1d6305476988160802f7e4f2d0. Date Accessed May 25, 2022.

Strachan, C., & Mitchell, J. (2014). Teachers' Perceptions of ESRI Story Maps as Effective Teaching Tools. *Review of International Geographical Education Online*, 4(3), pp. 195–220.

The World Bank (2021). Learning Data Compact – UNESCO, UNICEF, and the World Bank Unite to End the Learning Data Crisis. https://www.worldbank.org/en/news/factsheet/2021/06/30/learning-data-compact-unesco-unicef-and-the-world-bank-unite-to-end-the-learning-data-crisis. Date Accessed May 25, 2022.

Young, K., & Hammer, D. (2020). *Connecting Students to Real-World Investigations through Satellite Imagery. Projects in Action*. Buck Institute for Education. https://www.pblworks.org/blog/connecting-students-real-world-investigations-through-satellite-imagery. Date Accessed May 25, 2022.

6

Lifelong Learning for All
Lessons from the Columbia Climate School

Cassie Xu

With the world facing limited resources, continued population growth, and warming temperatures, we have a clear need to empower change and work collectively toward a sustainable future. One of the key ways this can be done is through initiatives that center on the idea of Education for Sustainable Development (ESD). UNESCO defines ESD as the process by which we can improve access to quality education, transform society by reorienting education, and help people develop the knowledge, skills, values, and behaviors needed for sustainable development (UNESCO, 2002). Specifically, this means including important concepts like earth systems science into formal and informal teaching and learning environments to better understand the importance of our individual and collective roles in creating a more sustainable world.

ESD goes beyond formal learning environments and is continuous. It is helpful to think about ESD as lifelong K-grey education that involves many audiences and stakeholders who aim to provide meaningful contributions to the development of a whole learner. Stakeholders involved in K-grey education efforts might include K12 students, parents and educators, industry professionals, non-government and community-based organizations, and informal learning organizations. Together, all of these connections form an important networked community that can organize for effective and efficient problem solving and concentrate all participants' strengths to create actionable results.

There is a need for training and educating future generations through ESD, particularly when providing access to quality content and innovative practices grounded in strong basic science through informal learning. The research on processes like climate change is changing rapidly, as are career prospects in the Science, Technology, Engineering, and Mathematics (STEM) fields. This increases the need for the teaching and learning in the space to follow suit. Learning for ESD can occur in many different environments and contexts and over other points in time. We do not stop learning just because we are outside of a traditional classroom, so it is essential to consider the different opportunities and circumstances that allow learners to be introduced to new science.

By offering opportunities for all to engage at different points in their lives and educational and professional careers, we can begin to normalize the idea that at any given moment, individuals are welcome to engage with new content and practices that empower them to play a role in achieving sustainability goals (Goodwill and Chen, 2021). Lifelong learning is an essential component of the UN's Sustainable Development Goals (SDGs), particularly from the perspective that the possibilities of lifelong learning will enable sustainable development processes and ensure the attainment of other SDGs.

This chapter will present two examples from the Columbia Climate School that will look at how lifelong learning opportunities are being facilitated for K-grey audiences. Through the examples, we hope to convey the idea that lifelong learning can take place in numerous settings and formats. Suppose we can foster a flexible structure where people from different backgrounds and stages in their educational and professional careers can converge to take part in new learning and training. In that case, we can leverage our unique strengths to elevate the importance of sustainable development practices.

Learning and teaching opportunities across K-grey levels will train and prepare future generations of learners to develop an agile growth mindset through science that can embrace lifelong learning outside of classroom walls, gain comfort with complexity, and set the ability to solve cross-cultural problems through teamwork. These informal learning opportunities provide learners with the capacity for creative invention and imagination, envision what is not there, and go forward with confidence.

The Columbia Climate School

Higher education institutions have a unique role to play in the ESD endeavor. The Columbia Climate School, which now encompasses the Earth Institute, provides a helpful example of how informal educational activities grounded in sound science, broad knowledge, and diverse perspectives can amplify the engagement of diverse audiences to motivate collective action. For the school, engaging in informal outreach activities channels knowledge derived from primary and applied research, contribute to developing an adaptive workforce in an ever-changing career landscape, motivate policy, influence decision-making, and empower individual action. The underlying premise is recognizing that solutions for a sustainable world and strategies for sustainable development require resources and brainpower beyond what any single sector of society can provide.

Many informal outreach activities existed before the formation of the school. The school structure allows us to establish a centrally coordinated office than can consolidate resources for content development, organize convenings, and become a resource for internal and external partners outside our formal degree programs. To this end, we have structured learning and engagement activities to collaborate. This means understanding what external stakeholders need and working with content area experts to design teaching and learning opportunities to meet specific needs.

The outreach efforts of the Climate School have established a significant footprint for developing innovative K-grey and educator training programs in the earth and environmental sciences. A special class of public outreach comprises community engagement programs that promote social capital through broadly based umbrella initiatives. For example, initiatives focused on alleviating social inequities through engagement with children in disadvantaged communities, with climate themes as foci, provide a structure for building social capital through goal- and solutions-driven interactions.

Another public outreach class is developing and delivering content and resources, which could be broadly shared and accessible to anyone who wants the information. Open online resources—developed in concert with other content modules—are now a hallmark of the school's approach to increasing accessibility to climate literacy—from videos to climate primers in multiple languages and formats.

This particular set of activities is where we will draw our two examples, and that includes our E.I. LIVE K12 E.I. Teach series.

Drawing on our hub and spokes model and our location in a city home to the largest school district in the country, the school is strategically set up to engage in this work. The human and organizational capacities for sustained educational excellence take decades to develop. In our case, this includes subject matter and pedagogical expertise, internal networks of collaboration and training, equipment and facilities, a repertoire of curriculum and appropriate research activities, ongoing connections to networks of educators and schools, partnerships with other "informal" educational programs, private funding sources, and a reputation for excellence with the federal funding agencies and reviewers.

E.I. LIVE K12

Our first example of public outreach is the E.I. LIVE K12 series. Named for the Earth Institute and implemented in April 2020 when the COVID-19 pandemic had reached New York City's doorsteps, the series started as a temporary way to supplement science learning for K12 students and educators who were now learning remotely.

Prior to the pandemic, the Earth Institute offered numerous informal opportunities through on-campus talks and outreach events, but there were not many online offerings. Many in-person learning activities centered on hands-on demonstrations for visitors in the New York metro area. The move online in April of 2020 forced us (in the best way possible) to get outside of our comfort zone to deliver quality and yet engaging science to broader audiences through a new modality.

Some talks and topics were not as well-suited to an online format. Therefore we curated content that could be covered over a short amount of time without any prior knowledge that numerous age groups could join in. In many ways, we are still testing out our content, as the demand for different science shifts with whatever else is happening in the world. We will also continue to adjust our formats and frequency of how/when these sessions are offered.

But one thing is for sure. Now, after more than 40 sessions that have reached over 10,000 individuals, the series is here to stay. Together with the E.I. LIVE platform, the series brings the science behind the climate crisis and sustainability to audiences nationally and internationally virtually. The K-12 channel features experts from around the Climate School to present relevant sustainability content in forty-five to sixty-minute live sessions for students, parents, and educators.

Each session has an appropriate targeted age range based on the topic, and the sessions vary between topical lectures, demos, and skills-based training. In addition to the videos, and whenever possible, we offer additional educational resources related to the content covered in these online sessions. The topics are decided on based on what our audience requests and the latest/most relevant science for this particular audience.

For each episode that has aired, a specific format is followed. Content area experts typically begin with an introduction/overview of a topic, share recent findings, and, if applicable, do a relevant hands-on activity. Once the content part is over, we open it up for Q&A with the audience, which is carefully facilitated to ensure that audience members have the time and space to have their questions addressed by our scientific experts. Following each session, recordings are shared with all viewers, along with additional reading material and activities where appropriate.

Each session is different in the content and speaker but follows a specific pattern. There is a strong focus on introducing the topic in a way accessible to the audience, so little jargon is used and real-world applications are emphasized. Most of the sessions do not require participants to have any prior knowledge of the topic, and for those that do require some previous knowledge, we ensure that learners can watch the last recording. Speakers use various tools, such as videos, music, images, and diagrams to communicate their science. By doing so, we are appealing to different learning styles and creating immersive experiences where participants are on a virtual journey with the scientists. The direct result of this is that participants are gaining a greater understanding of how the scientific evidence has been gathered and analyzed and how it connects to real-world experiences. An indirect result of these sessions has been an opportunity for participants to gain insight into *how* the science is done and the highs and lows that come with the territory of being a professional scientist. By getting a glimpse into the process of science, viewers get a behind-the-scenes look at the everyday lived experiences of the scientists.

The programming is often a delicate balance between traditional content lectures, hands-on activities, and demonstrations. The limited enrollment allows for an intimate environment that gives viewers the time and space to process the information and ask questions as learners regardless of the format. Given in Table 6.1 are just a few examples of the types of sessions we have aired in the last year.

Since April 2020, more than 3,000 individuals have tuned in to our E.I. LIVE K12 programming live and more than 7,100 views have been logged from the recordings that have been posted to the Earth Institute YouTube page.

E.I. Teach

Another educational offering that we believe is quite impactful is our remote E.I. Teach series that provides professional development opportunities for pre- and in-service educators. This online series began in the summer of 2020 and

Table 6.1 E.I. LIVE K12 Sessions

Session Title	Grade Level	Session Description
The Tip of the Ice Sheet	9–12	Participants go on a virtual adventure to traverse the West Antarctic Ice Sheet, measure how the ice flows, and learn about essential glaciology concepts.
Microplastics, Mega Impact	3–6	Microplastics have been found everywhere, from Arctic snow to the depths of the Mariana Trench. What are they exactly, where are they found, and why should we care about their emergence?
The Sound of What's Shaking	5–9	Learners explore seismology, the study of earthquakes, through seismic sounds. What do the sounds mean, and how are scientists using this information to understand earthquakes better?
Put a Ring on It	3–5	What can we learn about a tree's life and history by examining tree rings? Learn to analyze tree rings and how dendrochronologists use tree ring research to improve our understanding of past climate?
Sea for Yourself	7–12	Using a web-based app, students join scientists on an investigation to understand the sea level, why it changes, how it is changing, and the impacts.
I LavA Good Volcano	2–5	Learners explore different types of volcanoes, how volcanic eruptions happen, and the relationship between volcanoes and plate tectonics.
Communicating Climate Change	7–12	It's hard enough to get them to listen when we talk about something simple, so how do we get them to listen? Participants learn about the tools available for communication and how they can bring about real change.
How Global Climate Policy Works	9–12	What does climate change policy mean nationally and globally, and how can climate policies around the world protect our planet and help us take action?

has reached over 100 teachers across 12 states, 4 countries, and 5 time zones. We engaged with educators in numerous ways prior to 2020 in professional development opportunities, primarily through in-person professional development workshops on campus.

By being forced to move our learning opportunities for educators online, we expanded our reach in a way that was not possible before. Cultivating this online community for educators across different settings was genuinely impactful. Not only did educators attending the training walk away with content, but they also met and made connections with other educators that provided them with a learning community that could live beyond the training sessions. In this way, the online learning environment allowed them to network much more seamlessly and at a greater scale.

We see great value in making connections between scientific research and science education in school environments through scientific content (i.e., sea-level rise, ocean acidification) and scientific methods (i.e., data collection/analysis, communication).

Educators play a critical role in how future generations of learners will address the challenges of global sustainability and climate change. E.I. Teach joins the roster as our first program targeted primarily at educators of those students. Participation in E.I. Teach provides unparalleled access to experts from the school's numerous centers home to the world's leading climate scientists who are uniquely positioned to share their expertise with educators teaching in formal and informal learning spaces.

Because climate change is a relatively new subject area mandated in many schools, educators are often apprehensive about the content and the best practices. E.I. Teach aims to reduce the feelings of being overwhelmed by a new subject area by providing curricular ideas and ensuring that the content is integrated seamlessly into existing subjects.

To do this, E.I. Teach emphasizes that climate change education is a way of understanding the world that can benefit everyone. Climate change is in and of itself a systems problem that involves interconnected and dynamic processes, so our approach to teaching about it should also mimic that connectivity. It is not something that can only be taught as a science. By taking a systems approach to climate change education, students, and teachers alike can bring big ideas and integrated content across all curricular areas.

While each E.I. Teach session has different content goals, they follow a similar process. The sessions begin with a keynote speaker that provides foundational knowledge about a specific topic. In this keynote, which is often a lecture, we present the science and the facts that directly result from our research. We support findings with evidence and address questions about the science so that everyone has an opportunity to get on the same page and hook our learners with new knowledge.

After the keynote, the rest of the time is spent in sessions that focus more on translating new scientific research into activities that can be integrated into curricular units aligned to standards. During these sessions, presenters often share introductory content, but most of the time is spent sharing activity ideas with educators. The ideas range and can also be adapted for shorter versus longer lessons. Whatever the content or tool, the goal is to ensure students' engagement and connect the science idea to more extensive systems processes. In this way, teaching and learning become interdisciplinary. During this time, educators are also welcome to ask questions and participate in a discussion to share how they might adapt the content for their cohort of learners. This is also a time for educators to comment on their experiences of lesson planning and content delivery and learn from other educators in the room. Even though the educators come to hear from our scientific experts, their connections during informal discussions are a significant part of the experience. During this time, they learn about shared experiences in teaching and learning with other educators and often form essential connections with other participants who sustain their teaching careers.

The speakers who deliver a keynote versus those who focus on classroom-based activities are not the same. Everyone brings their unique strengths to the sessions, whether content knowledge or pedagogical expertise, which is an important piece of these sessions. One person alone cannot deliver everything that educators are looking for. Some educators might only want to hear the science, while others want to focus on lessons. In this way, these sessions are very much like classrooms, where learners have different curiosities and questions that they are after. So, we cannot have a one-size-fits-all approach and deliver content in just one way.

During the sessions that focus on classroom content, we train the educators as students. They are engaged in lifelong learning by seeking out professional development opportunities. The E.I. Teach sessions allow educators to learn and adapt to new content so that they are better prepared to deliver new science. The setup where educators become students again is an important one. The roles are switched in this setting, where they become students and hear from content experts. Educators can remove themselves from their typical teaching environments when this role reversal happens and become immersed in the content.

Gaining this perspective as a lifelong learner is a critical part of honing teaching and learning practices for educators. While the scientists are not pedagogical experts, they provide the educators with a chance to become a student, gain new content knowledge, and perhaps most importantly, engage in activities that bring real-world science research and data. Our ultimate hope is that when educators wrap up an E.I. Teach session, they are armed not only with lesson plans that are grounded in rich science but also perhaps more importantly, with the confidence to inspire a new generation of environmental stewards in their different teaching environments.

Findings and Best Practices

Education is an essential piece of the puzzle in our local and global response to climate change efforts. This generation of learners will feel the impacts of climate change more than any other. It is critical that every student is provided an opportunity to study and understand the climate crisis through a comprehensive and interdisciplinary lens across all subject levels and grades. Now more than ever, educators in different learning environments must be prepared to equip students with the knowledge, attitudes, and behaviors necessary to participate in sustainable global solutions.

The examples in this chapter are just a few anecdotal examples of outreach activities developed under the Columbia Climate School. It is essential to understand how we arrived at the design and implementation of these efforts. These programs have been shaped often by our ground-up and organic process and experiences. If we have picked our way toward increasingly useful programming, our guidepost has always been to center on the needs of learners, whether those learners are students or educators.

Here we outline some of the lessons learned from engaging in these activities, primarily from observations and anecdotal feedback from participants.

One of the most common things we hear from our audiences, from students to educators to parents and the public, is that these outreach opportunities provide them access to subject-area experts. Not everyone comes to these sessions to get resources or materials; they just want access to the experts so that they can learn from them and ask questions of them. We can incorporate this feedback into our planning for future programs. By having a better understanding of our audiences, their personal and professional goals for attending these educational sessions, and popular topics, we can sustain continued learning for our current audiences and engage new learners in lifelong learning as well.

We could not always pinpoint why individuals joined us for these sessions. We thought it was more about the resources that participants got to take away, but it went beyond that. The access to subject-area experts was fundamental to these learning opportunities because participants felt that they were able to directly engage with individuals and teams who are at the forefront of what they are doing. By creating a direct line and connection to end-users, we can contribute to a greater understanding of climate and strengthen climate literacy over time for various audiences. So, for us, it is not always about pieces of paper that we send them away with; it's about giving them different opportunities to engage at pivotal learning points with different content experts.

In line with this, when audiences can engage with content experts at a personal level, they become more comfortable with the science that can often feel distant from day-to-day experiences. By breaking down concepts that are seemingly complex, these informal learning opportunities allow learners to have fun and hear about content in a digestible format. This is very different than dumbing down the content in any way. It ultimately comes down to how things are communicated. Because we all know and understand science (and many other topics) differently, we need to think about how components of a seemingly complex topic can be shared differently.

Beyond offering audiences an accessible way to digest science, these outreach opportunities offer audiences the chance to learn about climate change together in real-time. That aspect of all being together in a shared learning environment opens up opportunities for us to learn from each other, not just the content experts. We have found that although these opportunities are promoted as K12 learning opportunities, we have a wide range of age groups joining us for these events. This signals that we are meeting different learning needs and that learning is happening at different times and stages for everyone.

We have heard very positive feedback from all of our participants about enjoying these opportunities. From elementary school students, we often hear about how they wished science was taught in this engaging way in their schools. From middle and high school students, we often hear about how these opportunities have inspired them to take action and do something about the impacts of climate change in their communities. We hear from educators (usually climate science novices) that our training has given them the confidence and expertise to incorporate climate science content into their classrooms. And broadly, we have heard from our adult learners that online learning has given them the ability to engage in lifelong learning. While many adults are not in the science/sustainability field, they have enjoyed learning with our experts and thinking more critically about their role in climate action. From this feedback, we realized that there was something for everyone to take away from these learning opportunities. Therefore, there is a need to continue offering these informal but equally important educational offerings.

Lastly, these outreach opportunities have created a convening space for K-grey audiences to tackle specific pieces of the climate science puzzle. The nature of covered topics spans both the physical and social sciences and coalesces around a central theme of systems thinking. Time and time again, the takeaway message for all viewers is that climate change goes beyond climate science. It does not simply exist in a stand-alone way in the sciences anymore, and, regardless of who we are, where we are, and how old we are, we are all going to witness (if we haven't already) the impacts of a warming planet. This clear message has allowed us to amplify our impact and link our science to awareness, education, impacts, and so much more.

We would argue that by interacting with world-renowned scientists (and each other), these opportunities have connected climate change to our biographies, stories, and lived experiences. They are an engaging way to facilitate a more holistic understanding of the climate system, specifically our role. By offering complex content in an informal setting where there are more personal interactions, we can start building a bridge between our individual stories and the complexities of climate change. These opportunities alone will not be enough, but they will start creating meaningful conversations and connections between global climate change and personal experiences.

Final Thoughts

When we started to offer these outreach opportunities, we set out with learning intentions primarily focused on content acquisition. While that has undoubtedly happened, we also believe that learners' success and understanding of the content have been strengthened due to the more nuanced, personal, and interpersonal connections that have shifted due to engagement with content experts.

This growth is harder to measure, but the learning opportunities through events such as E.I. LIVE K12 and E.I. Teach have made learners feel welcome. Ultimately, they have felt welcome because we have invited their interests and histories into our scientific and learning communities. We have been able to connect with them and gain their trust, and as a result, they have learned from us and with us.

These informal learning opportunities are crucial for lifelong learning by directly connecting with experts. Unlike Language Arts or Math, climate change is not always a topic K-grey audiences are learning and teaching in schools across all grade levels. Therefore, additional learning opportunities can play an important role in strengthening climate and scientific literacy across our citizenry.

In all of these remote learning sessions, we have tried to emphasize learning beyond performance expectations in a classroom. This is where these informal opportunities can have a lot of impact on bringing something learned in a traditional classroom environment to life and extending that learning. These outreach opportunities often force learners to think about complex processes and systems in crosscutting ways, and there is never an answer. We believe that it is dangerous to pigeonhole learners to think that there is always one correct answer in science. The point of this is to ensure that learners never have to choose one answer and that we are leaving it wide open for further exploration.

Alongside the benefits of these programs, there are also challenges. The first is the institutional barriers within higher education institutions around the idea of outreach. Our experts are first and foremost researchers, and their jobs are to do research. This often leaves little time to engage in these outreach activities, which can easily become overwhelming. Institutionally, there has not always been a culture for outreach that is sustained and for a general audience. Promotions and tenure acquisition add another layer of complexity to outreach. Most scientists are not promoted based on engaging with K-grey audiences in lifelong learning activities. They are offered job security and raises based on publications and grant dollars being brought in. While this is beginning to change, the idea that you should focus solely on publications and writing grants still dominates most science research organizations.

Despite the challenges, many feel the need to push onwards for lifelong learning opportunities for K-grey audiences across departments and schools. One of the main reasons driving this push is the idea that climate change will impact every aspect of society moving forward. Our goal with outreach is not to ensure that every learner becomes a climate scientist. It's the opposite. Through these learning opportunities that are accessible to different audiences, we are focused more on ensuring that everyone understands what is happening to our warming planet to apply that knowledge to their specific field.

The overarching goal of these outreach opportunities is aligned with the ESD framework of increasing access to and fostering inclusion within educational programming that facilitates lifelong learning. Education and outreach activities need to be formalized as institutional efforts to ensure that programs are well structured and offer reliable and meaningful learning opportunities for all audiences. We realize that collective action is required; what we need are systems-level changes and thinking if we will tackle the challenge of climate change. That starts with the education and training efforts of future generations. We hope that through our outreach opportunities, students will begin to see climate change as a systems problem and carry the weight of multidisciplinary thinking with them so that we will have a workforce in the future that understands broad global crises but be able to implement local strategies.

References

Goodwill, A.M., & Chen, S.H.A. (2021). *Embracing a Culture of Lifelong Learning: The Science of Lifelong Learning*. UNESCO Institute for Lifelong Learning, UNESDOC Digital Library. https://unesdoc.unesco.org/ark:/48223/pf0000377812?posInSet=1&queryId=04029ba5-690c-45ae-9e6d-c52696db00cf. Date Accessed May 25, 2022.

United Nations Educational, Scientific, and Cultural Organization (UNESCO) (2002). *Education for Sustainable Development*. Retrieved September 10, 2021 from https://en.unesco.org/themes/education-sustainable-development. Date Accessed September 10, 2022.

7

Building Cross-sectoral Education Programs for Sustainable Development

Design and Challenges

Niyati Malhotra and Yanis Ben Amor

Introduction

Education is often conceptualized as a tool for material well-being and economic growth because of its effect on improving human capital and its resulting contributions to the labor market, making it a cornerstone of Sustainable Development. While education necessarily develops these skills, it also has a crucial role to play in developing the holistic skills of children and young adults, especially in resource-constrained environments. Holistic development specifically refers to the interconnected development of intellectual, mental, physical, emotional, and social abilities in a child/adolescent so that he or she can face the demands and challenges of everyday life (Mahmoudi et al., 2012). This typically requires multifaceted approaches that do not solely rely on the education sector but ideally incorporate interventions from other complementary sectors such as health, gender, and infrastructure.

As such, school-based interventions can offer scalable and sustainable avenues for providing these holistic skills. In this chapter, we discuss our experience implementing two such programs in diverse contexts that emphasize consultative program design and innovative pedagogies to improve holistic outcomes for children.

Schools offer a unique setting where inter-sectoral programs to improve child outcomes can be situated and implemented. Schools are embedded features of local communities and provide a distinctive location where access to different types of education and services can be integrated and targeted toward children. Crucially, this also means that well-designed programs can integrate themselves into regular school activities and become sustainable community-oriented solutions. Many programs have successfully used schools for their implementation, notably school-based health promotion interventions (SHPI) that target improving health outcomes within educational settings (Bergeron et al., 2019). The Center for Sustainable Development at Columbia University's Earth Institute has developed interventions that expand the use of school-based programs to target Socio Emotional Learning, sexual and reproductive health awareness, and provide student-centered counseling to help students stay in school. Two of these programs, implemented as part of a strategy to reach the Sustainable Development Goals by 2030, are described in some detail below, along with our findings and lessons learned on implementing such programs in schools as companions to standard educational interventions.

Socio Emotional Learning in Uganda

The State of Children's Socio-emotional Well-being in Uganda

A key barrier to children's holistic development is the lack of access to socio-emotional education and reinforcement in school, particularly for girls. Socio-emotional challenges, such as a lack of self-esteem or self-efficacy, when combined with socio-cultural factors such as patriarchal norms, high rates of early marriage, and high incidence of teen pregnancy, may contribute to limiting the capacity of girls in coping with challenges that hinder educational attainment and school completion, thereby perpetuating a cycle of intergenerational disadvantage for women. But boys are also affected, and conditions for many children in Uganda do not create a facilitating environment for socio-emotional health. Large numbers of Ugandan children live in communities with chronic poverty, violence against women and children, depression, and communicable diseases such as malaria, tuberculosis, and HIV/AIDS (ICHAD, n.d.). The prevalence of anxiety-related disorders is also alarmingly high among Ugandan children, with 29.7 percent of girls and 23.1 percent of boys reporting anxiety in one survey of over 1,500 northeastern Ugandan adolescents (Abbo et al., 2013). Given this profile, children must be provided the tools that they need to rise above these challenges.

The *Eminyeeto* Girls Empowerment Program

To address the unmet need for Socio Emotional Learning (SEL) opportunities, our team of researchers developed the *Eminyeeto* Girls Empowerment Program to target holistic skill-building and subsequently healthy, financially independent lives for girls in Southwestern Uganda. *Eminyeeto*, which means "youth" in the *Runyankore* language, was a multidimensional program that aimed to strengthen the social, financial, and emotional empowerment of girls and young women in Uganda through a number of initiatives. Initiatives under *Eminyeeto* included establishing adolescent health centers, assistance for young women from the community to set up their own small businesses, and community-led mentorship programs for young girls. In addition to these programs, another initiative was implemented to focus exclusively on the socio-emotional status of young girls attending primary schools. This school-based initiative tailored an after-school SEL curriculum called the Girls and Young Women's Empowerment Curriculum for use in Ugandan primary schools based on existing universal SEL programs that have been shown to improve outcomes for school children in different contexts (Durlak et al., 2011; Collaborative for Social, Emotional, & Academic Learning, 2012; Morningside Center for Teaching Social Responsibility, 2012; Austrian and Ghati, 2010; REDI, 2012; Taylor et al., 2017). The program's immediate goal was to detectably improve socio-emotional skills in young girls attending primary schools, where the program was delivered to improve long-run socio-emotional development and mental health among participating students.

Curriculum Components

The Girls and Young Women's Empowerment Curriculum included lesson plans based on the five components of SEL identified by the Collaborative for Academic, Social, and Emotional Learning (CASEL): self-management, self-awareness, social awareness, relationship skills, and responsible decision-making skills. Each lesson was delivered through an hour-long session split between educational games followed by interpretation of the games into meaningful life lessons that targeted the components of SEL described in Table 1.

Lesson plans were structured to accommodate varying literacy levels to be used in low, high, or mixed literacy environments. Research has shown that effective SEL is Sequenced, Active-learning-based, Focused, and Explicit (SAFE) (CASEL, n.d.). The *Eminyeeto* curriculum implicitly focused on ensuring these components were incorporated into curriculum modules while offering teachers the flexibility to design class schedules that worked best for themselves and their students so long as the complete package of lesson plans was delivered. The SAFE components of the curriculum are described as follows:

Table 7.1 *Eminyeeto* Curriculum SEL Components and Descriptions

Topic	Description
Self-management	Lessons helped girls target their core beliefs and how these can affect their feelings and behavior and were designed to promote impulse control and stress management. Group members learned how to regulate their emotions to pursue goals and persevere through setbacks and frustration.
Self-awareness	Self-awareness lessons targeted encouraging participants to be in touch with their emotions, to have confidence in themselves, and use their awareness to harness new skills and talents.
Social awareness	Social awareness lessons targeted teaching participants the principles of empathy, understanding other perspectives, and interacting with others who may have different beliefs.
Relationship skills	Lessons targeted relationship skills that encourage participants to recognize, seek, and sustain healthy relationships. Activities targeted cooperation, communication, help-seeking, and help-providing behavior.
Responsible decision-making	Lessons targeted teaching participants how to evaluate their choices and possible courses of action, personal accountability, and encouraging participants to make ethical choices.

- The curriculum ensured *sequence* through closely tailored lesson plans that opened with ice breakers followed by connected activities that encouraged the development of specific SEL domain skills. For example, lessons targeting self-management sequenced activities that encouraged stress management followed by exercises designed to help equip girls with skills that encouraged control of the self and their environments. The combination of these activities was designed to encourage the regulation of emotions as well as to help children to develop goal-oriented thinking and actions.
- The curriculum used an *active learning pedagogical approach* to encourage the mastering of SEL skills through participation. Lesson plans primarily focused on encouraging girls to participate in play-based learning or encouraging them to share experiences and respond to hypothetical situations.
- The curriculum fostered a *focus* on developing specific SEL skills by equipping teachers with lesson plans identified by themes. Themes include confidence-building, effective communication, leadership lessons, trauma-

healing, cooperative learning, and critical thinking. These themes were used to guide teacher feedback, and student discussion after lesson activities were completed.
- The curriculum also delivered *explicit* lessons on specific SEL skills. Teachers were trained to deliver lessons to help students develop specific social and emotional abilities and were encouraged to use post-lesson debrief sessions to elaborate on what skills the preceding activities were trying to build in students.

In addition to ensuring that the curriculum met the standards of the SAFE approach, we also emphasized the importance of culturally adapting the curriculum to meet the specific contextual needs of Ugandan girls in primary schools. Research on cultural environments during childhood shows that these environments play a critical role in children's social and emotional development (Savina and Wan, 2017). Moreover, to implement the program in local public schools, we recognized that it was important to develop local support and partnerships so that the principles of the curriculum could be fully integrated into the school culture prevalent in primary schools. To achieve this, we started with a basic curriculum model. Through co-development and consultation with Ugandan public-school staff, including school heads and teachers, we customized lessons and determined the cultural relevance and adequacy of the final curriculum. The final syllabus was first delivered to female teachers from each of the schools selected for the program's initial rollout. They were subsequently invited to participate in training to deliver the curriculum's modules to their students. This two-step process was chosen because it served as an opportunity to improve the curriculum's cultural relevancy while also achieving buy-in to the curriculum's messaging from teachers.

Our impact study of the curriculum's effects, implemented in ten primary schools and compared with a control group of schools, showed that *Eminyeeto* significantly improved socio-emotional competencies in participating girls. The results from standardized SEL measurements showed that participating girls improved in self-efficacy and responsible choice-making and held more equitable views on the relative privileges and rights of men and women. Our study also showed that participating girls were less likely to exhibit indications of depression, which suggests that SEL can improve mental health outcomes (Malhotra et al., 2021).

The true impacts of socio-emotional well-being are diffuse and often appear much later in life, as seen in numerous studies of preschool programs in the

United States and elsewhere (Gray-Lobe et al., 2021). This means that our short-term study perhaps does not capture the full extent of the benefits of SEL for the participating girls. Yet, it points to the need to reinforce our schools with activities and lessons that target the development of holistic skills in children, which provide them with the necessary tools to be more resilient and successful adults. In the next section, we discuss another school-based program implemented in India to provide children in public schools with information on reproductive health to improve their literacy of sexual and reproductive health subjects to improve their reproductive decision-making capacity as adults.

"My Changing Body": Sexual and Reproductive Health Literacy in India

The State of Adolescent Sexual and Reproductive Health in India

Some of the leading causes of mortality and morbidity among adolescents globally can be attributed to risky sexual behaviors and lack of knowledge about sexual and reproductive health (SRH) (Khubchandani et al., 2014; Tripathi et al., 2013). In India, adolescent girls have 1.1 million unintended pregnancies, leading to 725,000 unsafe abortions and 1,400 maternal deaths (Murro et al., 2021). These figures suggest a significant unmet need for SRH education for adolescent boys and girls. SRH education can be essential in adolescence because of the critical nature of this life period for physiological and emotional development (Ismael et al., 2015).

Reproductive health education can give students the tools to know how to mitigate risks such as early pregnancy, as a national study has shown (Khubchandani et al., 2014). Still, the skills gained through SRH education can also be linked to socio-emotional development. Youth developmental assets such as responsible decision-making and self-confidence are not only critical stepping stones toward a healthier future but can also be protective factors against risky behaviors like unprotected sex (Oman et al., 2010). Therefore, teaching SRH alongside social and emotional skills can be beneficial for students at the crucial time of adolescence.

My Changing Body in India

My Changing Body (MCB) is a curriculum developed by the Institute of Reproductive Health at Georgetown University, covering several topics related to interpersonal relationships, sexual behavior, health, and literacy. Combining such issues as body literacy and fertility awareness aims to promote better SRH awareness in ten- to fourteen-year-old adolescents (Institute of Reproductive Health, 2011). Our researchers developed an integrated curriculum based on MCB for use through an after-school program in twenty-five public primary schools in a rural district in South India as a part of the *Yuva Nestham* ("friends of youth") Youth Empowerment Program.

Curriculum Components

This project's SRH component had two aims: (1) to increase participants' understanding of SRH through the implementation of a curriculum and (2) to improve participants' psychosocial well-being by creating a safe space to get their SRH-related questions answered by a professional (biology teacher or adolescent health expert hired by the project).

The broad themes covered by the curriculum included male and female puberty, fertility, sexual health, pregnancy, and interpersonal relationships. The MCB curriculum was delivered through a combination of in-class instruction, demonstration, and role-playing activities, which were facilitated by learning materials such as index cards, picture aides, and prepared dialogue that encouraged students to "act out" their questions about SRH topics.

The curriculum was tailored to work within the structure of the academic year in schools and conducted weekly with adolescents in grades six to eight from July to March for thirty-two to thirty-four sessions.

In order to adapt the MCB to the Indian context, our program team relied on building partnerships with district officials and schoolteachers:

- Consultative sessions were held with district officials, including the district education officers and sub-district officials responsible for managing local primary schools. These sessions were used to adapt the MCB curriculum to local needs. Formal approval for the curriculum's implementation was also obtained from the district collector's office.[1] Sub-district officials were also actively engaged to identify teachers from within public schools who could be trained to deliver the curriculum.
- Schoolteachers' input was sought to leverage their understanding of on-the-ground realities about fertility and reproductive health awareness. For example, specific myths around causes of infertility and menstrual hygiene were identified to be discussed during MCB sessions.

To assess the need and effectiveness of the MCB curriculum, we first implemented a pre-intervention assessment to study levels of knowledge among adolescents about menstruation, puberty, male and female reproductive systems, sexual intercourse, and pregnancy. Our findings suggested very low levels of comprehension among students, particularly on the subject of female reproductive systems. This helped us address significant gaps in knowledge, and our post-intervention assessments showed high levels of improvement in knowledge-based indicators of SRH topics covered in the curriculum.

In addition to focusing on knowledge outcomes, we also focused on the measurement of which topics students indicated an interest in discussing during in-class counseling sessions using a content analysis approach. We found that MCB counselors received questions specific to the sex identification of students. For example, adolescent boys generally showed interest in learning more about male reproductive systems. They had questions about erections, penis size, and wet dreams, whereas adolescent girls typically had questions about menstruation and its effects on the female body. Other general questions were related to the manifestations of puberty, such as the incidence of acne and body hair. That these questions were largely student-driven suggests a sizeable unmet need for SRH knowledge among children. Based on counselor feedback, students displayed curiosity and enthusiasm during classroom sessions, which was reflected in their questions about SRH topics. Counselors were often requested to stay after class to answer myriad follow-up questions.

A large part of the reason for the positive reception of our MCB curriculum as reported by facilitators was that it was delivered in the local language, culturally contextualized, and reviewed by local school staff and the district administration responsible for its deployment to government schools. This approach was critical given the potentially controversial nature of SRH topics and the danger of losing local support in a largely rural and culturally conservative region. In future studies replicating this program, we suggest a similar approach that prioritizes local support and contributions to program development. Also, thorough training must be prioritized because providers of services to adolescents should be specially trained to assess and respond to their unique needs in a targeted manner. Moreover, recognizing that the targeting of programs to the unique needs of adolescents is critical, programs should be demand-driven and their content should reflect the specific learning and other needs of adolescents.

Lessons Learned

Our experience leveraging school settings to deliver SEL and reproductive health literacy programs shows that schools can play a critical role in providing the setting for the holistic development of children by encouraging their socio-emotional development and reproductive health literacy. Since all programs that attempt to include these auxiliary learning outcomes for children are different, we compile some of the broad lessons from our implementation experiences that can help other programs adapt to diverse contexts.

School-based cross-sectoral programs should emphasize models that encourage the long-term adoption of practices. To achieve this, an integrationist approach to school-based programs is essential. While our programs in Uganda and India ranged in length from one to two years, we invested in a co-ownership model to ensure the sustainability of gains made when the programs were actively managed. For example, both programs relied on training existing schoolteachers to deliver programs instead of hiring external teaching staff. This helped us ensure that the curriculum would be available for schools to implement even after our active presence in program areas had concluded. Teachers with a sustained presence in schools who could model program behaviors were selected. Additionally, we also invested in consultations with district officials in India and council administrators in Uganda to discuss integrating SEL and SRH components into regular school programming to ensure the sustainability of school-based holistic learning opportunities for children. This was done keeping in mind evidence from implementing programs in another context that shows that the dosage and reinforcement of SEL concepts matter for their long-term effectiveness in improving student outcomes (Elias, 2010). The cultivation of partnerships with local governance institutions early during the implementation of programs can help trigger a process of cost-sharing and active adoption of program elements into school-level programming.

Standard curricula should be made culturally relevant through rigorous piloting and community consultations. A growing number of programs, strategies, and curricula that seek to prevent adverse outcomes and promote healthy development have emerged in recent years and provide a strong empirical base in socio-emotional and reproductive health education. These programs provide an important opportunity for replication in other contexts. To ensure that their potential positive impacts are realized, adaptations to these curricula should properly integrate cultural contexts and social environments. This can be done through intensive consultations with teachers, local community groups, and government authorities. *Eminyeeto*'s implementation teams consulted with schoolteachers, parents, and the local council chairperson to ensure that the curriculum that was implemented in schools was culturally coherent and understandable by local Ugandan school girls. In India, *Yuva Nestham* program officers created a rigorous review process involving schoolteachers, school heads, and the district collector's office in the district in which the program was delivered. Since the program involved sharing sensitive information about sexual health, it was essential to ensure that potentially fraught information on subjects such as menstruation, masturbation, and sexual intercourse was shared with students in a culturally sensitive manner. To achieve this, the original curriculum was discussed in meetings with district education officers, school heads, and schoolteachers to assess its appropriateness for the local context, and a consensus-based approach was used to identify adaptations and changes to the final curriculum. This consultative process, combined with an implementation that relied on training preexisting schoolteachers to deliver these programs, helped us ensure cultural relevancy and broad acceptance of the programs in local communities.

Investing in active learning and responsive teaching can maximize the impact of student-centered learning approaches. Active learning includes processes that focus more on "developing students' skills than on transmitting information and require that students do something—read, discuss, write—that requires higher-order thinking. They also tend to place some emphasis on students' explorations of their attitudes and values" (Brames, 2016). Since integrated programs like *Eminyeeto* and *Yuva Nestham* focus primarily on teaching practical life skills, an active learning pedagogical approach has helped students directly engage in positive behaviors and learning. *Eminyeeto* was implemented almost entirely through activities and games, followed by debriefing sessions that helped students focus on the intended SEL lessons of each activity. While *Yuva Nestham* relied more on classroom teaching, it also emphasized students' exploration of questions on SRH both in the classroom setting and through opportunities to ask questions privately. Both these programs emphasized student learning through nontraditional pedagogical means. Their active take-up by both teachers and students suggests that these methods effectively translate skills and knowledge.

Conclusions

Recent developments in the field of education have evolved the sector from solely teaching literacy and numeracy to expanding into critical aspects such as early childhood development, SEL, and generally instilling essential life skills. A successful education system teaches children and students to read, write, and count. Still, such a system should also provide children with the mental and emotional tools to become productive actors in society who are both tolerant and tolerated. Inter-sectoral programs are critical ways to develop curricula that expand the role of education and allow long-time experts in the sector to access new innovative tools and think "outside the box."

No change occurs overnight, and the most creative and useful education programs that teach children essential life skills outside the norm can face local cultural resistance during implementation. This is why the "top-down" approach in development programs, including education, needs to be replaced with community and stakeholder participation to promote constructive dialogue, opportunities for debates and critique, and improvement of the original ideas and their implementation. School-based programs offer a unique opportunity to do just that because of their embeddedness in their community and the opportunities they facilitate to actively and iteratively seek community input.

Note

1 A district collector is an officer who is in-charge of a district, the basic unit of administration, in India.

References

Abbo, Catherine, Kinyanda, Eugene, Kizza, Ruth B., Levin, Jonathan, Ndyanabangi, Sheilla, & Stein, Dan J. (July 10, 2013). Prevalence, Comorbidity and Predictors of Anxiety Disorders in Children and Adolescents in Rural North-Eastern Uganda. *Child and Adolescent Psychiatry and Mental Health*, 7, p. 21. https://doi.org/10.1186/1753-2000-7-21.

Austrian, Karen, Dennitah Ghati, and Population Council. (2010). Girl-Centered Program Design: A Toolkit to Develop, Strengthen & Expand Adolescent Girls Programme. *Population Council*. https://www.popcouncil.org/uploads/pdfs/2010PGY_AdolGirlToolkitComplete.pdf. Date Accessed May 25, 2022.

Bergeron, Dave A., Talbot, Lise R., & Gaboury, Isabelle. (November 1, 2019). Context and the Mechanisms in Intersectoral School-Based Health Promotion Interventions: A Critical Interpretative Synthesis. *Health Education Journal*, 78(7), pp. 713–27. https://doi.org/10.1177/0017896919833422.

Brame, Cynthia J. (2016). *Active Learning*. Vanderbilt University. https://cft.vanderbilt.edu/guides-sub-pages/active-learning/. Date Accessed May 25, 2022.

CASEL. SEL Approaches. https://casel.org/approaches/, Accessed July 30, 2021.

Collaborative for Social, Emotional, and Academic Learning. Effective Social and Emotional Learning Programs. https://casel.org/wp-content/uploads/2016/01/2013-casel-guide.pdf, Accessed May 27, 2021.

Durlak, Joseph A., Weissberg, Roger P., Dymnicki, Allison B., Taylor, Rebecca D., & Schellinger, Kriston B. (February 2011). The Impact of Enhancing Students' Social and Emotional Learning: A Meta-Analysis of School-Based Universal Interventions. *Child Development*, 82(1), pp. 405–32. https://doi.org/10.1111/j.1467-8624.2010.01564.x.

Elias, Maurice. (2010). Sustainability of Social-Emotional Learning and Related Programs: Lessons from a Field Study. *International Journal of Emotional Education* 2(1), pp. 17–33. https://oaji.net/articles/2017/4987-1496664657.pdf. Date accessed May 25, 2022.

Gray-Lobe, Guthrie, Pathak, Parag A., & Walters, Christopher R. (May, 2021). The Long-Term Effects of Universal Preschool in Boston. Working Paper. Working Paper Series. National Bureau of Economic Research. https://doi.org/10.3386/w28756.

Ismail, Shajahan, Shajahan, Ashika, Sathyanarayana Rao, T. S., & Wylie, Kevan. (2015). Adolescent Sex Education in India: Current Perspectives. *Indian Journal of Psychiatry*, 57(4), pp. 333–7. https://doi.org/10.4103/0019-5545.171843.

Institute of Reproductive Health. (2011). My Changing Body: Body Literacy & Fertility Awareness for Young People (2nd Edition). https://irh.org/resource-library/my-changing-body-body-literacy-fertility-awareness-for-young-people-2nd-edition/. Date Accessed May 25, 2022

International Center for CHild Health and Development. Child and Adolescent Mental Health Care in Uganda. https://brownschool.wustl.edu/News/Documents/Uganda-Combined-Policy-Brief-Report.pdf, Accessed July 21, 2021.

Khubchandani, Jagdish, Clark, Jeffrey, & Kumar, Raman. (July 2014). Beyond Controversies: Sexuality Education for Adolescents in India. *Journal of Family Medicine and Primary Care*, 3(3), pp. 175–9. https://doi.org/10.4103/2249-4863.141588.

Mahmoudi, Sirous, Jafari, Ebrahim, Nasrabadi, Hasan Ali, & Liaghatdar, Mohmmd Javad. (May 9, 2012). Holistic Education: An Approach for 21 Century. *International Education Studies*, 5(3), p. 178. https://doi.org/10.5539/ies.v5n3p178.

Malhotra, Niyati, Ayele, Zena Ewonetu, Zheng, Dandi, & Ben Amor, Yanis. (January 1, 2021). Improving Social and Emotional Learning for Schoolgirls: An Impact Study of Curriculum-Based Socio-Emotional Education in Rural Uganda. *International Journal of Educational Research*, 108, p. 101778. https://doi.org/10.1016/j.ijer.2021.101778.

Morningside Center for Teaching Social Responsibility. (2012). Teachable Moment Classroom Lessons. https://www.morningsidecenter.org/teachable-moment/lessons/911-anniversary-teaching-guide. Date Accessed May 25, 2022.

Murro, Rachel, Chawla, Rhea, Pyne, Souvik, Venkatesh, Shruti, & Sully, Elizabeth. (March 31, 2021). Adding It Up: Investing in the Sexual and Reproductive Health of Adolescents in India. https://www.guttmacher.org/report/adding-it-up-investing-in-sexual-reproductive-health-adolescents-india. Date Accessed May 25, 2022.

Obach, Alexandra, Sadler, Michelle, & Cabieses, Báltica. (April 2019). Intersectoral Strategies between Health and Education for Preventing Adolescent Pregnancy in Chile: Findings from a Qualitative Study. *Health Expectations : An International Journal of Public Participation in Health Care and Health Policy*, 22(2), pp. 183–92. https://doi.org/10.1111/hex.12840.

Oman, Roy F., Vesely, Sara K., Tolma, Eleni L., Aspy, Cheryl B., & La Donna, Marshall. (October 2010). Reliability and Validity of the Youth Asset Survey: An Update. *American Journal of Health Promotion: AJHP*, 25(1), pp. e13–24. https://doi.org/10.4278/ajhp.081009-QUAN-242.

REDI. (2012). Teaching and Learning. https://web.archive.org/web/20121102110351/http://www.deewr.gov.au/Schooling/Programs/REDI/professionaldevelopment/allREDI/competencies/Pages/lesson_plans.aspx. Date Accessed May 25, 2022.

Savina, Elena, & Wan, Kayan Phoebe. (2017). Cultural Pathways to Socio-Emotional Development and Learning. *Journal of Relationships Research*, 8. https://doi.org/10.1017/jrr.2017.19.

Taylor, Rebecca D., Oberle, Eva, Durlak, Joseph A., & Weissberg, Roger P.. (2017). Promoting Positive Youth Development Through School-Based Social and Emotional Learning Interventions: A Meta-Analysis of Follow-Up Effects. *Child Development*, 88(4), pp. 1156–71. https://doi.org/10.1111/cdev.12864.

Tripathi, Niharika, & Sekher, T.V. (August 9, 2013). Youth in India Ready for Sex Education? Emerging Evidence from National Surveys. *PLOS ONE*, 8(8), p. e71584. https://doi.org/10.1371/journal.pone.0071584.

8

Embedding Climate Science Research into Policy and Practice

IRI's Climate Services Academies Approach

Mélody Braun, Zain Alabweh, Ashley Curtis, Carmen González Romero, Amanda Grossi, Ezequiel González Camaño, Ángel G. Muñoz, Andrew Kruczkiewicz, Tufa Dinku, and John Furlow

Acknowledgments

This work is undertaken as part of the Columbia World Project "Adapting Agriculture to Climate Today for Tomorrow" (ACToday), Columbia University in New York, and supported by the SHMJRLEY Fund. Key partners of the National Academies mentioned in this chapter include the Bangladesh Meteorological Department (BMD), the International Maize and Wheat Improvement Center (CIMMYT), the Independent University Bangladesh (IUB) and the International Center for Climate Change and Development (ICCCAD) in Bangladesh; the Guatemalan System of Climate Change Sciences (SGCCC), National Institute of Seismology, Volcanology, Meteorology and Hydrology (INSIVUMEH), Institute of Agriculture, Natural Resources and Environment (IARNA), Rafael Landivar University (URL), International Center for Tropical Agriculture (CIAT) and International Union for Conservation of Nature (IUCN) in Guatemala; the Institute of Hydrology, Meteorology and Environmental Studies (IDEAM), Pedagogical and Technological University of Boyacá (UPTC) and Food and Agriculture Organization (FAO) in Colombia and the Ministry of Agriculture (MoA), National Meteorological Agency (NMA), Ethiopian Institute of Agricultural Research (EIAR), and the CGIAR Research Program on Climate Change, Agriculture and Food Security (CCAFS) in Ethiopia.

Introduction

With yearly new climate extreme records and a renewed urgency at the most recent climate negotiations (COP26) to support developing countries adapt to climate change and minimize associated loss and damage, it is critical to ensure that decision-makers from government officials to communities, especially in vulnerable sectors such as agriculture, energy, infrastructure, or public health, can rely on the best available climate information to inform their adaptation strategies.

A key challenge impeding the exploitation of climate information in different sectors is the persistent disconnect and lack of mutual understanding between the scientific community developing climate information and the practitioners' community designing climate adaptation strategies (Lemos et al., 2012). A shortage of capacity on what information exists, appropriately communicating complex climate information, developing products that support decision-making, and integrating such services within national systems hinder a country's ability to take adaptive action in an uncertain climate. Disaster risk reduction managers often lack appropriate training to execute these roles effectively (Biru and Dibaba, 2018). A mismatch persists between ambitious national policy frameworks and the reality on the ground.

These challenges call for a coordinated cross-sectoral approach to build the capacities of providers and users of climate information to develop reliable climate services tailored to decision-makers' practical needs. Climate services involve the production, translation, communication, and use of climate knowledge to inform climate-sensitive decision-making, policy, and planning (Climate Services Partnership, 2021). The recognition of the importance of climate services to support adaptation (WMO, 2019) has created a strong demand for comprehensive, high-quality training materials, and education curricula to strengthen climate services around the world. Leveraging decades of experience and over 500 professional development trainings in sixty-eight countries, the International Research Institute for Climate and Society (IRI) has been working with country partners as part of the Adapting Agriculture to Climate Today for Tomorrow (ACToday) project on the development of National Climate Services Academies to address these challenges by: (i) facilitating relationship-building between producers and users of information, (ii) developing comprehensive competency-based curricula, and (iii) ensuring the active engagement of local stakeholders from the first stages of the program design. The format of each National Academy is tailored to the particular context of each country. These National Academies are, in turn, informing the development of a Global Climate Services Academy aiming at connecting and supporting national and regional efforts. These efforts jointly contribute to transforming how countries provide and use climate services to support sustainable development and eradicate poverty.

Bangladesh—How Decision-centric Tools Help Bridge the Gap between Users and Providers of Climate Information

Climate Information for Preparedness in Refugee Camps

Background

In August 2017, outbreaks of extreme violence against the Rohingya minority in Myanmar led to THE MOVEMENT of almost one million Rohingya civilians into Bangladesh camps coordinated by United Nations groups. The Kutupalong-Balukhali Megacamp concentrated roughly 700,000 people in tarp and bamboo tents on steep hills that had to be rapidly deforested and terraformed (Goshal, 2020, Myat, 2018).

In early 2018, camp managers grew increasingly concerned about the potential impacts of the upcoming rainy season. Climate information products such as satellite data and maps were sent from all over the world. Unfortunately, a lot of it turned out to be of limited use because of its lack of translation into decision-relevant information and the lack of time and expertise of camp managers to compare and analyze them.

Methods

IRI collaborated with NASA and UN camp managers through Connecting Earth Observations to Decision-makers for Preparedness Actions (COMPAS). Instead of translating existing tools and datasets to camp managers, IRI's approach was to turn the problem around and first analyze decisions made by camp managers on the ground to identify inputs that would then help NASA tailor a tool to those identified needs.

Initial information was collected through news sampling, expert elicitation, focus group discussions, and a visit to the camps. These are critical to develop a trust relationship with camp managers, better understand concerns and priorities in the camps, roles, and responsibilities of different stakeholders, their constraints and limitations, and screen the available and/or used information.

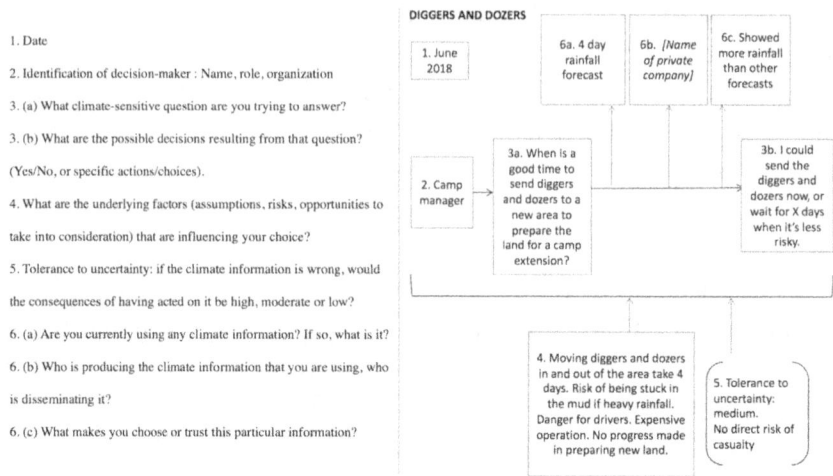

Figure 8.1 Decision-making flowchart model.

A descriptive diagram template called "Decision-making flowchart" (DMF) was developed to narrow down what specific inputs would be relevant. The DMF is a diagnostic tool that guides decision-makers through the communication of climate-sensitive decisions while extracting key elements—such as spatial and temporal scale, tolerance to uncertainty, data sources—that allow data providers to recommend appropriate climate inputs without an in-depth understanding of the context (Kruczkiewicz, Braun et al., forthcoming). Figure 8.1 displays the DMF questions along with a completed example.

Lessons Learned

Some DMFs directed decision-makers to specific information products; others provided inputs into the development of a landslide awareness tool for camp managers by NASA. They supported the dialogue between decision-makers and scientists through the extraction of decision-specific clues that guided the identification of relevant climate information. Over time, DMFs aim at capacitating users to better identify and express their information needs, facilitating the development of trusted relationships between stakeholders and supporting the design of tailored climate services.

DMFs should be adapted to the specific situation they are used for. Test-uses of DMFs in different contexts indicated different user preferences in language and format, varying with background, education level, and field of study. The content needs to include the clues that will guide the identification of useful climate inputs, but their framing can be adapted.

Building Capacity on Climate Services Through User-centered Interdisciplinary Training Dialogues

Background

Extensive coastal, river, and flash floods, sea-level rise, cyclones, and increasingly changing weather patterns combined with a low-lying topography and a very high population density threaten the livelihoods and food security of millions of people relying on climate-sensitive sectors such as agriculture and aquaculture (Auerbach et al., 2015; Goosen, 2018). Bangladesh has proactively integrated climate change into national policies and is renowned for its cyclone preparedness program. However, much of the focus has concentrated on long-term climate change scenarios and short-term weather forecasts. The Bangladesh Meteorological Department (BMD) has worked with IRI and other partners to improve the range and quality of information produced, including seasonal climate forecasts. In parallel, IRI, BMD, the International Center for Climate Change and Development (ICCCAD), and the International Maize and Wheat Improvement Center (CIMMYT) partnered to create the Bangladesh Academy for Climate Services (BACS), aiming at: (i) creating an interdisciplinary dialogue between providers and users of climate information; (ii) building their capacity to understand each other, and (iii) establishing a mechanism for sustainable collaboration and co-production of climate services.

Methods

BACS developed a five-day capacity-building training model divided into five modules (Figure 8.2), combining user-centered participatory exercises, educational sessions, collaborative learning and networking, and applied practice. In 2018 and 2019, BACS conducted two climate services trainings attended by forty participants from twenty-nine organizations.

The training approach focused on activating learning processes rather than simply transmitting knowledge, and followed principles from cognitive science, psychology and pedagogy, some of which as summarized here.

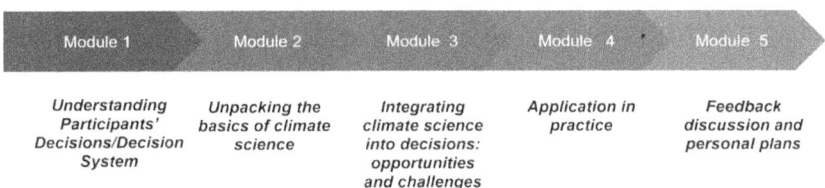

Figure 8.2 BACS training dialogue modules.

Inquiry-based learning—Following the principle that learning emerges from reflecting upon personal experiences and exploring a solution to a personal challenge instead of class-type settings (Oppl, 2016), DMFs were used as a pre-course exercise to identify climate-sensitive questions participants wanted to answer in their jobs. Each new concept introduced in training served as a tool to support their problem-solving goal, progressively building their capacity to develop a personalized plan to improve the integration of climate information into their decision-making process.

Two-way learning—Unlike traditional learning settings where information usually passes from the instructor to the student, two-way learning acknowledges that both parties have valuable knowledge to contribute to the learning process and promotes a culture of reciprocity, as illustrated by arrows in Figure 8.3 (Walsh, 2016).

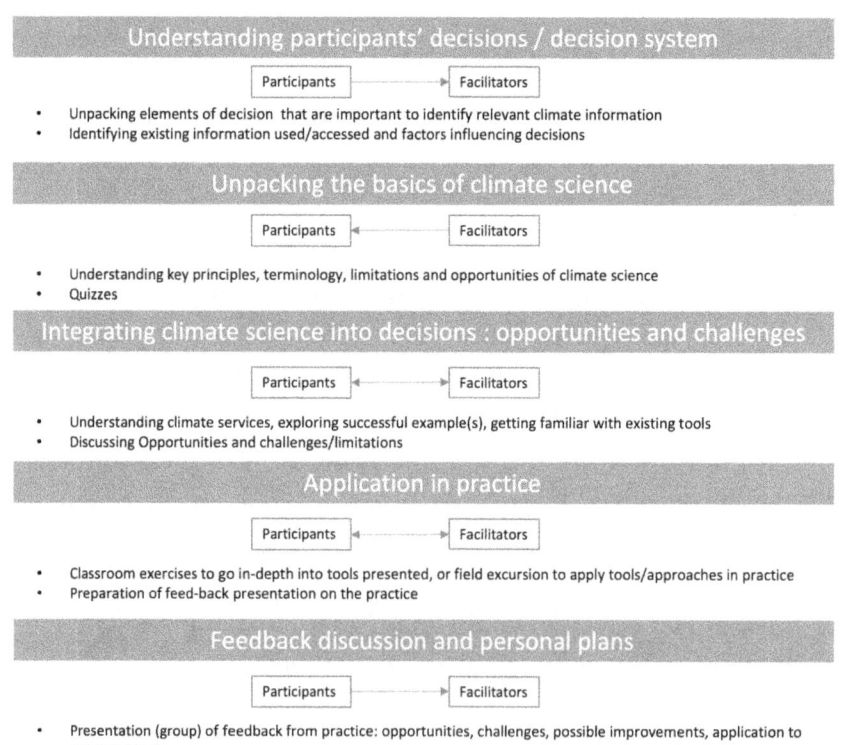

Figure 8.3 BACS training dialogue reciprocal learning approach.

Cooperative learning is enhanced in a collaborative context where individuals engage with others as part of their problem-solving efforts (Bandura, 1997). The divergence of perspectives within a group brings multiple new angles, stimulating cooperation toward developing a more holistic solution to the problem. Learning is then enhanced and fully appropriated in an individual activity. The BACS training format followed this principle by proposing group exercises and hands-on, collaborative practice and developing a personal plan for each participant.

Learning through practice—While theoretical concepts can appear clear and understood in a class setting, Freinet emphasizes that learning is enhanced by the obstacles encountered when trying to apply an idea (trial and error theory) in response to an actual need of the student (the questions self-identified in the pre-course DMF exercise) (Oppl, 2016). Success after trial and error will bring spontaneous memorization of the successful approach in similar situations and support the development of professional reflexes. BACS proposed hands-on practical exercises to integrate and apply new knowledge through field practice or testing tools in a practical exercise.

Information retention and knowledge assessment—The BACS approach included several knowledge assessments and retention mechanisms, including daily morning recaps of the previous day, daily evening takeaways, regular quizzes, and Q&As, along with a pre-and post-course participants' self-assessment survey.

Lessons Learned

Many participants recognized having little to no awareness of BMD and its products before the training and described the experience as eye-opening. In some instances, new partnerships were established between BMD and participants' organizations following the training to gain direct access and guidance on climate information. Many participants shared having never discussed the need for climate information in their field before the training. They started the week by identifying unrealistic information needs, which they self-updated. They gained a better understanding of current opportunities and limitations until they could self-identify what information was most relevant to them.

BACS aimed to conduct such training yearly. However, the COVID-19 pandemic prevented the organization of the 2020 and 2021 editions, and the highly interactive format was not readily convertible into online training.

Latin America and the Caribbean: A Community-based Decentralized Roundtable Approach

Background

Latin America and the Caribbean are highly vulnerable to climate variability and change due to specific geographical and socioeconomic characteristics. As of 2020, the agricultural sector represented 5.6 percent of the total national GDP (World Bank Data, 2019), with 54.6 percent of the labor force engaged in agricultural production in rural areas (Loukos and Arathoon, 2021). Some countries, like Brazil and Uruguay, have significantly increased productivity in the last decades due to economies of scale and capital-intensive methods. Others, like Bolivia or Guatemala, reported lower productivity mainly due to the preponderance of smallholder farmers and subsistence farming (Loukos and Arathoon, 2021). This heterogeneity makes the implementation of one-size-fits-all climate services unrealistic.

Methods

Farmers generally prefer making their decisions through group meetings reflecting local socioeconomic, environmental, and technological conditions rather than with individualized technical assistance (Loboguerrero et al., 2018). In Colombia and Guatemala, the implementation of the Mesas Técnicas Agroclimáticas (MTAs, "Agroclimatic Roundtables") enhanced capacity building through a dialogue with local stakeholders including specialists, scientists, NGOs, and private and public sector representatives (Giraldo-Mendez et al., 2021). Through these roundtables, farmers and local stakeholders generated a climate bulletin that was responsive to local agricultural and social needs while also fomenting critical interchange between sub-sectors that was invaluable in the construction of long-term sustainability and infrastructure.

The MTAs' focus on localized integration led by those most affected by environmental changes allowed for a facilitated community-based exchange of information. Indigenous knowledge of the environment can be a pivotal component of local education, alongside the discussion and implementation of new technologies, seeds, and/or practices. By bringing diverse stakeholder voices into the same decision-making environment, MTAs helped mitigate some of the existing social inequality in the agricultural sector, paving the way for a more inclusive climate response and education from the local level upward.

The MTAs started with an exercise to improve the participants' capacities to interpret climate information. The exercise actively engaged participants and accommodated different education levels. For example, a paper airplane exercise was used to explain forecast probability. Participants were asked to make paper airplanes and throw them toward a space divided into three sections: "above-," "below-," and "near-normal rainfall." Participants counted how many airplanes landed in each category and discussed the results. For instance, if six out of ten planes landed in the above-normal category, participants understood that the models suggested a 60 percent probability for above-normal rainfall.

This activity provided an excellent segue to discussing the climate forecast for the next three months in their region and its implications. Local experts recommended preparedness and response measures to the forecasted conditions in their sector from their expertise. For example, rain throughout September and October in Colombia can cause corn cob rot. MTA participants recommended using fungicide by maize farmers during the flowering period (Giraldo-Mendez et al., 2021). Recommendations were combined and shared in agroclimatic bulletins distributed by governmental agencies, NGOs, and farmers' associations using various communication channels (Figure 8.4).

Lessons Learned

Given the tremendous social, ethnic, and gender diversity throughout Latin America, climate education and capacitation are most efficient when implemented

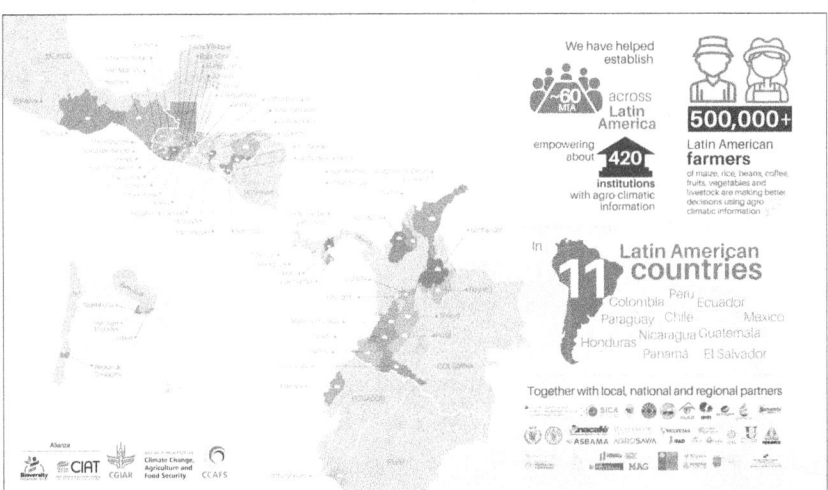

Figure 8.4 MTA implementation activities, Giraldo-Mendez et al. (2021).

through a participatory design matrix. Working from a community-designated meeting place, MTAs brought together farmers, scientists, and public and private organizations to reduce the gap between the generators of climate services and the users, developing solutions that respond directly to the problems faced by the community. This intersectionality of voices and the empowerment of traditionally underrepresented agroclimatic perspectives (i.e., women, ethnic minorities, indigenous people) was key to gaining a complete understanding of climate impacts with a dynamic, reciprocal, and collaborative capacity-building approach. MTAs generated and translated climate knowledge for dissemination in local communities and changed attitudes, knowledge, and abilities in participating stakeholders (Giraldo et al., 2021). MTAs sustainably empowered communities to make science-based informed decisions strengthening their resilience to agricultural and climatic challenges.

Due to its successful inclusion of minority voices and its utility in addressing local climate needs, the MTA approach has expanded throughout Latin America and the Caribbean into a network of at least fifty-three MTAs through 350 institutions (Giraldo-Mendez et al., 2021).

Ethiopia—Beyond Knowledge and Skills: How Systems Architecture Can Amplify Educational Impact

Background

In Ethiopia, the implications of a lack of foundational capacity around climate-risk management are especially pronounced in climate-sensitive sectors such as agriculture, which provides livelihoods to over 85 percent of the population (more than 70 million people) (USAID, 2021). Despite agro-ecology based interventions and climate-smart adaptation practices being identified as systemic bottlenecks in several national plans (EIAR, 2014; Eshete et al., 2020) (EIAR, 2014; Eshete et al., 2020), the 72,000 agricultural agents serving over 16 million farmers (Abate et al., 2020) are not capacitated to access and use historical, monitoring, or forecast climate information products available through the Spell out acronym first: National Meteorological Agency (NMA)[1] that would allow them to tailor their recommendations more appropriately. Similarly, professionals in the disaster risk reduction and management (DRR/M) sector lack adequate use and integration of climate information into decision-making processes.

This lack of capacity around climate-risk management presents problems for humanitarian action and longer-term sustainable development. Because of the multi-sectoral nature of the food system and DRR/M sector, it is also a challenge that permeates multiple institutions and every level of administration. However, to simply conduct capacity building in areas or with actors where gaps have been identified would be to ignore the systemic inefficiencies that gave rise to those gaps in the first place. Systems-level problems demand systems-level solutions.

The Climate Services Education (CSE) initiative of the ACToday-Ethiopia project approached the capacity-building needs of Ethiopia's food security and disaster risk management sectors from a systems perspective, with an eye toward sustainability. Rather than one-off trainings building foundational capacities at different institutions, it embedded co-produced curricula and training activities on climate-risk management within formal and informal educational ecosystems that mutually reinforced each other. Following the core principles of the academies, the approach was equally about strengthening relationships and trust among target beneficiaries as about building knowledge and skills. The social and educational architecture developed enables actors at all levels to meet present needs for climate-risk management and future needs as they evolve.

Methods

Stakeholders involved in the ACToday-Ethiopia CSE initiative are summarized in Figure 8.5. Targeted decision-makers included agricultural extension agents; university students; professionals (development actors, climate information providers); NGO staff; and farmers.

The capacity building of such actors was designed to reinforce capacities and maximize synergies among different stakeholders. Those trained in climate-risk management in agriculture at the university level may graduate and become inputs to the extension system, working as specialists guiding the development agents who work directly with farmers. Alternatively, university graduates, such as those at Bahir Dar University, may work for the National Disaster Risk Management Commission (NDRMC), the central government agency dealing with food security and disaster warning activities in Ethiopia. The benefits of capacity building at one level can thus cascade to other groups and areas of decision-making. To support such cross-pollination, curricula were co-designed with beneficiaries' institutions and those likely to employ them to ensure skills matching.

This same systems perspective can be implemented with professionals at the NMA or elsewhere. While professionals at the NMA are not necessarily inputs into the extension system or NGO sector, they must interact closely with them to ensure climate services are co-produced and useful, usable, and used.

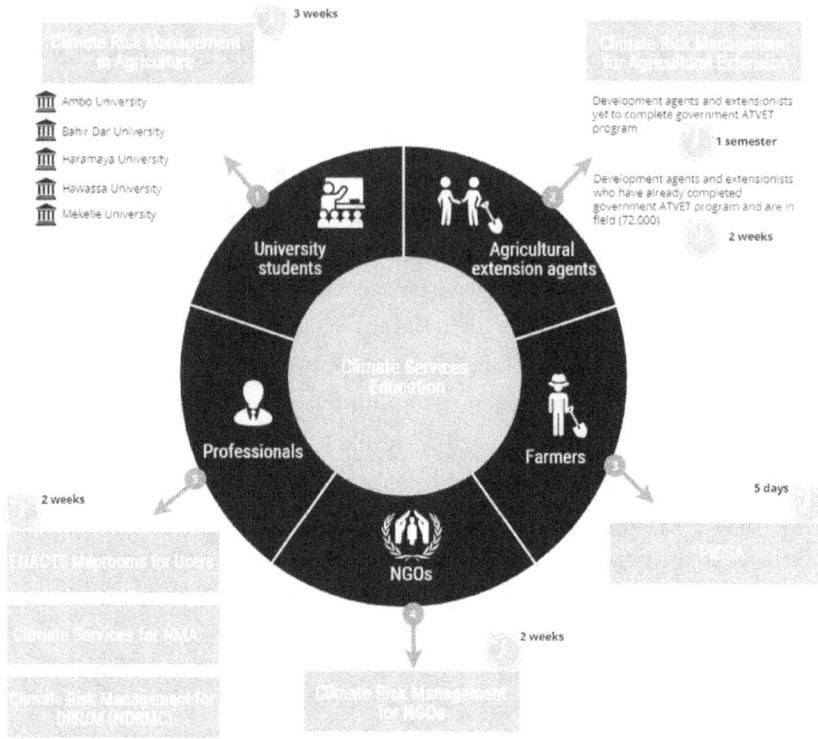

Figure 8.5 ACToday-Ethiopia CSE initiative.

Capacity building should thus be conducted not just to meet the immediate needs of the target decision-maker but to strengthen the relationships between that decision-maker and the rest of the system in which they operate. Moreover, capacity-building approaches must be embedded within educational systems—formal and informal, degree and non-degree—to ensure lasting impact, compliance, and responsiveness to evolving needs (Figure 8.6).

Lessons Learned

The following lessons have been identified so far:

- Co-designing curricula for climate-risk management should consider the entire system in which decision-makers operate to maximize synergies between different stakeholders in the climate services "ecosystem" (Goddard et al., 2020).
- Capacity-building efforts and curriculum development should be included within non-degree programs and educational systems, such as

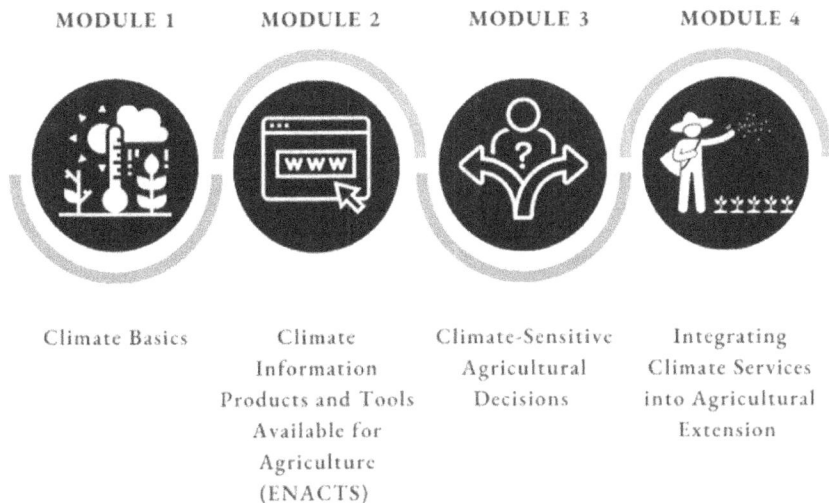

Figure 8.6 Example of a co-produced curriculum and topics. The modules shown here comprise the Climate-Risk Management in Agricultural Extension curriculum targeting extension staff.

the non-degree Agricultural Technical Vocational and Training (ATVET) program, which trains Ethiopia's extensive network of extension agents.
- In a context with highly structured administrative levels, a training of trainers (ToT) approach effectively cascades curricula from national to local levels. Twenty individuals directly trained by IRI will train 10,000 agriculture extensionists in the coming year, with all agricultural extensionists in the country—an additional 70,000 individuals—to be trained in the coming years by the MoA.
- Capacity-building efforts should ideally be codified through, complemented by, and aligned with policy to ensure that resources are allocated to sustain and embed within institutional and development practice.

The Way Forward: Climate Service Academies Go Global

Through these National Academies efforts, all ACToday countries demonstrated commitment and uptake of the Academies model. To expand and sustain this approach, IRI has since initiated Global Climate Academies launched in 2020 to act as a centralized hub of training programs for national and regional level academies, following four principles:

1. **Relevant and Comprehensive.** One-off ad hoc training efforts are not sufficient for genuine sustainable development. Developing a competency-based curriculum across the four pillars of climate services (generation, translation, communication, and use of climate information) enables a more comprehensive approach to disaster management and adaptation to climate change.
2. **Adaptable.** Not one size fits all. Capacity-building efforts apply best practices in design and the latest technology to adapt measures to local contexts and stakeholders' needs. This has allowed the IRI to meet the requirements of virtual training during the COVID-19 pandemic while maintaining high standards of quality and effectiveness.
3. **Fostering connections.** Recognizing the importance of connecting stakeholders within the climate services landscape to facilitate collaboration and avoid duplication of efforts, the global scale Climate Academies act as a hub for national and regional academies supporting professional development education, sustained through university engagement where viable.
4. **Professional and inclusive.** Capacity-building efforts integrate the IRI's globally recognized applied research and practice expertise in a culturally sensitive and respectful environment.

The $100 billion a year promised by developed countries to support developing countries' mitigation, and adaptation efforts have still not been delivered. As a result, it is critical to leverage South-South and South-North collaboration opportunities to ensure that decision-makers can access and use all the relevant climate information available. The academies model offers a coordinated approach across sectors to jointly identify competencies necessary to develop sustainable climate services and build the capacity of producers and users of climate information to respond to their climate and sustainable development challenges collectively.

Note

[1] http://213.55.84.78:8082/maproom/

References

Abate, G.T., Dereje, M., Hirvonen, K., & Minten, B. (2020). Geography of Public Service Delivery in Rural Ethiopia. *World Development*, 136, p. 105133. https://doi.org/10.1016/j.worlddev.2020.105133.

Auerbach, L.W., Goodbred, S.L. Jr., Mondal, D.R., Wilson, C.A., Ahmed, K.R., Roy, K., Steckler, M.S., Small, C., Gilligan, J.M., & Ackerly, B.A. (2015). Flood Risk of Natural and Embanked Landscapes on the Ganges-Brahmaputra Tidal Delta Plain. *Nature Climate Change*, 5, pp. 153–7.

Bandura, A. (1997). *Self-Efficacy: The Exercise of Control*. New York: Freeman, pp. 212–58.

Biru, D., & Dibaba, A.M. (2018). Assessment on the Operationalization of DRR System at Local Level. [Mission Report]. ASiST, European Commission.

Climate Services Partnership (August 20, 2021). What Are Climate Services? https://climate-services.org/about-us/what-are-climate-services/. Date Accessed May 25, 2022.

EIAR, MoA. (2014). National Strategy for Ethiopia's Agricultural Extension System: Vision, Systemic Bottlenecks and Priority Interventions. *Ethiopian Agricultural Transformation Agency*, Ministry of Agriculture. http://extwprlegs1.fao.org/docs/pdf/eth190334.pdf. Date Accessed May 25, 2022.

Eshete, G., Assefa, B., Lemma, E., Kibret, G., Ambaw, G., Samuel, S., Seid, J., Tesfaye, K., Tamene, L., Haile, A., Asnake, A., Mengiste, A., Hailemariam, S.N., Ericksen, P., Mekonnen, K., Amede, T., Haileslassie, A., Hadgu, K., Woldemeskel, E., & Solomon, D. (2020). Ethiopia Climate-Smart Agriculture Roadmap. www.ccafs.cgiar.org.

Ghoshal, A. (2020). Refugees and Human Security – A Study of the Rohingya Refugee Crisis. *IMPACT: International Journal of Research in Humanities, Arts and Literature (IMPACT: IJRHAL)*, 8, pp. 1–8.

Giraldo-Mendez, D., Navarro-Racines, C., Martínez-Barón, D., Loboguerrero, A.M., Gumucio, T., Martínez, J.D., Guzmán-Lopez, H., & Ramírez-Villegas, J. (2021). Mesas Técnicas Agroclimáticas (MTA): Una guía detallada sobre su implementación, paso a paso. 2da Ed. *Programa de Investigación de CGIAR en Cambio Climático. Agricultura y Seguridad Alimentaria (CCAFS)*. https://cgspace.cgiar.org/handle/10568/114605. Date Accessed May 25, 2022.

Glassman, M. (2001). Dewey and Vygotsky: Society, Experience, and Inquiry in Educational Practice. *Educational Researcher*, 30(4), pp. 3–14. doi:10.3102/0013189X030004003.

Goddard, L., González Romero, C., Muñoz, A.G., Acharya, N., Ahmed, S., Baethgen, W., Blumenthal B., et al. (2020). Climate Services Ecosystems in times of COVID-19. In: *WMO at 70 - Responding to a Global Pandemic. WMO Bulletin*, 69(2), pp. 39–46.

Goosen, H., Hasan, T., Saha, S.K., Rezwana, N., Rahman, R., Assaduzzaman, M., Kabir, A., Dubois, G., & van Scheltinga, C.T. (2018). Nationwide Climate Vulnerability Assessment in Bangladesh. Final Draft.

Kruczkiewicz, A., Braun, M., McClain, S., Greatrex, H., Padilla, L., Hoffman-Hernandez, L., Siahaan, K., Nielsen, M., Llamanzares, B., & Flamig, Z. (Forthcoming). Flood Risk and Monitoring Data for Preparedness and Response: From Availability to Use. In Global Flood and Drought: an AGU Monograph Series Book.

Lemos, M.C., Kirchhoff, C.J., & Ramprasad, V. (2012). Narrowing the Climate Information Usability Gap. *Nature Climate Change*, 2(11), pp. 789–94. https://doi.org/10.1038/nclimate1614.

Loboguerrero, A.M. et al. (2018). Bridging the Gap Between Climate Science and Farmers in Colombia. *Climate Risk Management*, Elsevier B.V., 22, pp. 67–81. doi: 10.1016/j.crm.2018.08.001.

Loukos, P., & Arathoon, L. (2021). *Landscaping the Agritech Ecosystem for Smallholder Farmers in Latin America and the Caribbean*. IDB. https://publications.iadb.org/en/landscaping-agritech-ecosystem-smallholder-farmers-latin-america-and-caribbean. Date Accessed May 25, 2022.

Myat, L. (2018). The Rohingya Refugee Crisis: Social, Economic and Environmental Implications for the Local Community in Bangladesh. Doctoral dissertation, Flinders University, College of Humanities, Arts and Social Sciences.

Oppl, Stefan. (2016). Adopting Concepts of Freinet Pedagogy in Higher Education – A Report on the Design and Evolution of a Didactical Experiment. Momentum Kongress 2017.

USAID (2021). Agriculture and Food Security—Ethiopia. United States Agency for International Development. https://www.usaid.gov/ethiopia/agriculture-and-food-security. Date Accessed May 25, 2022.

Walsh, B. (2016). *Two-Way Learning*. Harvard Graduate School of Education. https://www.gse.harvard.edu/news/uk/16/01/two-way-learning. Date Accessed May 25, 2022.

World Bank Data (August 24, 2019). Agriculture, Forestry, and Fishing, Value Added (% of GDP). https://data.worldbank.org/indicator/NV.AGR.TOTL.ZS. Date Accessed May 25, 2022.

WMO (2019). *State of Climate Services Report*. Geneva: WMO, ISBN: 978-92-63-11242-2.

9

Financial Education and Games in Weather-Index Insurance

Rahel Diro, Mélody Braun, Juan Nicolas Hernandez-Aguilera,
Souha Ouni, Max Mauerman, Yohana Tesfamariam Tekeste,
Nitin Magima, and Daniel Osgood

Introduction

With climate change, droughts and floods are projected to increase both in severity and frequency. Increased climate extremes will likely force smallholder farming and pastoral communities in low income countries to fall into perpetual food insecurity. Research shows that a 10 percent lower rainfall four to five years earlier had a 1 percent impact on future growth implying that welfare losses due to weather shocks in the absence of insurance or protection measures have long-term impacts (Dercon and Hoddinott, 2004). Furthermore, more frequent events also overwhelm such safety net programs. Transferring risk through financial mechanisms like insurance prevents long-term impacts. In addition, it creates an enabling environment for prudent risk-taking as creditors tend to be more comfortable lending to an insured borrower (Boucher, Carter and Guirkinger, 2008). Hence, mutually reinforcing measures may reverse asset erosion and a downward spiral can be reversed through access to financial mechanisms.

Smallholder agriculture by definition involves millions of farms producing different kinds of crops in small plots of land following heterogeneous practices. If an insurer were to cover the risk following traditional underwriting techniques, it requires adjustments after assessing the loss, which involves making adjustments after assessing the loss which involves huge substantial administrative costs. In addition, the insurer is exposed to moral hazard (where the insured is reluctant to prevent the loss) and adverse selection (where the insured is disproportionately exposed to the risk). This entails heavy transaction costs rendering the business unattractive for insurers.

Weather-index insurance is an innovative approach to insuring smallholder agriculture that overcomes all these challenges by underwriting the risk based on a weather variable that is highly correlated with a loss instead of the loss itself. In recent years, insurance products that are targeted to help the poor be resilient in the face of climate change are increasingly popular (Schaefer and Waters, 2016). Index insurance pilots and initiatives have been flourishing across the developing world, particularly in Sub-Saharan Africa (SSA). Impact assessment studies have demonstrated the promising potential of insurance in increasing productive investments. In Ethiopia, insured households increased their savings and grain reserves, while female-headed households benefited the most (Madajewicz, 2013). In Kenya, herders were more resilient to shocks (Carter, Janzen and Stoeffler, 2018; Bertram-Huemmer and Kraehnert, 2018). In Ghana, an RCT study showed relaxing risk had more impact than credit in improving productivity (Karlan et al., 2014). These findings demonstrate that insuring smallholder agriculture is a worthwhile investment.

Reliable weather data is a key prerequisite for designing and pricing weather index insurance products. Yet, weather station networks that report in real-time are sparsely distributed over many parts of the developing world, particularly in SSA. Even when weather stations are present they are located in major towns and cities, far away from agricultural areas. This leaves remotely sensed information (satellite data) as the most viable option for designing weather-index insurance products for smallholder agriculture in data poor regions of the developing world. Although success with satellites has allowed the expansion of index insurance programs (Stanimirova, 2013), it is not without its challenges. Remotely sensed data can conflict with on-the-ground observations and result in a mismatch between the payout triggered by the weather event and the actual loss, known as "basis risk." Basis risk is likely exacerbated where there is limited information on the extent of historical loss and damage triggered by a particular weather event.

Lack of understanding of a financial product is a key barrier to its adoption even in the context of a developed country like the United States (Bauhoff, Carman and Wuppermann, 2013). Financial literacy training is important to overcome any negative preconceived notions about the value of insurance. Continuous guidance to clients on product details and policy terms is helpful in minimizing inapplicable claims. There are plenty of examples in microinsurance where a lack of product awareness and financial education lead to client dissatisfaction. In Kenya, health insurance clients who are covered for permanent disability filed claims for broken arms and bruises because of confusion with the policy. Their claims rejection led to a negative perception of the value of the insurance and affected renewals (Cimon, Harnasch and Gross, 2013). Similarly, a low level of product awareness has been the main reason for non-renewal for clients in Guatemala (Herrera and Miranda, 2004).

Similarly, a key barrier to consider when implementing a weather-index insurance program is the level of farmers' understanding of the product. Even basic concepts like *"premium is not returned if payout doesn't occur"* can be challenging for farmers. Studies have shown that financial education and training play a very important role in determining the demand for index insurance (Gaurav, Cole and Tobacman, 2011; Dercon et al., 2014). Clear communication on what risks the insurance is covering, when payout is triggered, how the trigger level, and the amount of payout is determined, etc. are needed not only to entice demand but also to sustain it. There also needs to be a process in place to alert farmers and facilitate their re-enrolment. Farmers may not know the expiry date of their policies, simply forget to renew their policies, or may prioritize other goals.

The aim of this chapter is thus to provide some examples of novel education strategies that the authors have used to educate farmers on insurance and learn from farmers' experiences. Second section provides an overview of the Game Tools used to understand farmers risk management preferences. Third section presents interactive exercise methodology used in product design. Fourth section highlights some of the potential avenues to expand these approaches further using mobile technologies. The last section summarizes the paper and draws refined conclusions.

Farmers' Risk Management Games

Overview

For many farming communities and households around the world, the agricultural outputs of the year, which are closely tied to food security, rely on a combination of choices—about seed variety, inputs, time of sowing, etc. Each of these choices is made based on traditional knowledge, personal experience, context, and available information. Farmers are continuously performing mental cost-benefit analyses, weighing factors such as affordability vs higher yield or improved resistance to pests, or comparing the duration of a seed variety with the expected seasonal weather patterns.

Climate conditions play a considerable role in the success or failure of a crop, and farmers have developed agricultural strategies and calendars that are adapted to the climate in their area. In a changing climate, personal experience and traditional knowledge about the signs indicating the beginning of the rainy season, the typical duration of a season, and the frequency or magnitude of certain types of events might become less reliable, forcing farmers to make those choices with much more uncertainty, and with potential long-term severe consequences. A bad season or even a single extreme event occurring at the wrong time of the season, such as a prolonged drought after all seeds have been sowed, or a flood just before harvest, could lead to major losses of productivity and push farmers below the poverty line for several years. The fear of such a situation is sufficient to prevent farmers from investing in strategies that could help increase their income and resilience but are perceived as "too risky investment" in an uncertain climate.

By providing quick relief to farmers after a bad season or an extreme event, weather-index insurance can prevent farmers from having to make last-resort decisions with long-term impacts that would push them further into poverty or food insecurity, such as selling critical assets, skipping meals, taking kids out of school, and leaving their area. By transferring this risk, insurance also helps unlock new choices for farmers, such as inputs improving productivity, that may have been considered too risky without it. Those choices can in turn strengthen farmers' resilience to future climate challenges and progressively pull them sustainably away from the poverty line.

The farmers' risk management game is designed to unpack those choices, allowing simultaneously to build farmers' literacy around index insurance and its opportunities and limitations and to help researchers better understand the local context and farmers' preferences with regard to climate-risk management and agricultural options. In addition, the game promotes participation and inclusion of communities from the beginning of the project, supporting the development of trust and ownership, which has been shown to be a critical aspect of successful insurance initiatives.

Methodology

The game is designed to unpack how index insurance can impact farmers' choices and agricultural outcomes in a hypothetical upcoming season. It starts like this:

"Let's pretend we are all farmers from the same village, we are approaching the beginning of the season, and it is time to decide what we will plant for this the coming season." It can be played anywhere, from a classroom to a village center, to the shade of a tree. It only requires paper and a marker, and colorful tokens to represent the good and bad seasons—traditionally gum packets.

The game is divided into four rounds that progressively add new options for participants/farmers to choose from at the beginning of the season, bringing new layers of information into participants' decision-making processes. In each round, participants are asked to make a choice based on the options and information they have, without knowing if the upcoming season will be good or bad. In the case of a drought game, a normal season in the game means sufficient rainfall to support participants' crop growth, while a bad season implies a severe drought and complete agricultural loss. At the end of each round, the type of season is determined by blindly picking a colored packet of gums from a bag: a red packet represents a bad year, and a blue packet represents a good year. The game typically uses a probability of one bad year every five years. Each round represents a new start of the same season so that participants don't make choices based on gains or losses of previous rounds, just based on the information available in the current round.

In the first round, participants are asked to choose between "traditional" seeds or "improved" seeds. Improved seeds cost more (virtual) money, which in the game requires taking a loan, but have a higher yield in a good year. In a bad year, which in the game results in a complete crop loss, participants who chose to purchase improved seeds need to discuss how they can reimburse their loan. Seeds can also be described as or "low quality" and "high quality"—it is recommended to discuss with local partners about the preferred and most appropriate terms to use, or decide together what the most relevant input should be for the game so that it is not understood as a criticism of the quality of local seeds. In the second round, they are offered the option of purchasing an insurance policy to protect either choice of seeds. In the third round, the game introduces the notion of basis risk, that is, the risk that the farmers experience a bad season, but that the insurance does not trigger a payout. This can happen if the cause for a bad season is different than the risk insured, or if the pre-defined payout threshold is not reached. In the last round, participants who decide to purchase an insurance policy are offered the option to also participate in a community fund to protect them in the event of a basis risk situation. At the end of each round, participants are asked to explain their choices and discuss how they feel about themselves after seeing the result of the season.

Discussion

The use of a game to increase literacy around weather-index insurance allows participants to unpack complex concepts and explore "what-if" scenarios such as different choices and their impacts in good and bad seasons, in a fun and engaging way and without consequences in their real life. By recreating situations that farmers are familiar with, the game helps connect the new knowledge on insurance with the participants' personal experience and allows them to play out different scenarios to develop their understanding of the concepts. Because it does not require much written material and can be explained through symbols, the game is accessible to people whether they are literate or not. Facilitators are encouraged to discuss the way to best describe the game in the local language and be sensitive to the fact that the use of the term "game" in some languages only reflects children's game and may lead adults to believe that they are wasting their time or are being treated like children. On the other hand, the use of the term "exercise" is not as conducive to create a playful atmosphere and encourage participants to fully explore the "what-if" scenarios.

The game follows a specific structure but is designed to be adaptable to each context. In fact, tailoring the game to the specific context where it is going to be played, and adapting while it is played if necessary, can have a strong influence on how the game is received by local communities. For example, monetary values are adapted to the local currency and to realistic amounts. Crop variety and options of inputs can also be changed to reflect the local situation. The game can be played in teams or individually, collaboratively, or by introducing competition, to adapt to group size, local preferences, and the dynamic of the group. If it looks like participants all choose insurance "to please the facilitators" or insurance partners who may be present, it can be useful (and fun!) to insert co-facilitators in the game to play a skeptical, anti-insurance role and make people more at ease with their choices. The inclusion of underrepresented groups should be considered and discussed with local partners during planning. In some contexts, it is preferred to play separately with men and women, particularly if women are less likely to participate in the presence of men, and if they have different risk management strategies. For example, women may be less involved in agricultural decisions but more involved in microcredit programs that directly support agricultural choices.

The conversation part of the game, that takes place after finding out if the season was good or bad and going through the results of each group or participant's choice, is a critical part of the game that opens the floor for discussion on farmers' risk management preferences, accessible coping strategies, risk aversion, factors affecting decision-making processes, etc. Finding another source of paid income as a day laborer is often the first strategy that participants report, some reporting that they would simply find a job in a nearby city while others explain that they might migrate for the season in search of a paid opportunity elsewhere. In communities whose livelihood relies primarily on raising cattle, some participants have shared that they use their herd as a bank, and would sell cattle as a coping mechanism in a bad year and could buy it again later, while others emphasized the support they would give or get from other community members if the bad year affected some more than others—sparking conversations about group risk management strategies versus individual coping mechanisms. Farmers who are landowners would reluctantly sell part of their land, which would have negative consequences on their ability to grow food in the following years. In places where microcredit is very present and where families often have several ongoing microloans, many participants in the game chose to use microloans as a safety net to reimburse any loss during a bad year and reported that they could likely get a new loan to reimburse the previous one, opening the floor to discussions between participants about the sustainability of microcredit as a coping mechanism for a bad season. Through those conversations and scenarios, the game helps unpack and sometimes shift the understanding of risk: it is not uncommon that, at the beginning of the game, purchasing insurance be considered "the risky behavior" that implies spending some money on a service that may not pay out (in a good year), and that people choosing to purchase insurance in the game hope for a bad year to get a payout. As they explore the different what-if scenarios through the game, participants reassess the long-term risks and opportunities associated with each choice, and discuss the opportunity of insurance to act both as mechanism to provide immediate support after a bad season, and as a strategy to progressively build resilience to climate change and climate variability in the longer term.

The discussions triggered through the game and the exploration of the different scenarios are not only a powerful tool to develop farmers' literacy around insurance and promote their participation in the development of products, but it is equally an important opportunity for product development teams to understand risk management preferences that can help foster the development of locally relevant pro-poor insurance products, embedded in comprehensive risk management solutions.

Interactive Exercise Games

Overview

Involving farmers in index design has been fruitful in developing products that meet their needs. This is particularly important when dealing with satellite data. Satellite data doesn't exactly measure the weather on the ground, but estimates the weather events using algorithms based on a scientific relationship in the physical environment. For instance, the way rainfall estimates work is by capturing the development of rain clouds. But in reality, not all clouds would bear rainfall; or a cloud may pass some areas while bearing rainfall in a nearby location. Ground information is thus critical in order to establish a meaningful connection between satellite data and the actual event on the ground it is meant to represent.

In addition to historical rainfall data, other region-specific information on the agricultural practice is needed to design a weather index. The timing when the rainfall stress occurred is often more important for crop growth than the total rainfall amount over the season. Information on the type and variety of crops planted in the locality, when the crop is planted, when the different growth stages occur etc. are critical. This information is vital to understand the vulnerability of the crop to anomalous weather event. It will dictate the parametrization of the insurance and the appropriate coverage period. It'll also affect the demand for the product. Equally important is in historical loss information. The weather index needs to be calibrated using historical loss events. But similar to weather data, historical loss information for smallholder agriculture production in data poor regions, particularly in SSA, is not readily available. A fundamental challenge is yield data are often aggregated at administrative regions that encompass thousands of small fields. This makes it necessary to find innovative approaches to collate evidence of loss.

Farmers have intimate knowledge of their environment, which makes them an ideal source of ground information. They have knowledge of not only current conditions but also historical memory of their environment. Their livelihood is attuned to local environmental processes and they register changes to their environment as well as the risk it imposes on agricultural outcomes. Gathering information from farmers through field visits when designing an index insurance contract has shown to lead to robust products (Osgood et al., 2018; Stanimirova, 2013).

The interactive exercise game is an end-user-focused activity used throughout the process of index design and validation. The exercise is designed for index insurance (prospective) end-users. Farmers who subscribe to or are interested in subscribing to index-based insurance are invited to participate through an organized focus-group activity. Exercise facilitators divide a representative group of participants into two sub-groups. The representation in the exercise is important as it ensures an equal representation of women and men and a balanced presence of the different age groups in the visited community.

Methodology

When designing a weather-based index using remotely sensed data, there needs to be an end-user-centric process of validation in place to ensure that the remotely sensed data capture the reality on the ground (Brahm et al. 2019; Norton et al. 2014). The interactive exercise captures a set of information that is used in verifying the viability of an index design, monitoring the continued performance, and informing the parametric tuning/refinement of an index.

The exercise consists of two main sections, both interactive encouraging farmers to discuss among themselves and later between sub-groups. Section one is a cropping calendar-focused activity, conducted through a guided discussion about the typical agricultural practices that farmers have adopted in the community and the types of risk management resources currently available to them. The exercise discusses the types of crops grown by the farmers, the weather-related risks farmers face, and the risk management strategies utilized in their community and region.

Section 2 of the exercise is a bad year identification activity that guides farmers through a series of questions and discussions to determine key historical bad years experienced by participants. The end goal is to use the final list of worst historical years agreed upon by farmers to verify (1) if index insurance is a tool that can be helpful to their community in the case of a first feasibility visit (2) or if the performance of the index in capturing the reality on the ground in the case of a seasonal monitoring/validation visit.

Both sections of the interactive exercise serve as an activity to raise awareness on the specific role of index insurance and the existing climate-risk management strategies already in place in unlocking farmers' productivity.

Capturing of the Cropping Calendar

The exercise asks farmers about their typical agricultural practices: the types of crops they grow, when they plant, and when they harvest. Farmers are also asked when they typically experience seasonal onset and cessation of rainfall. This information is used to identify the critical and vulnerable phases of the cropping cycle and helps identify index windows of insurance coverage. It also helps identify the timing of the potential risks of late onset and early cessation of rainfall, which are typical perils experienced by farmers.

Bad Year Identification

Asking farmers about the bad years they have experienced due to a drought/critical deficit of rainfall is done through a focus-group recollection exercise in which farmers are asked to work together to remember and rank the worst drought years they've experienced in the past and help them validate these years by associating them to concurrent life events they or their community went through (elections/birth of a family member etc.). The worst years are tallied and ranked by the village. Bad years are essential in validating historical payout years triggered by an index.

Discussion

The interactive exercise serves as an activity to collect essential data on selected index insurance sites. Cropping cycle and bad year information is then used to identify which satellite product(s) and index parameters capture the farmers' information. The interactive exercise during the initial visit also serves as a "technical" introduction of index insurance to farmers (end-users). The exercise serves as an activity for farmers to understand how an index is designed and how information collected from their experience and practices can help tune an index to best cover their risks. Through the initial visit interactive exercise, farmers understand that the cropping calendar questions are used to understand the critical phases in their agricultural practices during the rainy season, as well as a way for them to verify that their personal experience of the rainfall patterns is taken into account when designing and validating an index. Additionally, farmers' recollection of drought years helps them think through the ways in which an index insurance can cover their risks, the frequency at which an insurance could trigger, and whether an insurance scheme is useful as a last piece of the puzzle in terms of climate-risk management. Typically, data collected from the field through interactive exercises become more accurate/precise with more data points collected, meaning, more visits, more farmers interviewed, and more neighboring villages visited. The initial visit, while it provides essential information, is usually followed by more visits at different stages of the design for further data intake and index communication.

The interactive exercise is also conducted during the mid-season and end-of-season monitoring visits. During the monitoring stage, in which the same set of data is collected, the interactive exercise serves as an activity for index validation and output communication. With an index already developed, the collection of a mid-season and an end-of-season cropping calendar focuses particularly on capturing the information on the ongoing season in order to track the performance of the index. Capturing when farmers experienced the onset of the rain, when they planted, and whether they've experienced significant rainfall pauses, helps index designers to better compare satellite data with farmer's accounts, and understand if a late onset or early cessation of rain occurred on the ground. Similarly, the bad year exercise is used to collect additional data on historical drought years to increase the sample size of ranked years.

At this stage of the index design process, facilitators present the index historical output, which represents the historical payouts generated by the index, in parallel with farmers ranked historical bad years. Farmers are invited to provide feedback on whether the level of matching between the index payouts and their recollection is satisfactory. The matching exercise serves as a way for index designers to assess the performance of the index and get feedback on/validation of key drought years. It also allows farmers to have a transparent overview of the way the index is capturing their risks and any potential basis risk they might experience. The active comparison represents a direct involvement of end-users in index validation and improvement making them central agents in the design process.

Digital Tools and Games

Overview

Rethinking education for sustainable development research, policy, and practice requires finding innovative ways to reach smallholder farmers in low- and middle-income countries. Advances in communication technologies represent an opportunity to scale, incentivize, and improve climate information and services access. Farmer data collection is usually limited to small-scale focus groups or participatory processes such as workshops, household surveys, and extensionist visits that require intensive facilitators' involvement.

Although these approaches provide local data, they are time-consuming, expensive, and limited in scope and frequency. Face-to-face encounters are constrained by the reduced possibilities of visiting communities because of specific security conditions, geographical access, physical distance, and travel restrictions (Hernandez-Aguilera, Mauerman, and Osgood, 2020). Moreover, smallholders are increasingly reluctant to participate in workshops and surveys where the incentives and benefits of generating and sharing information are not clear (Beza et al., 2017). There is a need to incentivize and extend crowdsourcing to thousands or millions of smallholders, and involve populations usually excluded from participatory and decision-making processes, such as young producers and women (Hernandez-Aguilera, Mauerman, and Osgood, 2020).

Building upon the games and interactive exercise presented in Sections 2 and 3, we are using gamification as a strategy to scale up focal groups and surveys to crowdsourcing at a low cost while engaging a large number of smallholders and reaching excluded populations (Hernandez-Aguilera, Mauerman, and Osgood, 2020). Gamification, which is defined as "the use of game design elements in non-game contexts" (Seaborn and Fels, 2015; Johnson et al., 2016) makes smallholders capable of transferring and translating climate knowledge, while simultaneously improving index insurance product design. Gamification is located at the intersection of three approaches: (i) serious games, as it engages and educates people through intrinsic motivation (e.g., competition and fun), (ii) persuasive technology, as it applies features that drive targeted behavior and incentive structures; and (iii) personal informatics, as it tracks individual behavior and self-reporting information using well-designed interfaces on mobile phones or similar devices (Cugelman, 2013; Johnson et al., 2016).

Methodology

We designed iKON (Climate&Society, 2021), an application named after KON—the Inca god of rain and wind—for gathering crowdsourced climate-risk data from across the world, with a focus on smallholder farmers. iKON uses gamified incentives and behavioral design elements such as competition to gather accurate historical loss data at a greater scale compared to conventional methods. iKON's specific design aspects include priming memory through the pairwise comparisons of years and incentivizing accuracy through a points-reward system. iKON works by showing players a pair of years (e.g., 2007 vs. 2008), and asking them to report which year was worse (or better) for a specific climate event (i.e., droughts and excess rain). Answers are scored based on their correspondence with remote-sensing data sources and other players' answers. Players' total points are then tracked on a public leaderboard. Over successive comparisons from thousands of players, the data from iKON can be used to estimate a ranking of years from worst to best—harnessing the wisdom of crowds. This ranking can be compared with what remote-sensing sources suggest. Simultaneously, farmers learn about relevant climate information sources that are used for designing insurance products such as satellites, weather stations, and community consent that reflect what is happening in their communities and localities (Hernandez-Aguilera, Mauerman, and Osgood, 2020).

iKON uses a freeware text messaging system (WhatsApp) or alternatively a web-based version, allowing to deploy the app anywhere in the world as long as the user has a smartphone (Figure 9.1). iKON's database collectively stores user responses from both versions and allows customization for different deployments, including language, localization, and sources for climate data based on specific regions' needs. iKON also incentivizes self-reporting and data generation by rewarding points to users for sharing the app with their family and friends. The experimental design of iKON involves testing behavioral aspects that affect the user's experience and interaction with the tool. Specific behavioral questions explored include whether providing memory triggers improves the accuracy of responses and the role of social comparisons and tangible end-goals for players—in particular, how emphasizing comparative feedback and information about the number of comparisons completed affect players' motivation, accuracy, and attrition.

Discussion

iKON has been piloted with rice and coffee growers in Colombia. Preliminary results suggest that farmers' information corroborates remote-sensing sources when there is a convergence of evidence and adds novel local-level information when primary remote-sensing data sources yield ambiguous results (Hernandez-Aguilera, Mauerman, and Osgood, 2020). In addition, there is an important ratio of engagement and shareability of the game even when the conditions for gathering information are not optimal (i.e., national strike with roads closed). We are also designing and evaluating a new generation of games using digital tools and devices. For instance, Noki, in contrast with iKON, focuses on current and future climatic and agricultural information. Noki incentivizes farmers to generate information such as the expected start and end date of the season, observed and expected rainfall, and other elements critical to improving

Figure 9.1 Crowdsourcing climate risk data with gamification and digital tools. iKON WhatsApp version.

the design of climate-risk management instruments. Noki induces habits of journaling about climate information while educating farmers about basic aspects of climate forecast and modeling.

Overall, technologies of this century can expand the scope and validity of alternative approaches and games in agriculture. However, a systematic literature review of games and fieldwork in agriculture between 2000 and 2020 shows that this integration is still underdeveloped compared with other sectors (Hernandez-Aguilera, Mauerman, et al., 2020). The integration of new technologies and games will require better connectivity conditions and researchers with the skills to make this happen. The lack of investments and fixed costs of new technologies can undoubtedly constrain digital tools and games in agriculture in less developed regions. Nonetheless, 70 percent of the poorest 20 percent in low- and middle-income countries have access to a mobile phone, and one in three people have internet access (The World Bank, 2016; Deichmann et al., 2016; Fabregas et al., 2019). Although connectivity prevails in urban settings, it has also spread to rural areas, where the ratio of farmers to extension workers exceeds 1,000 to one (S. Fielke et al., 2020; The World Bank, 2016; Deichmann et al., 2016; Fabregas et al., 2019). In the end, the connectivity of humans and technologies in agricultural knowledge and advice networks is most likely to keep growing. It is estimated that digital tools and devices could help to reach more than 170 million small-scale farmers around the world, improving their decisions based on better knowledge and information (S. Fielke et al., 2020; Steiner et al., 2020; Hernandez-Aguilera, Loboguerrero, et al., 2020).

There are, however, significant gaps that constrain the adoption of new technologies and digital tools in agriculture, which goes beyond connectivity and farmers' access to smartphones (Hernandez-Aguilera, Loboguerrero, et al., 2020). Specifically, conducting games and fieldwork in agriculture demands managing complex relationships between parties and presenting and communicating ideas and innovation to lay individuals (J. A. List and Metcalfe 2014; John A. List 2011). These challenging environments define researchers' value-leading games and fieldwork in agriculture to respond to today's challenges of rethinking data generation and literacy approaches for climate change and climate resilience.

An additional concern related to the massive use of digital tools is the lack of transparency and clarity around data ownership, portability, privacy, trust, and liability in the relationships that govern digital agriculture. Many farmers are wary of becoming data laborers that are progressively displaced and deskilled without any consideration of their identity, traditional knowledge, and networks. Moreover, the increasing number of alternatives, including applications and web-based platforms is difficult to track, classify, and evaluate (Eastwood et al., 2019; S. J. Fielke et al., 2019; USAID, 2018; Hernandez-Aguilera, Loboguerrero, et al., 2020). For instance, it is estimated that there are approximately 140 digital services provided just in Ethiopia, but their usage is low. Existing tools tend to generate information that is not decision-relevant to smallholders, and tools' design and implementation are often made unilaterally by NGOs or researchers without including key incentives and agents with substantial agricultural extension networks and experience (Raithatha and Tricarico, 2019; Ventocilla et al., 2020).

Translating climate information to farmers' context and realities is essential so that the development of digital tools does not evolve quicker than their use. The experience with advisory and digital tools for coffee production and climate risk provides an interesting example. Typically, top-down approaches and advisory tools for coffee production alert the global effects of climate change on the land suitable for cultivation. However, the implications of those advisory tools and models at the farm level are not clear. Based on different greenhouse gas concentration trajectories and assumptions, diverse models conclude that suitable coffee cultivation areas could drop on average 50 percent by 2050 (Adhikari et al., 2020). In Africa, a 39 percent to 65 percent reduction in suitable present-day land is predicted, predominantly in Ethiopia, with the worst-case scenario resulting in a 90 percent to 100 percent loss of land between 2080 and 2099 (Davis et al. 2012; Moat et al., 2017). Nonetheless, advice for specific and tailored practices and adaptation strategies is minimal. Recommendations do not consider the farmers' economic constraints, and the adaptation practices and investments required are not always feasible considering farmers' production costs and income. To connect the economics and climate of coffee, and with the support of the Columbia World Project ACToday, a group of researchers at the International Research Institute created MyCoffeeFarm (Ventocilla et al., 2020). MyCoffeeFarm is a customized dynamic advisory tool that integrates farm-level climate information and profitability, "translating" the economic costs of climate shocks and specific adaptation strategies. This bottom-up approach improves farmers' decision-making while supporting and informing specific policies based on microeconomic foundations and feasibility.

In conclusion, increased physical restrictions and the limited scope of extension services and traditional workshops clash with the need to reach and engage with farmers. Games, digital tools, and devices may represent a turning point for climate and agriculture research and operations while improving access for farmers and other key stakeholders to climate services and education. There are, however, cultural and methodological gaps that compromise games and digital tools' proliferation in agriculture and require a more comprehensive approach. Even if infrastructure and education barriers are overcome—as has been progressively happening—there are deeper concerns that might compromise games and digital tools acceptance from farmers. Twenty-first-century communication technologies provide an exciting opportunity to improve climate services for agriculture; however, technology per se is not sufficient. Creativity and imagination should also recreate a more inclusive and attractive environment and interfaces that contribute to rethinking and revolutionizing sustainable agriculture.

Conclusion

Millions of people worldwide depend on rainfed agriculture for employment and food supply and their livelihood is increasingly threatened by climate change There is plenty of evidence showing that empowering farming households to better deal with weather shocks has far-reaching implications in improving their welfare in the short-term and for long-term economic growth (Hill, 2010). The provision of agricultural insurance services has proved to be one means to reduce household vulnerability to weather shocks in the face of increasing climate change. However, only 20 percent of smallholder farmers worldwide have access to agricultural insurance (ISF Advisors and Microinsurance Network, 2022). The estimate is staggering for SSA where 97 percent of smallholder farmers are uninsured.

Implementing agricultural insurance, particularly in the context of smallholder agriculture, has so many challenges. The heterogeneity of practices and scarcity of data (be it weather or yield) make insurance design a challenge. On top of that, low levels of financial literacy limit the menu of agricultural insurance products that can be extended to smallholders. Successful implemented index insurance programs often employ innovative financial education and games to close the knowledge and information gap on-demand side as well as to improve product offering on the supply side. In order to ensure the insurance product is inclusive and tailored to client needs, the insurance product needs to be intentionally designed to incorporate farmers' perspective on the local environmental conditions and their historical experiences.

Growing mobile penetration rates makes it increasingly possible to crowdsource product design information as well as facilitate awareness in index insurance. A game-like interactive platform, like iKON - where farmers themselves are incentivized to provide ground information that would improve the insurance products - are critical innovations that would take index insurance forward. Furthermore, such innovations will help to reduce costs and improve the effectiveness of training programs. For instance, one can send an SMS explaining the product to the farmers in a language that they understand. This provides greater autonomy to the farmer on the purchase decision. The use of mobile technology to promote the product vastly increases the likelihood of reaching many people. As use of mobile phones becomes ubiquitous, it is provides opportunities to reach marginalized groups such as women-headed households who are less likely to be invited to training sessions.

References

Adhikari, Mira, Isaac, Elizabeth L., Russell, R., Paterson, M., & Maslin, Mark A.. (2020). A Review of Potential Impacts of Climate Change on Coffee Cultivation and Mycotoxigenic Fungi. *Microorganisms*, 8(10), p. 1625. https://doi.org/10.3390/mic roorganisms8101625.

Bauhoff, Sebastian, Carman, Katherine, & Wuppermann, Amelie. (2013). Financial Literacy and Consumer Choice of Health Insurance: Evidence from Low-Income Populations in the United States. *SSRN Electronic Journal.* https://doi.org/10.2139/ssrn.2326756.

Bertram-Huemmer, Veronika, & Kraehnert, Kati. (2018). Does Index Insurance Help Households Recover from Disaster? Evidence from IBLI Mongolia. *American Journal of Agricultural Economics*, 100, pp. 145–71. https://doi.org/10.1093/ajae/aax069.

Beza, Eskender, Steinke, Jonathan, van Etten, Jacob, Reidsma, Pytrik, Fadda, Carlo, Mittra, Sarika, Mathur, Prem, & Kooistra, Lammert. (2017). What Are the Prospects for Citizen Science in Agriculture? Evidence from Three Continents on Motivation and Mobile Telephone Use of Resource-Poor Farmers. *PLOS ONE*, 12(5), p. e0175700. https://doi.org/10.1371/journal.pone.0175700.

Boucher, Stephen R., Carter, Michael R., & Guirkinger, Catherine. (2008). Risk Rationing and Wealth Effects in Credit Markets: Theory and Implications for Agricultural Development. *American Journal of Agricultural Economics*, 90, pp. 409–23.

Brahm, Manuel, Vila, Daniel, Martinez Saenz, Sofia, & Osgood, Daniel. (April, 2019). Can Disaster Events Reporting Be Used to Drive Remote Sensing Applications? A Latin America Weather Index Insurance Case Study. *Meteorological Applications*, https://doi.org/10.1002/met.1790.

Carter, Michael R., Janzen, Sarah A., & Stoeffler, Quentin. (2018). Can Insurance Help Manage Climate Risk and Food Insecurity? Evidence from the Pastoral Regions of East Africa. In *Climate Smart Agriculture* (pp. 201–25). Cham: Springer.

Cimon, E., Harnasch, B., & Gross, P. (2013). *Removing Obstacles to Access Microinsurance*, p. 43.

Climate&Society, IRI. (2021). *IKON: Playing to Adapt.* https://youtu.be/jMXJ5shoPD4.

Cugelman, Brian. (2013). Gamification: What It Is and Why It Matters to Digital Health Behavior Change Developers. *JMIR Serious Games*, 1(1), p. e3.

Davis, Aaron P., Gole, Tadesse Woldemariam, Baena, Susana, & Moat, Justin. (2012). The Impact of Climate Change on Indigenous Arabica Coffee (Coffea Arabica): Predicting Future Trends and Identifying Priorities. *PLOS ONE*, 7(11), p. e47981. https://doi.org/10.1371/journal.pone.0047981.

Deichmann, Uwe, Goyal, Aparajita, & Mishra, Deepak. (2016). *Will Digital Technologies Transform Agriculture in Developing Countries?* Policy Research Working Papers. The World Bank. https://doi.org/10.1596/1813-9450-7669.

Dercon, S., & Hoddinott, J. (2004). Health, Shocks, and Poverty Persistence. In S. Dercon (Ed.), *Insurance Against Poverty* (pp. 124–36). Oxford: Oxford University Press. https://doi.org/10.1093/0199276838.003.0007.

Dercon, Stefan, Hill, Ruth Vargas, Clarke, Daniel, Outes-Leon, Ingo, & Taffesse, Alemayehu Seyoum. (2014). Offering Rainfall Insurance to Informal Insurance Groups: Evidence from a field Experiment in Ethiopia. *Journal of Development Economics*, 106, pp. 132–43.

Eastwood, Callum, Ayre, Margaret, Nettle, Ruth, & Dela Rue, Brian. (December, 2019). Making Sense in the Cloud: Farm Advisory Services in a Smart Farming Future. *NJAS - Wageningen Journal of Life Sciences*, 90–91, p. 100298. https://doi.org/10.1016/j.njas.2019.04.004.

Fabregas, Raissa, Kremer, Michael, & Schilbach, Frank. (2019). Realizing the Potential of Digital Development: The Case of Agricultural Advice. *Science*, 366(6471). https://doi.org/10.1126/science.aay3038.

Fielke, Simon J., Garrard, Robert, Jakku, Emma, Fleming, Aysha, Wiseman, Leanne, & Taylor, Bruce M. (December, 2019). Conceptualising the DAIS: Implications of the 'Digitalisation of Agricultural Innovation Systems' on Technology and Policy at Multiple Levels. *NJAS - Wageningen Journal of Life Sciences*, 90–91, p. 100296. https://doi.org/10.1016/j.njas.2019.04.002.

Fielke, Simon, Taylor, Bruce, & Jakku, Emma. (April, 2020). Digitalisation of Agricultural Knowledge and Advice Networks: A State-of-the-Art Review. *Agricultural Systems*, 180, p. 102763. https://doi.org/10.1016/j.agsy.2019.102763.

Gaurav, Sarthak, Cole, Shawn, & Tobacman, Jeremy. (2011). Marketing Complex Financial Products in Emerging Markets: Evidence from Rainfall Insurance in India. *Journal of Marketing Research*, 48, pp. S150–S162.

Greatrex, Helen, Hansen, James, Garvin, Samantha, Diro, Rahel, Le Guen, Margot, Blakeley, Sari, Rao, Kolli, & Osgood, Daniel. (2015). Scaling up Index Insurance for Smallholder Farmers: Recent Evidence and Insights. *CCAFS Report*.

Hernandez-Aguilera, J. Nicolas, Loboguerrero, Ana Maria, Herrera, Alexandra, & Baethgen, Walter. (August, 2020). Harnessing Digital Tools for Climate and Agriculture. *Research Program on Climate Change, Agriculture and Food Security, CCAFS*. https://ccafs.cgiar.org/blog/harnessing-digital-tools-climate-and-agriculture. Accessed 25 August 2020.

Hernandez-Aguilera, J. Nicolas, Mauerman, Max, Herrera, Alexandra, Vasilaky, Kathryn, Baethgen, Walter, Loboguerrero, Ana Maria, Diro, Rahel, Tekeste, Yohana Tesfamariam, & Osgood, Daniel. (2020). Games and Fieldwork in Agriculture: A Systematic Review of the 21st Century in Economics and Social Science. *Games*, 11(4), p. 47. https://doi.org/10.3390/g11040047.

Hernandez-Aguilera, J. Nicolas, Mauerman, Max, & Osgood, Daniel. (2020). Playing to Adapt: Crowdsourcing Historical Climate Data with Gamification to Improve Farmer's Risk Management Instruments. SSRN Scholarly Paper ID 3639580. Rochester, NY: Social Science Research Network. https://doi.org/10.2139/ssrn.3639580.

Herrera, C., & Miranda, B. (2004). CGAP Working Group on Microinsurance Good and Bad Practices Case Study No. 5 - Columna, Guatemala. CGAP.

Hill, R.V., & Viceisza, A. (2012). A Field Experiment on the Impact of Weather Shocks and Insurance on Risky Investment. *Experimental Economics*, 15, pp. 341–71. https://doi.org/10.1007/s10683-011-9303-7.

ISF Advisors and Microinsruance Network (2022). State of the Sector: Agri-Insurance for Smallholder Farmers: A global stocktake of an evolving Industry. ISF and microinsurance Network, 2022.

Johnson, Daniel, Deterding, Sebastian, Kuhn, Kerri-Ann, Staneva, Aleksandra, Stoyanov, Stoyan, & Hides, Leanne. (November, 2016). Gamification for Health and Wellbeing: A Systematic Review of the Literature. *Internet Interventions*, 6, pp. 89–106. https://doi.org/10.1016/j.invent.2016.10.002.

Karlan, Dean, Osei, Robert, Osei-Akoto, Isaac, & Udry, Christopher. (2014). Agricultural Decisions after Relaxing Credit and Risk Constraints. *The Quarterly Journal of Economics*, 129(2), pp. 597–652.

List, John A. (2011). Why Economists Should Conduct Field Experiments and 14 Tips for Pulling One Off. *Journal of Economic Perspectives*, 25(3), pp. 3–16. https://doi.org/10.1257/jep.25.3.3.

List, John A., & Metcalfe, R. (2014). Field Experiments in the Developed World: An Introduction. *Oxford Review of Economic Policy*, 30(4), pp. 585–96. https://doi.org/10.1093/oxrep/grv005.

Madajewicz, M. (2013). *Managing Risks to Agricultural Livelihoods: Impact Evaluation of the HARITA Program in Tigray, Ethiopia, 2009–2012.* Oxfam America.

Mercy, Corps. 2016. *A 2016 Zambia Ecosystem Review and Strategic Perspective on Digital Financial Services for Smallholder Farmers.* A white paper prepared by Mercy Corps AgriFin Accelerate Program for The MasterCard Foundation. zambia_white_paper_0.pdf (raflearning.org).

Moat, Justin, Williams, Jenny, Baena, Susana, Wilkinson, Timothy, Gole, Tadesse W., Challa, Zeleke K., Demissew, Sebsebe, & Davis, Aaron P. 2017. Resilience Potential of the Ethiopian Coffee Sector under Climate Change. *Nature Plants*, 3(7), pp. 1–14. https://doi.org/10.1038/nplants.2017.81.

Norton, M., Osgood, D., Madajewicz, M., Holthaus, E., Peterson, N., Diro, R., Mullally, C., Teh, T.L., & Gebremichael, M. (2014). Evidence of Demand for Index Insurance: Experimental Games and Commercial Transactions in Ethiopia. *Journal of Development Studies*, 50(5), pp. 630–48. https://doi.org/10.1080/00220388.2014.887685.

Osgood, D., Powell, B., Diro, R., Farah, C., Enenkel, M., Brown, M.E., Husak, G., Blakeley, S.L., Hoffman, L., & McCarty, J.L. (2018). Farmer Perception, Recollection, and Remote Sensing in Weather Index Insurance: An Ethiopia Case Study. *Remote Sensing*, 10, p. 1887. https://doi.org/10.3390/rs10121887.

Raithatha, Rishi, & Tricarico, Daniele. (2019). Mobile Technology for Rural Climate Resilience: The Role of Mobile Operators in Bridging the Data Gap. *Mobile for Development* (blog). https://www.gsma.com/mobilefordevelopment/resources/mobile-technology-for-rural-climate-resilience-the-role-of-mobile-operators-in-bridging-the-data-gap/. Accessed August 24, 2020.

Schaefer, Laura, & Waters, Eleanor. (2016). *Climate Risk Insurance for the Poor & Vulnerable: How to Effectively Implement the Pro-Poor Focus of Insuresilience.* United Nations University Institute for Environment and Human Security.

Seaborn, Katie, & Fels, Deborah I. (February, 2015). Gamification in Theory and Action: A Survey. *International Journal of Human-Computer Studies*, 74, pp. 14–31. https://doi.org/10.1016/j.ijhcs.2014.09.006.

Stanimirova, R. (2013). Using Satellites to Make Index Insurance Scalable. In *Encyclopedia of Global Warming & Climate Change*. Thousand Oaks: SAGE Publications. https://doi.org/10.4135/9781452218564.n384.

Steiner, A., Aguilar, G., Echeverria, R., Gandhi, R., Hadegaard, C., Holdorf, D., Ishii, N., Quinn, K., Ruter, B., & Loboguerrero, Ana Maria. (February, 2020). Actions to Transform Food Systems under Climate Change: Reduce Food Loss and Waste. *CCAFS Policy Brief*. https://cgspace.cgiar.org/handle/10568/107235. Accessed May 15, 2020.

The World Bank (2016). *World Development Report 2016: Digital Dividends*. Washington, D.C.: World Bank Publications.

United Nations University. (2015). Climate Risk Insurance for the Poor & Vulnerable: How to Effectively Implement the Pro-poor Focus of Insuresilience, p. 208.

USAID (2018). Digital Tools in USAID Agricultural Programming Toolkit. Feed the Future, USAID.

Ventocilla, Maria Claudia, Grossi, Amanda, Nicolas Hernandez-Aguilera, J., Dinku, Tufa, Recha, John, & Ambaw, Gebermedihin. (November, 2020). Brewing Resilience for Ethiopia's Smallholder Coffee Farmers: A Closer Look at Ethiopia's Coffee Sector to Help Address Climate Information Gaps. https://cgspace.cgiar.org/handle/10568/110123. Accessed December 10, 2020.

10

Building Child-focused Community Resilience Utilizing a Community-based, Multi-Modal Educational Approach

Jeff Schlegelmilch and Jonathan Sury

Introduction

The case study presented explores the disaster literacy facets of the Resilient Children/Resilience Communities (RCRC) Initiative. The community-based project aimed to build the capacity of six unique communities in the United States and its territories. The RCRC aimed to build a model of child-focused community resilience through a community mobilization approach. The community mobilization approach seeks to engage a broad range of sectors, groups, and individuals across a given community to facilitate change. In this case, the approach was focused on building disaster knowledge, providing evidence-base for child-focused preparedness at the institutional level, enhancing disaster planning, and supporting local and national advocacy for the unique needs of children in disaster. The following case study provides the theoretical underpinnings behind the model and demonstrates the educational outputs throughout the entire initiative. The model presented is not one-size-fits-all but aims to illustrate how community-driven and contextually appropriate disaster preparedness and resilience programming can lead to significant improvements in disaster planning and an enhanced culture of preparedness.

Background

Children and Disasters

Disasters affect children differently than adults. Children are more likely to experience post-traumatic stress disorder and other impacts after a disaster, which may manifest in different ways for different age groups. For instance, younger children may display increased dependence, become more emotionally volatile, and may regress with bedwetting and other behaviors. Older children may be less interested in social activities and suffer from eating disorders, confusion, and lack of concentration. Children are also more physically vulnerable to illness, injury, and death. Additionally, children are more sensitive to disruptions in education. Often disasters will impact education institutions and resources, leading to a poor academic performance with cascading impacts on the child's economic conditions and situations can also exacerbate these vulnerabilities at home (Peek, 2008).

It has also been demonstrated that children are the bellwethers of disaster recovery (Abramson et al., 2010). Children are dependent on a multitude of community members, institutions, and services and are thus linked with the overall recovery of the community. They are dependent on both direct and indirect systems of support. Direct services include structured programming such as child care, K-12 schooling, and support services such as social services. Their health and well-being are also tied to informal support services and networks such as family and friends in social capital, community organizations that may support the entire family unit, and even access to green space and public utilities.

Children are also unique in that they lack the agency to advocate for themselves in a community setting. As such, the needs of the children are often left out of the broader preparedness processes. For example, the drafting and revision of disaster plans are typically led by government agencies, such as Emergency Management, that coordinate across multiple responding agencies, and rarely seek public input, especially that of children. These responders may include police, fire, public health, or emergency medical services who are tasked with the immediate preservation of life and property and public health and who also track disease, injury, and aims to curtail the physical and mental health sequelae both during and after a disaster. While there is a greater shift toward "Whole Community" planning (FEMA, 2011), the legacy of Emergency Management agencies is often with the military or first-responder agencies and the embedded traditions. Within the sphere of preparedness planning at the governmental level, children are often not planned for as a unique population, but rather are grouped in with the general population or are not included at all (Peek, 2008; National Commission On Children And Disasters, 2010). During and after a disruptive event, such as a disaster, those they depend on may also be dealing with the trauma and complexities of recovery that may range from injuries, lost jobs, damaged property, and housing uncertainty, among other challenges (Abramson et al., 2010). Integrating child-serving institutions with emergency management structures through inclusive planning should be a standard practice at the community level (Institute of Medicine, 2014; National Commission On Children And Disasters, 2010).

These challenges are well described; however, various sectors of civil society are often poorly coordinated to meet the needs of children in the aftermath of disasters and complex emergencies. As a result, children are often not central to recovery planning, are lumped into broader categories of "special populations," or are left out of the planning thought process entirely. And while there have been increasing efforts to address the unique needs of children in disasters, the education, awareness, and connectivity of communities to adequately address these requirements warrants deeper integration and agency-level commitment. Ongoing efforts should be made to better understand the impact of disruptive events experienced by children in disasters and how to appropriately and adequately plan for and to respond before, during, and after a disruptive event (Peek et al., 2018; National Commission On Children And Disasters, 2010).

Community Mobilization

Community organizing is often used as a tool to gather support for a cause at a grassroots level. It is citizen-led and often in collaboration with mission-focused community-based organizations that rally around a specific community-identified issue. Community coalitions have long been used as a community mobilization method to collate many community stakeholders. If effectively organized and managed, community coalitions can provide a powerful tool for collective efficacy within a community. Inherently, there is a recognition in a coalition that it "takes a village" to solve a problem and coalitions bring the village to the table. Coalitions are informal and may be composed of government agencies, community-based organizations, the socially conscious private sector, the mandated private sector, concerned citizens, and ultimately (and ideally) the beneficiaries of the coalition's mission. Coalitions can be effective change agents to address child-focused community-wide disaster planning (Institute of Medicine, 2014).

Community mobilization, when implemented in partnership with an academic institution, may take several forms. They may take the grassroots bottom-up approach, and top-down researcher-driven approach such as the Community Betterment Model, or somewhere in between as seen in

Participatory Action Research (PAR) or Community-Based Participatory Research (CBPR) methods, which value local knowledge coupled with academic rigor. Another approach that places power in the hands of the community members as opposed to academics is the Community Empowerment Model (CEM) (Kim-Ju et al., 2008). CEM places decision-making power, coalition leadership, and action plan implementation in the hands of community members with supporting action from academic partners. The model aims to build partnerships that expand and strengthen social networks thereby increasing social capital leading to a more coordinated and connected disaster response across a community.

When designing any type of intervention, regardless of the specific approach to community mobilization, the researcher's role is a critical reality that should be at the forefront of a reflective process centered on the concept that local context matters (Tremblay et al., 2014). The values and experience a researcher brings to a local community context may differ from those of the community with which they intend to work. This potential incongruence, and power differential, is not incompatible with effective and productive interaction but should be done so in a thoughtful and reflective, or reflexive, manner. Reflexivity is the act of double-loop learning which requires the active review of programmatic goals, frameworks, and approaches to be actively assessed and adjusted to fit within a changing social context. Within global health, there is a concept of a "travelling model" or a model developed within a specific set of contextual factors, which implementers think will apply to every context (e.g., geographic region) in which they work (Olivier De Sardan et al., 2017). This assumption is misled and ill-informed and can be dangerous. There are many contextual factors that affect program implementation in any community, some of which include governance structures, culture, historical trauma, prior disaster exposure, colonization, language, and social norms, to name a few. Relying on local leaders and integrating with community members themselves will help mitigate potentially destructive and culturally insensitive approaches to community mobilization efforts. Most importantly, working within a local context takes time, and change does not happen overnight (Wessells, 2015). Ongoing iterative learning, with an openness to acknowledge when certain actions do not lead to the desired result, should not be seen as negative but as an opportunity to collectively learn, adapt, and improve (George et al., 2018). Community mobilization efforts require a long-term commitment that must be developed from, created within, and levered existing structures such as preexisting coalitions, public partnerships, or any other formal or informal structure which shares a similar vision, mission, or values.

In focusing on the impact on children as the downstream beneficiary, this model was focused on community leaders and organizations that serve children, and/or would be responsible for their well-being in a disaster situation. The application of this model is described in more detail later, but the grounding principles of enhancing existing community capacities through fostering connectedness and providing technical assistance are fundamental to the approach.

Disaster Literacy and Health/Risk Communication

Disaster literacy (see definition below) is a fairly understudied topic itself but draws from the well-established health literacy literature (Brown et al., 2014). The field of health literacy, which pre-dates the field of disaster literacy and is focused on an individual's capacity to access and utilize information to make informed health decisions, provides a blueprint for the notion of disaster literacy. Health literacy research has demonstrated that individuals with poor health literacy cannot effectively understand and act on health information which affects their health outcomes. Brown et al posited that the same applies to disaster literacy in that, poor health outcomes are expected post-disaster if individuals cannot appropriately understand their risk, emergency communication messages, or navigate the complex aid systems in a post-disaster context. Çalışkan and Üner extend the model proposed by Brown et al, which primarily focused on an individual's disaster-related decisions, to that of "accessing, understanding, appraising, and applying disaster-related information" (Çalışkan and Üner, 2020). Most importantly, their model (Figure 10.1) connects contextual and individual factors to social/community factors. This connection suggests a transfer of knowledge and information throughout a community and its bidirectional influence on disaster-related outcomes of preparedness, response, recovery, and mitigation. They then propose a new definition of disaster literacy which states the following:

> Disaster literacy is individuals' capacity to access, understand, appraise, and apply disaster information to make informed decisions and to follow instructions in everyday life concerning mitigating/prevention, preparing, responding, and recovering/rehabilitation from a disaster in order to maintain or improve quality of life during the life course. (Çalışkan and Üner, 2020)

At the root of most disaster literacy models is the ability to access, understand, appraise, and apply information before, during, and after a disaster. The

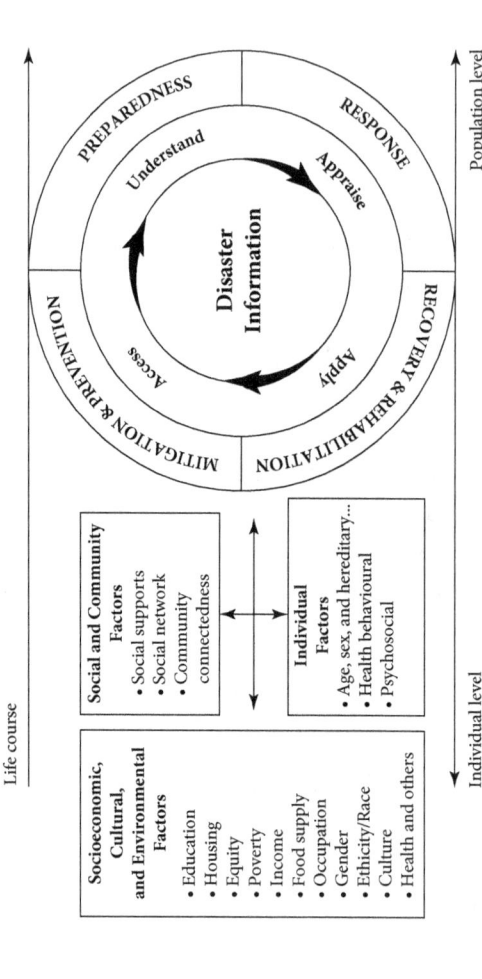

Figure 10.1 Integrated Disaster Literacy Model (Çalışkan and Üner 2020). Image copyright held by the Society for Disaster Medicine and Public Health, used with permission.

community coalitions through community mobilization initiatives when centered on preparedness and planning can serve to help all stakeholders improve their collective ability to follow this process of processing disaster-related information. Each stakeholder provides their own expertise and ability to translate knowledge culturally, professionally, and in an age-appropriate way. Building upon community strengths to share this information adds fluency in discussing these topics in a contextually relevant manner. The notion of improving disaster literacy is not simply to provide stronger knowledge of disasters, but with that knowledge to better inform key decisions, preparedness actions, and advocacy efforts than in the absence of enhanced disaster literacy. Understanding the long-term effects of disasters on children after, for example, disruption of education, extended lack of community child care services, temporary relocation, protracted displacement, excess household stressors, or navigating disaster relief aid, highlights the importance for families and organizations to have plans for continuity of education, mental health and psychosocial support, and other community support mechanisms. Understanding the common stress reactions of children to disasters can also prevent misdiagnosis of behaviors in ways that can be detrimental to recovery.

Building a Child-focused Community Preparedness and Resilience Model

The RCRC Initiative

In 2015, the National Center for Disaster Preparedness (NCDP) at Columbia University's Earth Institute and Save the Children (STC) formed a new partnership through a grant from the global healthcare company GSK. This partnership called the RCRC Initiative focused on creating a model of child-focused community resilience by strengthening community-based preparedness plans (National Center for Disaster Preparedness, 2015). A central feature of this partnership was its ability to strategically and effectively communicate the value of child-focused community resilience through evidence-based concepts in disaster research and humanitarian response. Phase-I of the project occurred between 2015 and 2018 in Washington County, Arkansas, and Putnam County, New York, and focused primarily on pre-disaster resilience building, often described as "blue sky" times. These locations were chosen because they present different demographic, geographic, and hazard profiles. They were also chosen because of the preexisting relationships with pilot projects either with NCDP or STC and the successful history of collaboration necessary for the initial refinement of this approach and trusted entrée into a community. Phase-II of the initiative was led by NCDP under a follow-on grant from GSK and conducted for two and a half years from 2019 through the first half of 2021. The communities identified for Phase-II were selected by their recent exposure to a major disaster and were looking to integrate child-focused resilience building into recovery strategies. These communities included Robeson County and New Hanover County of North Carolina, recovering from Hurricane Florence, and the Mayagüez and Humacao regions in Puerto Rico (as well as Puerto Rico-wide through the centrally operated Puerto Rico Children and Youth Task Force), recovering from the devastation of Hurricane Maria.

Project Framework

Theory of Change

The RCRC Initiative focused on meeting the needs of children in disasters by supporting community-based institutions that either serve children, parents, and caregivers, or those that are otherwise responsible for supporting the needs of children as part of community-wide responsibilities. While many preparedness programs provide education at the individual or household level, which may include children or adults, this project chose child-serving institutions as the target of the intervention. This approach aimed to build institutional capacity in a systemic fashion. These benefits would ultimately trickle downstream to benefit children, their caregivers, and institutional staff. They would furthermore bolster community resilience by promoting community-wide steps to helping children return to normalcy post-disaster. It should be noted that a return to normalcy in this context is not necessarily a pre-disaster normal, but can be a *new normal* buttressed by newly established routines and structure in a child's life.

Building on existing research, the model is child-centric (see Figure 10.2) which places children as the center-point and primary beneficiary (Schlegelmilch and Sury, 2019). The operations component and primary intervention point of the project was the Community Resilience Coalition (CRC). Utilizing a coalition model allowed a diverse set of community-identified stakeholders to assemble around a common goal—improving the safety and well-being of children during and after disasters. The CRCs were organized to include all child-serving institutions in the community with a unique emphasis on the inclusion

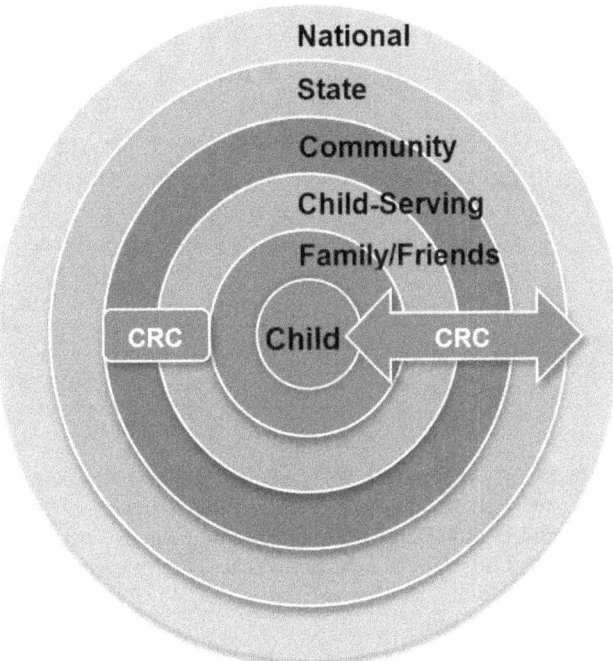

Figure 10.2 RCRC Initiative key stakeholders and Community Resilience Coalition (CRC) Reach. CRC rectangle depicts CRC members and arrows depict CRC reach.

of emergency management as a central figure. Each CRC identified a local "Community Champion" to serve as a community liaison and focal point of this initiative. Through participation in the initiative, the CRCs were connected with the existing evidence-base provided by NCDP base in academia, and national policy discussions, with the goal of building a scalable and replicable model for child-focused community resilience (see Figure 10.3).

Integrating community through partnership reduces silos and builds capacity through disaster literacy and fluency which has primarily been observed in two directions. The first is local emergency management and first-responder infrastructure gaining literacy about child development—in other words how the stages of development change agency and ability to comprehend and act on emergency information, the intricacies of the delivery of services for children, and the value of service providers and their contribution to the entire community (National Center for Disaster Preparedness, 2016). This may also be extended to children who may have disabilities, access, or functional needs and their need to be appropriately included in emergency plans and most importantly first responder and staff training and education on the proper protocols and equipment necessary

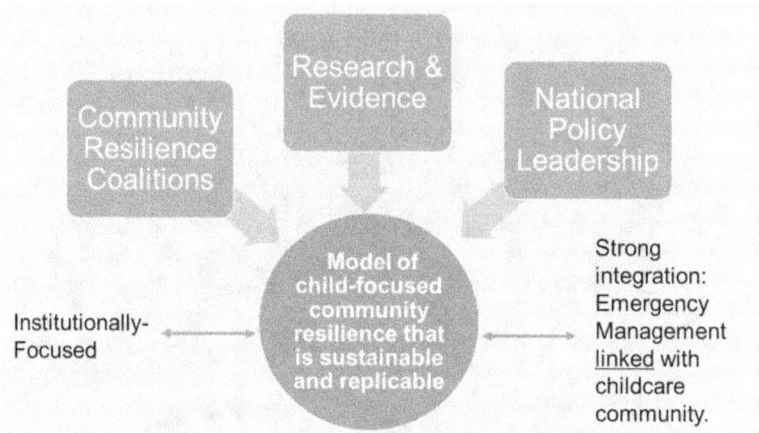

Figure 10.3 The RCRC Initiative Model. The model combines Community Resilience Coalitions, Disaster Recovery and Preparedness Research, and National Policy Leadership through a board of experts. The targets of the interventional child-serving institutions and linked closely with Emergency Management agencies.

to appropriately care for these children in disaster settings. This would integrate into more all-hazards and general population planning than children are often captured within but without these nuances included (although there are some pediatric-specific medical protocols and other targeted exceptions in planning). And the other direction, child-serving institutions learning about emergency management policies and procedures (e.g., emergency management response structure, the difference between Emergency Response Plans and Continuity of Operations Plans), preparedness beyond fire drills and evacuation, and understanding the response capacity limitation of emergency services during a large-scale emergency (i.e., emergency responders cannot be everywhere at once and needs will be prioritized according to the scope and scale of the event). Ultimately, the greatest learning occur when there is a multi-directional understanding of the interconnectedness between these systems to ultimately build a more resilient community enabling children to return to normalcy by quickly re-establishing routines through a community. One notable example is during two separate tabletop exercises (a discussion-based disaster simulation) in different communities, child-serving institutions indicated they would immediately call first-responder agencies for help, and first-responder agencies indicated they would be too overwhelmed to respond unless it was an immediate life-safety situation, and even then could be delayed, and that they were relying on child-serving organizations to have plans to function without their assistance for a time.

Measuring Progress

Public Health Preparedness and Response Core Competencies and Capabilities have been primarily focused on issues relating to public health preparedness and its workforce, but very few tools, if any, have been developed to measure or evaluate community-level preparedness for child-serving institutions (Ablah et al., 2019, Centers for Disease Control and Prevention, 2018). In 2014, STC and the NCDP developed an expert-validated and community-piloted tool called the Community Preparedness Index (CPI). This tool was designed to assess a jurisdiction's (i.e., county) ability to meet the specific needs of children during and after a disaster. The measure intends to serve as a proxy for a communities' resilience by demonstrating its readiness to systemically protect children in disasters. To the authors' knowledge, the tool has only been deployed in its piloting during development and within the context of this project. This initiative has deployed the tool twelve separate times for a baseline and follow-up (i.e., the end of a project phase) in the six RCRC communities.

The CPI evaluates the preparedness leadership, policies, guidelines, and best practices across eight child-serving sectors which may be grouped into the following three domains: (1) sectors that take care of children during the day—child care/day care centers, home-based family child care (aka family child care homes), public schools, private schools, foster care; (2) where many children receive care during an emergency which includes Emergency Shelters and Hospitals; (3) the sector which is responsible for coordinating all the sectors during a disaster which is considered the community-wide organization and is functionally lead by the jurisdiction's emergency management agency. Additionally, up to ten lead organizations identified who set the standards, generally, the licensing authorities or regulatory bodies, both formal and informal, receive a separate lead organizations survey (data excluded from this analysis). Eight different elements of preparedness are evaluated sector by sector. The elements are evacuation, sheltering in place, communicating with parents/guardians, emergency responders, and staff before, during, and after emergencies, pediatric emergency medical situations, emergency mental/behavioral health services for children, facility Continuity of Operations Planning (COOP), conducting exercises and drills, and the needs of children with disabilities, access, and functional needs in a disaster (Berg et al., 2014). Through the scoring algorithm, unique sector scores are provided and an overall average score is calculated for the entire community. Scores are presented in three major categories such as needs improvement, moderate—some improvement necessary, and strong—well positioned.

Educational Methods

Education outputs have been developed with different target audiences and different approaches. These can generally be categorized into Project team-led, Community-based, Community-leader led, and Social Interactions.

Project team-led training was those proposed and delivered by the core project team from NCDP and/or STC. An example of this includes the adaptation of NCDP-developed COOP training for human services organizations that was previously developed under funding from the US Centers for Disease Control and Prevention as part of broader public health preparedness efforts. COOP is one of eight key elements of preparedness measured for improvement in the CPI. The initial baseline deployment noted a deficiency of this particular element. This training focuses on the key elements of COOP that smaller businesses and not-for-profit organizations entities can focus on, who have more limited resources than larger corporations or government agencies. Based on community identification of the significant need for COOP for child-serving organizations, this training was adapted and delivered in multiple communities in-person and online. It was also revised and delivered as a webinar at the start of the COVID-19 pandemic, in anticipation of prolonged continuity challenges for this and all sectors. Similar training was conducted on themes related to disaster communications and disaster funding, among other topics that were deemed important by the community partners.

An additional training program deployed was the STC "Prep Rally." These prep-rally-style events took place at schools and childcare facilities and directly engaged youth to teach key principles of preparedness that they can take home to their families. This training was a critical part of early efforts to move from the planning stages to being to implement programs and generating enthusiasm among community partners, as well as the youth participants in the rallies. The Prep Rallies also bridged Project team-led activities to community-based education.

The project team also led a series of tabletop and full-scale exercises to help test planning efforts to meet the needs of children in a simulated environment, as well as to conduct an after-action analysis from real-world COVID-19 response efforts. Advocacy efforts were also sponsored including a congressional briefing and meetings with federal agencies and legislators. Each of these activities was led by the project team, but co-designed and focused on community-derived objectives, findings, and talking points.

Community-based education consisted of events, trainings, and engagements that were rooted in community institutions and events. These included community fairs where booths included materials on personal and family preparedness, keynote and sessions at local and state conferences, and participation in talk shows and other local media coverage. Two examples from Arkansas exemplify this approach. As part of community engagement for a local minor league baseball team, nonprofit organizations in the community were sponsored and would hand out materials at their home games. For one of these games, a core community partner for the RCRC Coalition included personal preparedness flyers and messaging as part of the materials at the game. Additionally, a cross-section of the project team and coalition members were featured on a live call-in talk show on the state public television station to talk about preparedness for children in disasters, and to answer viewer questions.

These educational activities were important opportunities to meet members of the community where they were. In utilizing these opportunities, the format and scope of the engagement were not always under the control of the coalitions, but it provided key access to dialogue with various segments of the community at events and through mediums that they have already engaged with.

Community-leader-led education utilized local leaders for communications to the public as well as to support the identification and adaptation of Project team-led training (e.g., COOP training) were prioritized by local emergency management officials and integrated into their goals and priorities. Some examples include town-hall-style events with elected officials where panels would discuss experiences related to children in disasters, followed by officials discussing efforts to improve readiness and to hear from constituents. Videos of officials discussing priorities and the value of the work were captured and developed around key themes. Additionally, formal communications structures, such as agency social-media accounts were used to raise awareness, especially during key designated timeframes, such as preparedness month and the start of hurricane season. Project data and reports were also disseminated through these official channels as well as community-based and informal channels. The engagements of community leaders provided a greater legitimacy to the efforts of the coalitions and were an important complement to the grassroots efforts of the coalition members.

In one coalition, members organized a local advocacy event centered around local and state leaders, as well as representatives from the state's congressional delegation to discuss issues around children in disasters in a town-hall-style format. For this event, the project team led the invitation and agenda development, with the project team supporting the facilitation and recruitment of panelists with experience working with children in disasters. Another community opted instead of a local policy event, to host a local mini-conference for child-serving institutions. This event included panelists from academia, nonprofit organizations, as well as local officials. The event then went into breakout sessions where participants could choose between educational sessions focused on the mental health needs of children or COOP for community human service organizations.

The coalitions also recognized and valued the role of less formal social interactions in reaching community members. Initial community buy-in was critical to the success of this initiative, and these relationships began at the beginning of the project before formal public kickoff meetings were held. Key community stakeholders were engaged to discuss the project aims, address concerns, and learn more about the community and the constellation of partners responsible for meeting the needs of children in disasters. Initial outreach was guided by the CPI sectors, and by community partner input. Individual meetings in less formal settings also provided a forum for partners to share ideas and express concerns, as well as to provide insights into social and political dynamics that they would be less able/willing to share in a formal group setting. Frequently, time was set aside before and/or after coalition meetings for individual conversations. These were particularly bidirectional educational opportunities with the project team both learning and educating. Significant investment of the project in the time to accommodate these types of interactions was a key factor in the success of the more formal educational approaches described earlier.

Project team-led events were primarily focused on child-serving institutions and/or community-wide organizations. Some exceptions, such as the "Prep Rallies", engaged the institutions and children directly. Policymakers were also engaged at strategic milestones throughout the project when a critical mass of sharable knowledge was reached. Community-based and community-led events, as well as social interactions also reached these audiences but extended further to parents and caregivers in the broader community. For communities seeking to engage in similar work, resources curated by the coalitions, editable templates, and links to public events were all provided free of charge (National Center for Disaster Preparedness Earth Institute Columbia University, 2021) (https://rcrctoolbox.org).

As a result of the work of the CRC, including the educational approaches described earlier, a total of 183 child-serving organizations were reached across the six communities through the Community Resilience Coalitions. Community self-reported cumulative reach of CRC member organizations ranged within each coalition's reach from 16,184 to 212,091 additional community members gaining access to disaster-preparedness resources. Improvements to resilience as measured through the CPI described in the following occurred across this breadth of community reach.

Baseline CPI scores were collected upon the start of each project phase. The same instrument was re-administered upon the completion of each respective phase of the project across all six communities ($n = 6$). Scores are presented on a scale of 0–100 in the following three categories: 71–100, reflects a high level of preparedness policies and activities already in place; 41–70, suggests there may be areas for improvement by making moderate improvements to activities and policies; 0–40, indicates opportunities to improve and enhance planning efforts and relationships. In the examination of the baseline and follow-up score comparisons, a paired t-test revealed a statistically significant ($p < 0.001$) difference in scores with an average improvement of fifteen points across all sectors. The baseline mean score was approximately 39 (33, 44; 95 percent CI) and the follow-up mean was approximately 54 (46, 62; 95 percent CI) despite a large standard deviation. Due to the small sample size and the nature of the instrument, these data are highly promising. Figure 10.4 depicts the baseline and follow-up scores by sector and compiled across all six communities. In general, a noticeable improvement was seen across most sectors with some exceptions. Both school sectors proved challenging for integration into the CRCs and were bound by limitations posed by management structures, political challenges such as the responsibility to school boards, resource limitations of staff, and staff time. Major improvements were seen community-wide (i.e., Emergency Management), which their central role in this initiative can partially explain.

Lessons Learned

Among the toughest challenges of supporting the identification and expansion of community capacities as an outside institution is balancing the need to provide structures and models for convening, while not imposing preconceived solutions on a community, and being truly inclusive of community participation in decision-making. An approach that provided options, rather than mandates to community coalitions seemed to have catalyzed action, fostering more community-based and community-led events. In this regard,

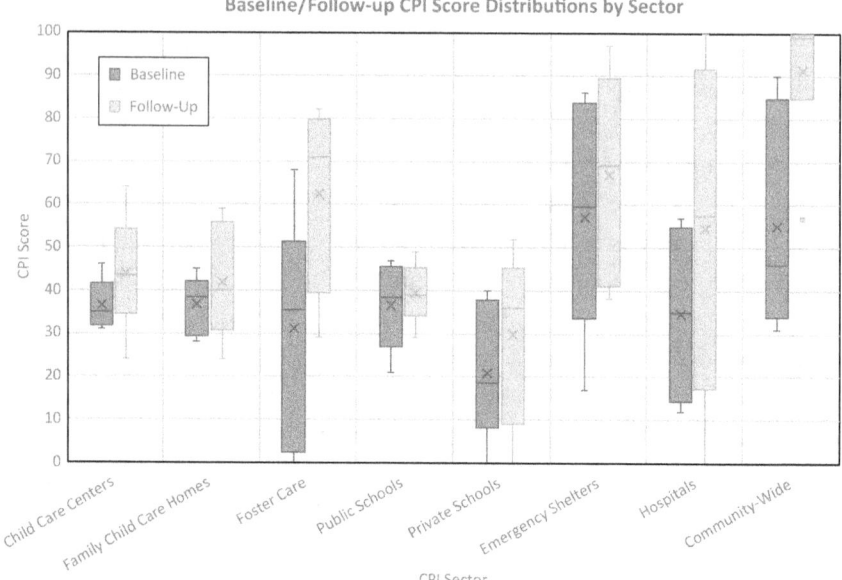

Figure 10.4 Composite Community Preparedness Index (CPI) scores from six RCRC communities ($n = 6$) by sector depicted using a Box and Whisker chart. The chart shows baseline and follow-up scores with medians (horizontal line in each box) and percentile distributions.

the importance of reflexivity in community programming, with an evidence-based framework for evaluating success (in this case, the CPI), was essential for striking this balance.

At the conclusion of each phase, the CPI scores showed a significant increase across multiple sectors, far in excess of the original program target of increasing two sectors by 25 percent or more. This demonstrates success in the model in achieving increased resilience. Additionally, the largest increase in scores can be attributed to changes in answers from "don't know" to key staff being able to answer questions and being aware of existing plans and protocols. This further suggests the importance of a multifaceted educational approach to build resilience by increasing the reach of existing capacities within the communities.

Each community was also in different places in terms of sectors ready to initiate action, and others that required more lead time, or that otherwise had inertia from institutional, political, or other factors. Working with community partners to demonstrate success early on, often led to additional ownership by that sector (e.g., childcare), and provided community-based demonstrations that other sectors (e.g., schools) could follow.

As the project grew, and more communities began participating, opportunities for sharing best practices, lessons learned, and general experiences across peers in different communities began to emerge, suggesting that as more communities participate in the initiative, there was an opportunity for greater peer support. The development of robust peer support mechanisms has the potential to further catalyze community-level change, by bridging peers across communities for mentorship and knowledge-sharing. Although beyond the project's evaluation focus on institutions, programs for direct youth involvement were utilized by some of the child-serving institutions. Examples include the deployment of STC's Prep Rally program to generate enthusiasm between adults and children for preparedness. The RCRC Toolbox also features tools for supporting conversations with children of different age groups and a webinar on curricula available to engage older youths in preparedness learning and service projects. While these resources were provided, they were not systematically evaluated but could serve as inspiration for future projects that are designed to be focused more on the child-adult relationship and interactions.

Enhancing tools like the CPI for greater usability independent of the relationship with NCDP was also identified as a way to further bring the successes to other communities. And while much of the successes were able to be captured by the CPI, improvements in social capital and community cohesion were widely reported anecdotally but lacked a rigorous evaluation instrument. Thus, it is likely that improvements in other sectors that may appear more slowly on the CPI were in fact achieved but not quantified due to the lack of a suitable measurement framework.

In a departure from the typical disaster literacy individual agent, this initiative has created a new approach to disaster literacy by creating institutional fluency about children and disasters. Through this enhanced disaster literacy approach, the ability to understand child-specific and community-wide risk and translate that into pre-disaster planning and educational activities has built not just sector-wide improvements but also woven the topic of disasters into the fabric of everyday life. Integrating new learnings from this initiative into everyday practice and the ability to make decisions differently than before this intervention demonstrates its efficacy and ultimately its sustainability within each community.

References

Ablah, Elizabeth, Weist, Elizabeth McGean, McElligott, John E., Biesiadecki, Laura A., Gotsch, Audrey R., Keck, C. William, & Gebbie, Kristine M. (2019). Public Health

Preparedness and Response Competency Model Methodology. *American Journal of Disaster Medicine*, 14(4), p. 8. doi:10.5055/ajdm.2019.0338.

Abramson, D. M., Park, Y. S., Stehling-Ariza, T., & Redlener, I. (2010). Children as Bellwethers of Recovery: Dysfunctional Systems and the Effects of Parents, Households, and Neighborhoods on Serious Emotional Disturbance in Children after Hurricane Katrina. *Disaster Medicine: Mitigation, Preparedness*, 4(Suppl 1), pp. S17–27. doi:10.1001/dmp.2010.7.

Berg, Bridget M., Musigdilok, Visanee V., Haro, Tamar M., & Myers, Paul. (2014). Public-Private Partnerships: A Whole Community Approach to Addressing Children's Needs in Disasters. *Clinical Pediatric Emergency Medicine*, 15(4), pp. 281–8. https://doi.org/10.1016/j.cpem.2014.10.003.

Brown, Lisa M., Haun, Jolie N., & Peterson, Lindsay. (2014). A Proposed Disaster Literacy Model. *Disaster Medicine and Public Health Preparedness*, 8(3), pp. 267–75. doi:10.1017/dmp.2014.43.

Çalışkan, Cüneyt, & Üner, Sarp. (2020). Disaster Literacy and Public Health: A Systematic Review and Integration of Definitions and Models. *Disaster Medicine and Public Health Preparedness*, pp. 1–10. doi:10.1017/dmp.2020.100.

Centers for Disease Control and Prevention (2018). *Public Health Emergency Preparedness and Response Capabilities: National Standards for State, Local, Tribal, and Territorial Public Health*. U.S. Department of Health and Human Services. https://www.cdc.gov/cpr/readiness/00_docs/CDC_PreparednesResponseCapabilities_October2018_Final_508.pdf. Date Accessed May 25, 2022.

FEMA (2011). *A Whole Community Approach to Emergency Management: Principles, Themes, and Pathways for Action*. FEMA. https://www.fema.gov/sites/default/files/2020-07/whole_community_dec2011__2.pdf. Date Accessed May 25, 2022.

George, Asha S., Lefevre, Amnesty E., Schleiff, Meike, Mancuso, Arielle, Sacks, Emma, & Sarriot, Eric. (2018). Hubris, Humility and Humanity: Expanding Evidence Approaches for Improving and Sustaining Community Health Programmes. *BMJ Global Health*, 3(3), p. e000811. doi:10.1136/bmjgh-2018-000811.

Institute of Medicine (2014). *Preparedness, Response, and Recovery Considerations for Children and Families: Workshop Summary*. Edited by Theresa Wizemann, Megan Reeve and Bruce M. Altevogt. Washington, DC: The National Academies Press.

Kim-Ju, Greg, Mark, Gregory Y., Cohen, Robert, Garcia-Santiago, Orlando, & Patty, Nguyen. (2008). Community Mobilization and Its Application to Youth Violence Prevention. *American Journal of Preventive Medicine*, 34(3 Supplement), pp. S5–S12. doi:10.1016/j.amepre.2007.12.005.

National Center for Disaster Preparedness (2015). *The Resilient Children/Resilient Communities Initiative*. Earth Institute, Columbia University. https://ncdp.columbia.edu/rcrc. Date Accessed May 25, 2022.

National Center for Disaster Preparedness (2016). *Evolutions in Emergency Management: Linking Emergency Management and Childcare Providers*. Earth Institute, Columbia University.

National Center for Disaster Preparedness Earth Institute Columbia University (2021). The RCRC Toolbox. https://rcrctoolbox.org.

National Commission On Children And Disasters (2010). *2010 Report to the President And Congress*. Edited by Agency for Healthcare Research and Quality. Rockville, MD: Agency for Healthcare Research and Quality.

Olivier, De Sardan, Jean-Pierre, Aïssa Diarra, & Moha, Mahaman. (2017). Travelling Models and the Challenge of Pragmatic Contexts and Practical Norms: The Case of Maternal Health. *Health Research Policy and Systems*, 15(S1). doi:10.1186/s12961-017-0213-9.

Peek, Lori. (2008). Children and Disasters: Understanding Vulnerability, Developing Capacities, and Promoting Resilience — An Introduction. *Children, Youth and Environments*, 18(1), pp. 1–29.

Peek, Lori, Abramson, David M., Cox, Robin S., Fothergill, Alice, & Tobin, Jennifer. (2018). Children and Disasters. *Handbook of Disaster Research*, pp. 243–62. Springer.

Schlegelmilch, Jeff, & Sury, Jonathan J. (2019). From the Ground Up: Building Child-Focused Community Resilience. *Research Counts, Special Collection on Children and Disasters*, 3 (SC18).

Tremblay, M. C., Richard, L., Brousselle, A., & Beaudet, N. (2014). Learning Reflexively from a Health Promotion Professional Development Program in Canada. *Health Promotion International*, 29(3), pp. 538–48. doi:10.1093/heapro/dat062.

Wessells, Michael G. (2015). Bottom-up Approaches to Strengthening Child Protection Systems: Placing Children, Families, and Communities at the Center. *Child Abuse & Neglect*, 43, pp. 8–21. doi:10.1016/j.chiabu.2015.04.006.

Acknowledgments

The authors would like to thank the project team and initiative participants in the development and implementation of the RCRC Initiative. This includes the core team from the NCDP at Columbia University—both staff and graduate students, STC US, and members of the National Children's Resilience Leadership Board. And a special thanks to the six CRCs, their respective Community Champions, and community partners in Washington County, Arkansas, Putnam County, New York, New Hanover and Robeson Counties, North Carolina, and the work of the central Puerto Rico Children and Youth Task Force as well as resilience coalitions in the municipios of Mayagüez and Humacao for their past and continued efforts to meet the needs of children in disasters. We are also grateful for five years of grant support from GSK, without which this project would never have been possible. We are also appreciative of additional support from Children's Health Fund.

11

Spaces for Youth Perspectives through Communication and Arts for Education for Sustainable Development

Haein Shin

Youth eco-activism—seeking diverse solutions through engagement in social or political campaigns to prevent damage to the environment (Kraja, 2018) by young people—has become an integral part of environmental literacy, environmental education, and climate change education in recent years. Surrounding academic, political, economic, and social spheres are the voices of youth, represented by individuals like Greta Thunberg at the local and global levels, ranging from individual classrooms, town halls, all the way to the United Nations and beyond. The youth perspectives and voices represented in these spaces are not merely trends; rather, they suggest the critical need to include youth perspectives in the learning processes and the global movement on environmental and climate actions worldwide.

Suppose education can be seen as an enabler of transformations. In that case, participatory youth learning that builds environmental literacy, which can also help sustain the global eco-activism momentum for change, becomes a necessity. While creating educational spaces where youth can learn, collaborate, and sustain momentum for environmental action is not limited to one particular method, this chapter aims to illustrate one case where youth engagement has been able to build momentum with communication and arts as one of the key components in New York and New Jersey through Columbia University's Eco Ambassador network.

The chapter first cites the rise of the youth movement with communication and arts as key strategies in recent years. It then shows how such elements have been incorporated and found in environmental education programming and events, along with potential motivations that could affect how youth engage in eco-activism, which may give some considerations and guidance for replication in the future for other contexts.

Why and How Youth Message on the Environment Is Gaining Ground

For decades, young people have been talking about climate change. In 1962, Rachel Carson's *Silent Spring* condemning the overuse of pesticides, which linked to human health consequences, sparked the modern environmental movement. This period was also marked by the rise in personal automobile ownership and industries in the United States, affecting air pollution. Subsequent years included strings of environmental protection measures, including the Clean Air Act of 1963; the Water Quality Act of 1965; Endangered Species legislation in 1966, and rising conversations on overpopulation and self-sustainable living in 1968. In 1969, youth and young college graduates were recruited to direct a national "teach-in" about environmental issues, leading to the first Earth Day in 1970. Along with the civil rights movement of the 1960s in the United States, people of color started the Environmental Justice Movement when the placement of toxic facilities in urban ghettos and poverty areas exposed people of color and Native-American reservations to health dangers (Trevathan, 2019). Although environmental campaigns and eco-activism are not new, the estimated 1.6 million youth in 125 countries protesting in the footsteps of Greta Thunberg in March of 2019 demonstrate a new scale and intensity of a coordinated youth movement (Marris, 2019). Communications experts attribute this new level of activism to a few factors, ranging from youth's moral authority, social-media savviness, and the conviction to key issues which are seen as ethical and justice issues (Marris, 2019). Communication tools via the prevalence of technology have played a key role. The visibility of the youth movement on social media and in the press has created a feedback loop whereby youth get so much attention that it draws even more youth into the movement (Marris, 2019). Added to this digital communication platform is a fundamental change in the framing of climate change and environmental issues; rather than an issue that is purely environmental, many youth environment activists and climate campaigners problematize climate change from a justice perspective (Han and Ahn, 2020). This translates to not just being concerned about one environmental threat but also recognizing the human-environment connection and its implications for the most vulnerable people on Earth (Marris, 2019). The media coverage does not showcase the many other youth environmental activists beyond Greta Thunberg, who use their voices and actions for eco-activism.

Xiuhtezcatl Martinez (United States) is one of the twenty-one youths suing the US government to secure the constitutional right to life and liberty by demanding action on climate change and fossil fuel reduction. Mayumi Sato (Japan), speaks about environmental issues such as social, race, and conflict issues, as she works in Thailand, Laos, Nepal, and beyond on the social impacts of deforestation, landscape restoration, and climate mitigation. Alexandria Villasenor (United States), a supporter of Greta Thunberg's school strikes in Stockholm, has founded Earth Uprising, a climate education group. Ghislain Irakoze (Rwanda), founded a mobile app called Wastezon that connects the consumer to the recycling industries after noticing the overflowing landfill in his hometown and learning about the 50 million tons of electronic global waste. His company has helped send 460 tons of electronics to recyclers in Kigali. Felix Finkbeiner (Germany) founded a tree-planting nonprofit at the age of nine, and now has an army of over 93,000 "climate just-tice ambassadors" who are activists in their communities (Parker, 2020). Some of the other youth activists include Isra Hirsi (daughter of Ilhan Omar), Autumn Peltier (Wikwemikong Unceded Territory in Canada), Bruno Rodriguez (Buenos Aires), Helena Gualinga (Ecuadorian Amazon), and Mari Copeny (United States) (Trevathan, 2019).

As a result of this new wave of youth eco-activism, youth voices are indeed being heard. One study from a longitudinal survey of adults in the United States reveals that the adult population is getting more receptive to the youth strikers' message and increasingly getting concerned since 2015 (Marris, 2019). Across the United States, United Kingdom, Portugal, and Australia, studies show adults' concern about climate impacts on their children and future generations. The adults simultaneously perceive the integrity of youth concerns, who do not have financial incentives or motives, or professional hindrances, to share their direct message of concern for climate change and related environmental issues that have implications for the future. Messages by youth at various debates, and political and social forums, are being viewed millions of times, making it into the news with its drama, novelty, authenticity, and catastrophe (Marris, 2019).

Youth messaging on climate and environmental issues can take multiple forms, and the use of an artistic expression has been one of the key mediums utilized, with terms like "artivism" on the rise. Artivism stems from the "Action Art" movement of 1960s anti-cultural movements in Europe (Rodal et al., 2019). The Action Art movement is thought to have elicited social networks by exposing young audiences to artistic creation, which has also had strong linkages to civil protest movements (Rodal et al., 2019). More specific to environmental artivism, eco-art emerged in the 1970s; however, the medium was more often marked by individuals working on specific and local issues and lacked a message linked to the art form. The prior version of eco-art looks different from the variety of forms that environmental art has evolved to today (Moore, 2021), especially where targeted message linked to visuals with wide reach is more common. In the current era of Instagram, Twitter, and hashtags, the social network has expanded, globalized, and delocalized networks. In the current age, the art+activism terminology shows that "beyond transcending national territories, new, significant geographies are continually being reconstructed" (Rodal et al., 2019, p.23). Beyond the social networks created through art, youth voice, messages, and expression, the artistic medium embodies spatial impacts and experiences that can be utilized as a strategic tool. Art has the "capacity to foster cultural, cognitive and psychological change" (Sanz and Rodriguez-Labajos, 2021, p. 41) and is also capable of inclusion, bringing together wide-ranging demographics, and enhancing public participation in decision-making to result in education, social cohesion, and expression of ideas (Sanz and Rodriguez-Labajos, 2021).

Climate Education Youth Summit Design and Eco Ambassador Network Experiences

Recognizing the power of youth voice and perspectives, the NY & NJ Climate Education Youth Summit hosted by the Eco Ambassador Program network of the Center for Sustainable Development (CSD) of Earth Institute, Columbia University in February 2021 sought to bring together youth perspectives with youth as key organizers, moderators, speakers, and facilitators of the Summit. The aim was not a single event where youth would merely be represented but also to begin the calendar year with youth being the primary voices in sharing their initiatives and perspectives on current environmental issues, which can further guide environment education programming for the year. The summit was both a culmination of the prior year's partnerships and programming and a means to foster new networks to identify potential areas of collaboration and support the sustaining of environmental education efforts for sustainable development while focusing on youth initiatives as the core element.

The broader program, Eco Ambassador Program, began in 2019 at CSD to apply the knowledge and research of Lamont-Doherty Earth Observatory

(LDEO) scientists of the Earth Institute to science curricula of schools and community centers in schools in developing countries where CSD works. In the process, however, it soon became clear that regardless of context and setting, every community of learners can benefit from environmental and sustainability education in homes, schools, businesses, and communities (CSD, 2021). The program started with a summer project pilot where youth observed their surroundings and identified environmental issues[1]. Based on their topic of choice, research and action-planning began, consulting with LDEO scientists, teachers, experts, and practitioners for guidance alongside youth-led projects. The project scope was wide-ranging, including reducing microplastic waste in schools, engaging local businesses to reduce single-use plastic utensils, testing for microplastics in local tap water, reducing waste by making and selling reusable masks at the onset of COVID-19 and donating proceeds to a local volunteer organization, creating a safe electronics disposal program, and sharing the findings through peer-to-peer learning workshops and even presenting ideas at local town halls. Action plans and potential solutions were also presented at an international conference, workshops, schools, and local businesses of the Eco Ambassador Program network.

As the program grew and youth began sharing their interests, the role of communication and developing communication skills and the usage of diverse mediums, such as the arts, became clearer. For the Eco Ambassador Program network, the timing and partnership aligned well to enable the incorporation of concrete communication tips and considerations into the programming. Columbia University's Earth Institute had created an "Initiative on Communication and Sustainability to boost the capacity of scientists, journalists, educators, students and growing in recognition and in citizens to communicate in ways that can speed progress toward a more sustainable relationship between our species, our planet and each other" (Earth Institute, 2021). Access to such initiatives enabled workshops with journalists and staff from the initiative on effective communication and messages to youth. This process importantly facilitated also hearing what youth were doing to share their messages in their own time and in their communities. Some youth were motivated to go beyond their existing passion projects to create their podcasts to share the environment message. Others were engaged in their communities by communicating with local businesses, schools, and political leaders. These diverse experiences were encouraged to be shared at the Youth Summit and event partners' youth experiences.

Experiences Shared at the Climate Education Youth Summit

With around 200 participants attending each day for the 5-day summit, the range and depth of experiences related to the environment, shared by youth, showed the impressive levels of dedication, knowledge, and commitment that individual and collective youth gave to environmental issues. Beyond the scope of utilizing communication and arts to effectively deliver messages about the environment, some youth read an entire 544-page book, *Age of Sustainable Development* authored by Professor Jeffrey Sachs, to understand the macro-level picture of global sustainable development in order to ask questions about the book during the summit session. As moderators of various panels, the youth asked about how communication, arts, and music can be used for environmental messages and climate justice issues; local township successes in pushing forth pro-environment policies; how to incorporate curriculum content for effective learning on environment content; community organizing through storytelling for advocacy; and how teachers are teaching environment and climate topics.

In the summit, which was heavily moderated and led by youth participation and presentations, key elements were observable across the various youth presenters and participants. The key themes can be summarized in the diagram (Figure 11.1). This chapter suggests that the key elements found from youth eco-activism displayed during the summit relate to the elements of Dunn and Dunn's learning style model and Maslow's theory of motivation, as explained as follows.

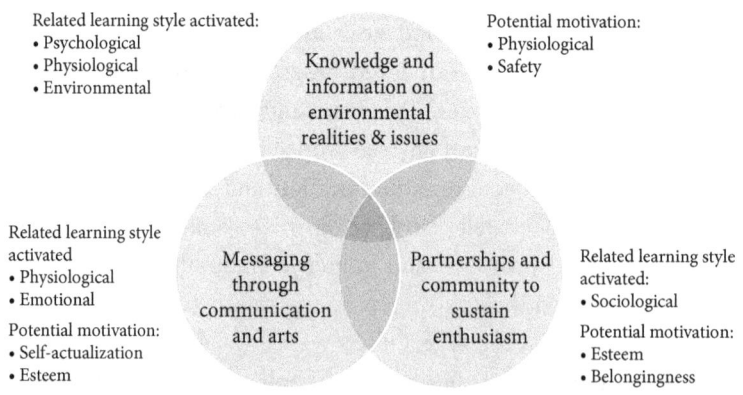

Elements across youth eco-activists' work observed from Summit

Figure 11.1 Elements observed across youth work presented in the summit merging learning styles and potential motivation. Self-elaboration, 2021.

Dunn and Burke's (2005) learning style model shows that learners learn with a combination of characteristics and elements: environmental, emotional, sociological, physiological, and psychological. Observing how youth have engaged through communication and arts not only for dissemination of information but also for their learning, expressions, and sharing, it can be postulated that their overall learning and activism experience has activated the diverse elements and styles in which information is learned and applied. While the environmental facts may be learned by activating the physiological and psychological elements, as youth engage and share information through communication and arts in their communities, the emotional and sociological learning elements may be activated. Additionally, Maslow's theory posits that different needs lead to motivation, starting from physiological needs (food, water), to safety needs (security), belongingness (relationships, friendships), esteem needs (feeling of accomplishment), and self-actualization (reaching potential, including creative activities) (McLeod, 2020). Youth engagement and activism growing through arts and communication can potentially be motivating for youth, in ways that range from their concern of very physical and physiological well-being of themselves, their environment, and society, merged with the self-actualization of creatively reaching their potential and accomplishments while feeling a sense of belongingness in the common cause.

Communication and Arts Strategies

The youth understands the power of communication and arts, and their understanding goes beyond posting an environmental message on social media. Specific movements that have been catered to highlight the power of communication and arts, such as the one that Extinction Rebellion Youth NYC shared at the summit, define their mission as "youth organizers who use grassroots tactics like mutual aid, community care, and Non-Violent Direct Action to advocate for climate justice. In every action we take and community we build, there is a backbone of art." The youth also understands foundational human psychology beyond using communication as tools; for example, the youth organization uses the expression "love & rage" as a signature motto. This is to express the anger that is felt "toward the destruction of our planet and continued disinterest over fixing our mistakes," and on the flip side, the love "for our community, for people, for the world. It means that we understand that both of these emotions are necessary to fuel a movement" (Extinction Rebellion, 2021).

The in-depth understanding of youth on how certain concepts can align to their environment mission leads to creating effective communication strategies that can easily be captured, digested, and disseminated, accurately showing and spreading the group culture and mindset.

The youth reiterate what is found in literature about the artistic medium being able to also create a community beyond the built momentum. While the content of the arts in the movement is about celebrating and sharing messages through mediums such as physical, performance, music, dance, and video, the sharing process also creates a community around art and climate advocacy that more firmly establishes the movement. The art form has taken many creative shapes. From the Extinction Rebellion's example alone, there were methods of utilizing fashion, poetry, writing, research, and editing skills to spread environmental messages. The youth shared that their goal in hosting a fashion show using recycled materials with a sustainability message was to prove to people and industries that beauty didn't have to be sacrificed to be environmentally conscious and sustainable. The youth work using art as communication tools for climate action embodies youth's passion and belief that important messages can be communicated through the arts and understanding of the underlying communication strategies and factors that can make their messages shareable and impactful.

Knowledge with Activism

The concept of activism has often had a negative connotation of actions without theoretical backing (Reis, 2020). Still, the youth showed that they were also studying their topics of interest in addition to raising their voices on environmental issues. For example, the extent of the knowledge youth had on their key issues enabled them to lead hour-long, information-driven workshops during the week-long summit. During the sessions, some youth shared that they were often unable to learn the topics of their specific environmental interests in schools. That sometimes served as motivation for youth to create their clubs, where groups can learn and share more about the topics. Students concerned about water quality and single-use plastics were conducting their own research to test on the local water sources, local waterways, and beaches and consulted an expert on microplastics. Students who were interested in fashion were studying the fashion industry's waste and production. Students who were interested in the extinction of species were studying biodiversity. Rather than problematizing environmental issues, the youth studied and researched information to know more and share it with peers.

In the case specific to the theme of communication and arts, the youth workshop facilitators also showed that they have a deep understanding of the theoretical background and the deeper aim that is meant to be cultivated with their tools of art and communication. In the Extinction Rebellion session, the facilitators shared that their work goes past "the stereotype of only learning from books and theory and open the door to reflection from artistic mediums. By placing sensibility at the core of our reflection, we offer a communal base to our learning" (Extinction Rebellion, 2021, p. 14). The creation of communities and communal bases for learning also suggests that these spaces can ultimately help sustain the youth movement for the environment beyond one-time events and campaigns.

Partnerships to Sustain the Enthusiasm

Although many talented individuals have started their initiatives, what seems to help sustain the initiatives is the partnerships fostered along the way. While the scope of respective youth's work varied, the youth initiatives shared at the summit had either co-founders or other individuals, schools, or organizational involvement and partnership that then leads to meeting others in the shared network and sustaining the work. From a programmatic level, the summit itself showed how such partnerships matter. Even though the Eco Ambassador Program is a program on its own and its network, the extent to which the summit was able to elicit the participation of various youth who have diverse backgrounds and experiences with environmental initiatives, came as a result of the partnerships fostered in organizing and bringing together the event. The partnerships helped bring various organizers, panelists, and participants and helped with communicating and promoting the event. With youth organizers, the usage of social-media platforms became even more crucial to spread the word and bring more youth to be involved. While the scope of New York and New Jersey gave a specific geographical reference to bring the local youth, educators, and experts together, the youth and the program extended the invitation to its global network, knowing that the themes of communication and arts will have universal relevance for youth globally. Individual presentation and youth perspectives shed light on their specific local initiatives, yet the experience shared was more global in scale. As one program alone, sustaining the participants' interests and continual engagement may have been a challenge. However, the interactions and discussions can be sustained, scaled, and diversified further with close and continued partnerships and with individuals from wide and diverse networks.

Further, the connections within the wider network of individuals display the importance of youth-adult partnerships in the process. While youth activism facilitates the attention and momentum, the parents, adults, educators, local business owners, and local leadership play a critical role in supporting and mentoring the youth. In the case of the Eco Ambassador Program, parents played an active role in partaking in online sessions, asking questions, giving feedback to youth presentations, and educating the youth about environmental issues experienced in their locales and experiences. More organized groups or experts from local business, environmental, and educational organizations, shared knowledge with youth and often provided a bigger platform for youth to share their perspectives by engaging the organization and community partners. While much knowledge-sharing and activism take place with the critical help of partnerships and community, the linkage to schools and educational spaces should not be forgotten. As an organized learning space, schools can play bigger and stronger roles in both providing a designated space for youth to both learn and share knowledge and perspectives, as well as to foster stronger academic training, knowledge transfer, and practice of the arts and communications with messaging grounded in social and community connections of the schools.

While the summit was a one-time event, the summit spoke for the prior groundwork that needed to precede the event, which is the identification and partnerships centered on programs and initiatives centered on youth perspectives and youth activism for environmental issues. As literature cites, the communication and arts utilized by youth to convey the environment and climate issues are not mere strategies to draw the audience to the broader cause. The summit experience showcased how the active youth have a genuine concern for these issues from moral and justice perspectives. They have gone beyond the passion to research and study and create their initiatives to learn and share more about the issues. Communication and arts play key roles in bringing their messages to the forefront and cultivating broader communities surrounding the shared interests.

Reaching beyond the confines of formal school classrooms, youth have found ways to deliver, carry, and sustain their environment messages using various mediums of communication and arts, along with their technology savviness, creating spaces for their learning and education. The current youth activism phenomena illustrate a powerful picture of how education, specifically environmental education, should be designed. Many youths are already "out in the streets" and "out in the world" sharing and disseminating the messages on the environment, climate, and sustainability. The level of initiative, engagement, and participation of youth show much promise; however, it may also signify where schools and educational institutions may have fallen short in responding to youth's magnitude of interest and desire for eco-activism. Educational institutions can play a critical role in providing information and platforms for communicating the environmental messages from school to homes and community while fostering a culture of communal action. The key is to bring these voices together in sustained ways, past social-media posts. The advocacy using communication, arts, and social media has grabbed the attention of the world. As educators, the momentum built can continue by further supporting the community and networks established due to effective communication and arts strategies, and by keeping meaningful partnerships alive and sustained, where the cross-organizational and peer-to-peer learning continue.

Note

1 Feel-Imagine-Do-Share method of Design for Change.

References

Center for Sustainable Development (CSD) (2021). Eco Ambassador Program. www.csd.edsd.columbia.edu.

Dunn, Rita, & Burke, Karen (2005). *Learning Style the Clue to You*. LSCY: Research and Implementation Manual. https://webs.um.es/rhervas/miwiki/lib/exe/fetch.php%3Fmedia%3Dlscy_rimanual_v1.pdf. Date Accessed May 26, 2022.

Earth Institute (2021). Initiative on Communication and Sustainability. https://sustcomm.ei.columbia.edu/content/about-initiative. Date Accessed May 26, 2022.

Extinction Rebellion (2021). Artivism. *Youth Climate Summit Slides*, pp. 1–25.

Han, H., & Ahn, S.W. (2020). Youth Mobilization to Stop Global Climate Change: Narratives and Impact. *Sustainability*, 12, p. 4127; doi:10.3390/su12104127.

Kraja, E. (2018). *Eco-activism: What it is and Why it is Relevant. Sustainable Development, Climate Justice (Policy Work), Climate Action, News, the Netherlands*. WECF International. https://www.wecf.org/eco-activism-what-it-is-and-why-it-is-relevant/. Date Accessed May 26, 2022.

Marris, E. (September 18, 2019). Why Young Climate Activists Have Captured the World's Attention. *Nature*, 573, pp. 471–2. https://doi.org/10.1038/d41586-019-02696-0. Date Accessed May 26, 2022.

McLeod, S. (2020). Maslow's Hierarchy of Needs. *Simply Psychology*. https://www.simplypsychology.org/maslow.html. Date Accessed May 26, 2022.

Moore, K. (2021). *The Evolution of Environmental Artivism*. UNTE. https://www.utne.com/arts/the-evolution-of-environmental-activism/. Date Accessed October 17, 2021.

Parker, L. (March 25, 2020). Greta Wasn't the First to Demand Climate Action. Meet More Young Activists. *National Geographic: Earth Day Issue*.

Reis, P. (2020). *Environmental Citizenship and Youth Activism*. Chapter 9, Conceptualizing Environmental Citizenship for 21st Century Education. Gewerbestrasse: Springer. pp. 146–55.

Rodal, B., Castillo, P., Sanchez, S., & Popelka, R. (April 1, 2019). From Action Art to Artivism on Instagram: Relocation and Instantaneity for a New Geography of Protest. *Catalan Journal of Communication & Cultural Studies*, 11(1), pp. 23–37 (15).

Sanz, T., & Rodriguez-Labajos, B. (June, 2021). Does Artistic Activism Change Anything? Strategic and Transformative Effects of Arts in Anti-Coal Struggles in Oakland, CA. *Geoforum*, 122, pp. 41–54.

Trevathan, E. (2019). Greta Thunberg vs. the Thousands of People Who Came before her. RubicOnline. https://www.rubiconline.com/greta-thunberg-v-s-the-thousands-of-people-who-came-before-her/. Date Accessed May 26, 2022.

12
Conclusion

Radhika Iyengar and Ozge Karadag Caman

We end this book at the heels of the United Nations Climate Change Conference (COP26), where ministerial agreements on climate education were just framed.[1] There are eight commitments from the co-chairs of the Education and Environment Ministers Summit as a part of COP26. The group of international ministers agreed that climate education needs to be integrated into the core curriculum and examination and teacher training. The group agreed to enhance cross-sectoral collaborations between the education sector, environment sector, and others. It was a re-affirmation that actions toward meeting the Paris Agreement are urgent and education is a key pathway toward meeting its targets. The group also agreed that all types of education (informal, nonformal, and formal) are needed to create public awareness and professional training on climate action. However, there is no discussion on structural issues that need to be addressed first. How can education be the instrument to highlight the systemic factors that deepen economic, social, and health disparities? COP26 needed to recommit to Sustainable Development Goal (SDG4.7). The ministers needed to commit to using Education for Sustainable Development (ESD) and Global Citizenship Education to re-establish the balance between the people and the planet.

Let us revisit Stafford Ocansey's civic-literacy framework (in Chapter 2). Justice and sustainability elements that she uses need to be the lens that the Ministers of Education and Environment should prioritize. Global citizenship education requires an inclusive approach toward sustainable development. Schlegelmilch and Sury's chapter on disaster preparedness discusses child-centered resiliency plans. Children should be included in created grounds-up strategies for disaster risk mitigation. Community comes first; which is demonstrated in Braun et al.'s discussion on bringing in key stakeholders and local decision-makers for an evidence-based dialogue on climate adaptation. The chapter touches on breaking hierarchies of power and creating pockets of knowledge which is very aligned to the peace education pillar in Ocansey Stafford's framework. Diro et al. use sophisticated financial modeling and directly communicate with the farmers to safeguard them against weather changes. Iyengar, van Geen, and Munson discuss female power, breaking gender stereotypes through their work on citizen science in Central India. The chapter is aligned with environmental justice on the water quality issue, which is a basic human right for every individual. The chapter is an example of empowering the community to become aware of their environmental issues and creating agents of change to demand basic human rights.

The social and emotional learning aspect in Stafford Ocansey's framework forms the core of the chapter by Malhotra and Ben Amor, who urges the schools to include long-term health interventions to focus on holistic growth. These cross-sectoral linkages foster social-emotional learning in children and not just cognitive. The twenty-first-century skills component in Stafford Ocansey's framework speaks to Shin's arts and communication skills. Shin uses youth voice amplified through arts and communication as a form of climate activism. The knowledge and skills needed for ESD are the foundation of the book. This is also reflected in multiple chapters including Stafford Ocansey, Schnarr, Layugan, and Werner's chapter on education planning using GIS mapping. The authors use technology and data to conduct education planning which is cross-sectoral. Xu's chapter provides every learner a chance to enhance their knowledge and skills and become more aware of local and global climate change issues. Ethridge and Rabiee provide an outlet for individuals to StoryMaps as a medium to narrate their local SDG stories and amplify their voices. They help to connect the local to the global.

In all these chapters, it is clear that communities have a story to tell, communities can identify their own problems and find unique solutions. In relation to this, communities need empowerment and need to be updated with scientific data and evidence to adapt and plan better for an uncertain future. These teaching and learning exercises are not restricted to only schools, but scientists and social scientists can reach out to various segments of the population directly through nonformal and formal means to plan better for the future. Many more dialogues are currently in progress where there is a reciprocal exchange between the community and researchers. These case studies from the Earth Institute/Climate School also demonstrate that the learnings from the ground-up are integrated into various interventions. The role of the researchers in these chapters is to provide the best possible evidence, real-time updated data, and ask the stakeholders to deliberate solutions together. These plans take shape with a mix of cultural, social, and contextual confounding factors which make them locally relevant.

There are two strands that cut across all the chapters. The premise of the book is that ESD is not restricted to classrooms and schools alone. Through these case studies, the book is able to take education directly in the communities and out of institutions. As technologies advance, there is a nonlinear learning path that communities take. They are able to learn across the board and realize the lifelong SDG goal through various mechanisms. These mechanisms are discussed in the book. Technology plays a significant role in making this possible. Second, open access to data that the communities themselves curate builds in more accountability and transparency in the local processes. Across all these case studies, access to data, data analysis, and communication of the analysis form a key role in transformative education.

The book is able to answer questions such as—How does ESD look like in practice? How do cross-sectoral strategies play out in the field-based setting? What constitutes climate justice? How should we include the community as a key stakeholder? What role does technology play in ESD? The purpose of the book is not to transplant these interventions to other countries or to scale up these interventions out of context, but to get a flavor of various topics that we include in our wider definition of what constitutes ESD. ESD should not be treated as teaching about the environment exclusively, it is also getting connected with the people, culture, values, and belief systems. The book provides various case studies that show that education is an important tool for sustainable development. It also provides an opportunity to foster multidisciplinary collaborations to address key sustainable development topics.

This book shows the potential of education in leading the path toward sustainable development. Education does not only mean schools and colleges but also what the farmers need for sustainable agricultural practices. Education is also for the educational planners to read maps, and for preparing the communities for the upcoming natural disasters. Education is also the climate information the refugees need in their camps; it is the health interventions that are often neglected, especially for adolescent girls. Education is needed for residents to know if the water they drink is safe and there are also free climate education classes for retirees and community leaders on a digital platform. The book helps to look at ESD and its different pathways and opens the education community to a wider set of possibilities to ensure "lifelong learning" (SDG4) is possible through inter-sectoral collaborations including community involvement.

This book also shows us that there are some gaps that need to be addressed. For instance, much more work needs to be done on ESD as a tool to discuss climate justice. Education for climate justice is an underexplored field due to many reasons. Climate justice is a topic that makes less headway in schools, communities grapple with the topic on a daily basis, but the pedagogical tool to uncover these topics is largely absent. Some curricula may include the topic, however, it is at a very superficial level. Field-based interventions on ESD, curricula in schools and colleges, and open-source curricula on climate education that do not address climate justice issues are not examining the root cause of the climate change issue. These root causes need to be addressed in all ESD interventions and curricula to make a dent in the system. "Who is excluded?" and "Why?" need to be part of ESD.

This book has been able to open the field of ESD to a much wider array of topics and treatments, and it also points out that climate justice is the missing piece of the puzzle that needs to be addressed urgently. In our view, ESD research and practice must attempt to delve deeper into the intersection of climate justice and social justice; the impact of climate change on the most marginalized and ways to mitigate it; how intersectionality should be emphasized in education modules, and finally, why climate education needs to be a priority climate change mitigation strategy. We hope that this book can be a new beginning for some readers, while it motivates other readers to build more on this topic.

Note

1 https://ukcop26.org/co-chairs-conclusions-of-education-and-environment-ministers-summit-at-cop26/

Index

accessibility   45, 47, 48, 53–5, 77
action civics   13–16
action plan   14, 24, 40, 44, 144, 165
agency   2, 5, 8, 10, 11, 17, 68, 142, 149
agents of change   2, 174
agroclimatic   110–12
anti-racist education   2, 8
applied learning   62
applied research   77, 116
aquaculture   107
arctic warming   66
art-based educator   2
artivism   163, 164
arts   2, 16, 18, 30, 85, 161, 165–71, 174

behavioral design   130
bias   9
biodiversity   51, 56, 62, 168
bottom-up approach   134, 143
Box and Whisker chart   156
bureaucratic   22

capacity building   38, 107, 110, 112–16
case study   3, 21, 65, 141
child-centered   4, 173
child-focused   4, 141, 143, 147–9
citizen science   5, 21–9, 31, 32, 67, 70, 174
civic action   18
civic education   7–15, 17, 18
civic engagement   9–11, 13, 16–18
civic equality   13
civic knowledge   8, 12, 13, 16
civic-literacy   6, 8, 173
civic mission   2, 8, 11, 18
civic spaces   2, 8
civil society   14, 15, 18, 62, 143
climate activism   2, 15, 174
climate adaptation   3, 104, 173
climate literacy   77, 84
climate resilience   133

climate risk   4, 112–15, 122, 127, 128, 132
climate-risk management   112–15, 122, 127, 128, 132
climate science   84, 85, 103
climate scientist   81, 86
climate-sensitive decision-making   104
climate services   103–7, 110, 112–14, 116, 134
climate variability   110, 125
collaborative mapping   68
collective rights   9
colonialism   8, 9
colonization   7, 144
communication   2, 4, 8, 9, 23, 27, 29, 53, 54, 57–9, 64, 80, 81, 92, 104, 106, 111, 116, 121, 129, 134, 145, 152, 153, 161, 162, 165–71, 174, 175
communities of color   10
community-based education   4, 5, 152, 153
community-based participatory research (CBPR)   144
community coalition   143, 147, 155
community collaboration   6
community empowerment model (CEM)   144
community engagement   12, 77, 153
community health worker   23, 30
community involvement   5, 21, 175
community leader   145, 152, 153, 175
community mobilization   141, 143, 144, 147
community ownership   5
community preparedness index   151, 156
community resilience   4, 141, 147–50, 154
confidence-building   5, 92
cooperative learning   93, 109
corporatization   7
counseling   4, 90, 96

covid-19   3, 5, 9, 10, 48, 54, 56, 58, 72, 78, 109, 116, 152, 165
creativity   8, 9, 57, 134
criminal justice   7
critical thinking   2, 8, 9, 57, 93
cross-pollination   113
cross-sectoral   3–5, 41, 89, 97, 104, 173–5
crowdsourced data   48–9
cultural diversity   2, 7, 56
culturally relevant   4, 97
culture of peace   1, 7
culture of reciprocity   108
curriculum   11, 13, 14, 16–18, 30, 31, 62, 63, 77, 91–8, 114, 116, 166, 173

data analysis   15, 38, 40, 44, 49, 175
database   23, 25, 131
data-driven decision-making   26, 35–9
data-driven storytelling   57, 62, 67, 71, 72
decentralized roundtable approach   110
decision-making flowchart   106
democracy   13, 14, 17
demographic data   3, 38
dental fluorosis   23, 24
development sector   1
digital access   48, 49
digital divide   48, 54
digital education   48
disadvantaged minority groups   12
disaster literacy   4, 141, 145–7, 149, 157
disaster preparedness   2, 4, 5, 141, 147, 149, 154, 155, 173
disaster research   4, 147
disaster risk reduction   104, 112
discourse   8, 18
disinformation   13
drinking water   21, 22, 62, 70
drive-time analysis   65
Dunn and Burke's learning style model   166, 167

eco-activism   161, 163, 171
eco ambassador   14, 62, 63, 161, 164, 165, 169, 170
eco-art   164
economic development   1, 55
economic growth   7, 53, 89, 135
educational games   4, 91
education equity   48

education reform   10
education systems   7, 11, 14, 18, 30, 49, 50, 71
empathy   9, 12, 92
empowerment   5, 13, 14, 17, 90, 91, 95, 112, 144
engineering   10, 22, 75
environmental action   25, 161
environmental art   164
environmental education   8, 161, 164, 171
environmental justice   2, 8, 9, 164, 174
environmental literacy   161
environmental racism   8, 58, 60
ethical framework   9
ethics   9
evidence-based   4, 36, 147, 173

fertility rate   1
field-based intervention   4, 176
financial literacy   4, 120, 135
fluoride mitigation   5
food security   107, 113, 121
formal education   1, 4, 30, 154
forth mandate   17
free education   5

gamification   4, 130, 132
gender equality   1, 7
gender equity   44
gender power dynamics   5
gender stereotypes   174
geodatabase   38
geographic literacy   56, 70
geophysicist   2
geo-reference   3, 23, 26, 35, 38, 54, 69
geo-referenced infrastructure   3, 38
geo-referenced map   3, 23
geospatial data   35–41, 43–5, 47–50, 55–9, 68, 71
geospatial literacy   53, 62, 69, 70
geospatial mapping   3, 44
gis-based storyteller   2
gis education   69, 70
global citizenship   1, 2, 7–9, 173
global competitiveness   10
globalization   7, 56
government   3, 30, 31, 36–8, 44, 45, 56, 62, 70, 96, 98, 104, 111, 113, 142, 143, 152, 163

Gray literature   13
grid and cloud computing   25
groundwater   23
Group Empathy Theory   12

health education   5, 94, 97
health intervention   4, 174, 175
health literacy   94, 97, 145
health promotion   90
health system   10
higher education institutions   5, 14, 18, 76, 86
high school   10, 14, 15, 62, 63, 68, 84
history   7, 11, 17, 80, 148
holistic development   4, 89, 90, 97
human dignity   8, 9
humanitarian response   4, 147
human rights   1, 7–10, 174
human rights education   2, 8–10
hypothesis   25

ice breaker   92
imperialism   8, 9
inclusive approach   173
indicator   3, 21, 35, 96
indigenous knowledge   110
individual rights   9
industrial revolution   7
infant mortality   1
infographic   59
informal education   31, 76, 77, 113
informal learning   75, 76, 81, 84, 85
injustice   2, 8–10
inquiry-based learning   108
intellectual   4, 21, 26, 89
intellectual property   26
interdisciplinary   5, 26, 64, 82, 83, 107
inter-sectoral   1, 3, 30, 39, 45, 89, 99, 175
intervention study   29, 31
interview   13, 29, 30, 39, 45, 128
iterative learning   144

jargon   79
journalism   71
journalist   68, 165
junior   47
jurisdiction   151
justice   2, 162, 166, 167, 170, 173–6

k-12   13–16, 18, 30, 62, 71, 78, 142
key lessons   22, 31
keynote   81, 82, 153
k-grey education   75
kickoff meeting   154
kit   21, 26, 31
knowledge-sharing   157, 170

lawmakers   15
laypeople   25
leadership development   15, 16
learner engagement   13
learning through practice   109
legal rights   2
legislative change   16
lifelong learning   1, 5, 75, 76, 82–6
living planet   15
lobbying   15
local environment   3, 5, 126, 135
local government   5, 31, 36, 37
local-level adaptation   3
low-income schools   13

marginalized groups   11, 12, 135
maslow's theory of motivation   166
math   10, 75, 85
measurement   3, 93, 96, 157
media campaigning   15
media literacy   9
microcredit   124, 125
minority groups   12
misconception   23
movement   3, 11, 16, 105, 161–4, 167–9
multidisciplinary thinking   87

national education policy   3, 40
national policies   3, 4, 107
natural sciences   8
network   16, 26, 63, 77, 81, 112, 115, 120, 133, 142, 144, 146, 163, 164, 169–71
nonformal educator   2
non-violence   1, 7
nonviolent direct action   15

online session   78, 170
open-source data   48
open-source mapping   48
oppression   8, 9

outreach   4, 5, 15, 25, 26, 76–8, 83–7, 154

pandemic   3, 5, 7, 10, 48, 54, 55, 72, 78, 109, 116, 152
participatory action research (PAR)   144
participatory approach   38
participatory budgeting   14
participatory community mapping   55
partnership   3, 24, 53, 64, 70, 77, 93, 95, 97, 109, 143, 144, 147, 149, 164–6, 169–71
peace   1, 2, 7–10, 173
peace education   2, 8, 9, 173
pedagogical   14, 17, 18, 77, 82, 92, 98, 103, 176
peer-to-peer learning   165, 171
personal informatics   130
persuasive technology   130
planet care   16
plastic pollution   3
play-based learning   92
polarized societies   10
politically motivated decision-making   44, 49
political participation   9
political scientists   17, 18
population-based indicators   3
poverty   7, 90, 105, 122, 146, 162
prep rally   152, 157
preprimary education   42
professional development   14, 15, 17, 79, 80, 82, 104, 116
public health   2, 9, 10, 22, 104, 142, 151, 152
public health preparedness   151, 152
public outreach   77, 78
public school   15, 93–5, 151
public support   15

race   9, 10, 12, 163
racial equality   16
racism   8, 9, 15, 58
rallies   15, 16, 152, 154
real-time data   3, 53, 55
reciprocal learning approach   108
reflexivity   144, 156
regenerative culture   16
relationship skills   91, 92
remote sensing   131

resilience   4, 9, 112, 121, 141, 147–51, 154–6
responsible decision-making   91
risk communication   145
risk management   112–15, 121, 122, 124, 125, 127, 128, 132
role-playing   95

satellite imagery   68
schooling   1, 56, 142
science-based training   5
science communication   53, 58, 59
science-driven   4
scientific knowledge   3
SDG tracking   3
secondary education   1, 36, 47
security   1, 10, 66, 130, 167
self-actualization   166, 167
self-awareness   92
self-management   91, 92
sense of belongingness   167
serious games   130
service-learning   12, 13
sexual and reproductive health   4, 90, 94
skills-based training   78
social abilities   4, 89
social assessment   39
social awareness   8, 91, 92
social capital   9, 30, 77, 142, 144, 157
social change   2, 10
social cohesion   164
social determinants of health   10
social development   1
social emotional learning   2, 4, 8, 9, 174
social inequities   77
social media   12, 13, 15, 153, 162, 167, 169, 171
social responsibility   8, 9, 91
social scientist   15, 174
societal inequities   9
socioecological   8
sociopolitical   9
spatial analysis   57
spatial distribution   28, 56
spatial skills   71
spatial variability   26
storymap   55, 58–68, 71, 174
storytelling   3, 15, 53, 55–9, 62, 63, 71, 72, 166

structural inequalities   2
student agency   17
student-centered   4, 13, 90, 98
student engagement   67
survey   16, 28, 39, 64, 90, 109, 129, 130, 151, 163
sustainable development   1, 2, 5–8, 15, 21, 22, 30–2, 35, 38, 48, 53–9, 62, 63, 67–72, 75–7, 89, 90, 105, 112, 116, 129, 161, 164, 166, 173, 175
sustainable lifestyles   1, 7
sustainable society   7
systems approach   81
systems thinking   9, 85

tabletop exercise   150
technology   3, 5, 10, 30, 32, 37, 49, 53, 54, 57, 62, 68, 71, 75, 116, 130, 134, 162, 170, 174, 175
theater   28–30, 54
theory of change   148
toxicant   21
training course   15
training of trainers (TOT)   115
trial and error theory   109
twenty-first-century skills   8, 9, 174
two-way learning   108

underrepresented groups   124
underserved communities   13
universal access   8
user-friendly   3, 62

values   2, 8, 13, 75, 98, 144, 175
virtues   12, 17
volunteer   24, 25, 165

water testing   5, 28
weather-index insurance   4, 5, 119–22, 124
weather prediction   5
weather-related risks   4, 127
well-being   9, 11, 54, 89, 90, 93, 95, 142, 145, 148, 167
well-resourced schools   18
"whole community" planning   142
workshop   3, 36, 38, 39, 43–5, 49, 63, 64, 66, 80, 129, 130, 134, 165, 168, 169

youth activism   15, 170
youth-adult partnership   170
youth climate activism   2, 15
youth leaders   15, 16
youth-led   16, 165
youth organizations   15

www.ingramcontent.com/pod-product-compliance
Lightning Source LLC
Chambersburg PA
CBHW061831300426
44115CB00013B/2326